A Master Catalogue of the Manuscripts and Published Editions of the Works of Mirza ‘Abdul Qadir-e Bīdel

A Master Catalogue of the Manuscripts and Published Editions of the Works of Mirza 'Abdul Qadir-e Bīdel

Compiled by

Prof. Sharif Husain Qasemi

INDIAN COUNCIL OF WORLD AFFAIRS

PENTAGON PRESS LLP

First published in 2023 by

PENTAGON PRESS LLP
206, Peacock Lane,
Shahpur Jat New Delhi-110049,
India Contact: 011-64706243

Composed by Abdur Rehman Qureshi

Typeset in Times New Roman, 12 Point and
Lotus and Mitra (Persian), 13 Point

Printed by Aegean Offset Printers, Noida

ISBN: 978-93-90095-72-8 (HB)

از صفحه کلکِ وحشتِ ما پیشرفته است

امـروز هـم ز نسـخهٔ فـردا نوشـتهایـم

در زنـدگی مطالعـت دل غنیمـت اسـت

خواهی بخوان و خواهی مخوان، نوشتهایم

The pen of my wilderness runs beyond the paper on which I write,
Even today I write from the book of tomorrow,
In life it is important to read the heart,
Whether you read or not, I write.

Contents

Abbreviations

Aḥsan	*Fehrist-e Makhṭūṭāt, Ẕakhīreh-e Aḥsan*, M.A. Library, A.M.U., Aligarh, 1983.
AMU	Aligarh Muslim University, Aligarh U.P., India.
Āṣafīya	*Fehrist-e Kotob-e 'Arabī, Fārsī-o-Urdū, Kitābkhāna-e Āṣafīya*, Hyderabad, 1332 A.H.
ASB	*Concise Descriptive Catalogue of the Persian Manuscripts in the Collection of the Asiatic Society of Bengal*, First Supplement, Calcutta, 1927.
Banaras	*A Descriptive Catalogue of the Persian Manuscripts in the Banaras Hindū University Library*, Varanasi, U.P.
Browne	*A Descriptive Catalogue of the Oriental Manuscripts Belonging to the Late E.G. Browne*, Cambridge, 1930.
Bohār	*Catalogue of the Persian Manuscripts in the Bohār Collection*, National Library, Calcutta, 1982.
Curzon	*Concise Descriptive Catalogue of the Persian Manuscripts in the Curzon Collection*, Asiatic Society of Bengal, Calcutta, 1926.
Deoband	*Ta'aruf-e Makhṭūṭāt-e Kotobkhāna-e Dārul 'Ulūm*, Deoband, 1973, Vol. II.

Ethe	*Catalogue of Persian Manuscripts in the India Office Library and Records, Foreign and Commonwealth Office*, London, 1980.
Ḥabībganj	*A Catalogue of Manuscripts in Ḥabībganj Collection*, M.A. Library, AMU, Aligarh, 1981.
Ḥamīdiya	*Fehrist-e Noskhehā-e Khaṭṭī-e Kitābkhāneh-e Sho'beh-e Teḥqīq-o-Ishā'at-e Kashmīr-o-Kitābkhāneh-e Ḥamīdiya Bhopal*, Persian Research Centre, Iran Culture House, New Delhi, 1364 H.S./ 1986 A.D.
Hardayāl	*Fehrist-e Noskhehā-e Khaṭṭī-e Fārsī of Hardayāl Public Library, Delhi*; Persian Research Centre, Iran Culture House, New Delhi, 1377 H.S./ 1999 A.D.
Ivonow	*Concise Descriptive Catalogue of the Persian Manuscripts in the Curzon Collection*, Asiatic Society of Bengal, Calcutta, 1926.
Jāmia	*Fehrist-e Noskhehā-e Khaṭṭī-e Fārsī of Dr. Ẕākir Ḥusain Library*, Jāmia Millia Islāmīa, Persian Research Centre, Iran Culture House, New Delhi, 1377 H.S./1999 A.D.
Jawāhar Museum	Fehrist-e Makhṭūṭāt, Ẕakhīreh-e Jawāhar Museum, A Collection in M.A. Library, AMU, Aligarh.
Khodā Bakhsh/ Bānkīpūr	Catalogue of the 'Arabic and Persian Manuscripts *in the Khodā Bakhsh Oriental Public Library*, Patna, 1988.
Khushgū	Safīneh-e Khushgū.

Lucknow	*Catalogue of Oriental Manuscripts in the Lucknow University Library*, Kālī Prasad, Lucknow, 1951.
Madras	*A Descriptive Catalogue of Islamic Manuscripts in the Government Oriental Manuscripts Library*, Madras, 1950.
Monīr-e 'Ālam	*Monīr-e 'Ālam Collection in the Maulānā Āzād Library*, Aligarh Muslim University (AMU), U.P., India.
Monzavī	*Fehrist-e Moshtarak-e Noskhehā-e Fārsī-e Pakistan*) (*A Union Catalogue of Persian Manuscripts in Pakistan*), Iran-Pakistan Institute of Persian Studies, Islamabad, Pakistan, 1987.
Mozzammil	*Descriptive Catalogue of Arabic, Persian and Urdū Manuscripts of Mozzammil Library, Aligarh*, Patna, 1995.
Nadva	*A Catalogue of Persian Manuscripts in the Library of Nadva-tol 'Ulemā, Lucknow*; Persian Research Centre, Iran Culture House, New Delhi, 1365 H.S./ 1986 A.D.
Rampur	*A Catalogue of Persian Manuscripts in Rampur* Razā Library, Rampur, Vol. I, 1996, Vol. II, 1998.
Rieu	*Catalogue of the Persian Manuscripts in the British Museum*, London, 1879-83.
Sālār	*A Descriptive Catalogue of Persian Manuscripts in Sālār Jung Museum and Library*, Hyderabad, 1980.
Sharaf-ul Molk	*A Hand-List of Arabic, Persian and Urdū*

Library	*Manuscripts in Sharaf-ul Molk Library*, Chenā'ī (not published but available in the library).
Shīfta	*Fehrist-e Makhṭūṭāt, Ẕakhīreh-e Shīfta*, A Collection in M.A. Library, AMU, Aligarh, 1982.
Sobḥānallāh	*Sobḥānallāh Collection in M.A. Library*, AMU, Aligarh.
Solaimān	*Solaimān Collection in M.A. Library*, AMU, Aligarh.
Sprenger	*A Catalogue of Arabic, Persian and Hindūstāny Manuscripts in the Libraries of the Kings of Oudh*, Calcutta, 1854.
Tājīkistān	*Fehrist-e Nosakh-e Khaṭṭī-e Fārsī-e Institū-e Āthār-e Khaṭṭī-e Tajikistan*, Tehran, 1376 H.S./ 1997 A.D., Vol. I.
Tonk	*Maulānā Āzād Arabic and Persian Research Institute Rajasthan*, Tonk.
University	A Collection in M.A. Library, AMU, Aligarh.
Upsala	ACTA Bibliotheca R. Universalities Upsaliensis.

Scheme of Transliteration

ا، أ، آ	Ā, ā	ص	Ṣ ṣ
ب	b	ض	Ẓ ẓ
پ	p	ط	Ṭ ṭ
ت	t	ظ	Ż, ż
ث	th	ع	‘
ج	j	غ	gh
چ	ch	ف	f
ح	Ḥ ḥ	ق	q
خ	kh	ک	k
د	d	گ	g
ذ	Ẕ ẕ	ل	l
ر	r	م	m
ڑ	Ḏ ḏ	ن	n
ز	z	و	u, ū (Occasionally o)
ژ	zh	ه	h
س	s	ء	‘
ش	sh	ی	ī
ـَ	a		
ـِ	i (Occasionally e)		
ـُ	u (Occasionally o)		

Preface

The social historians, following thorough, have concluded that the cultural achievements of the Mughals in India were not exclusively an Indian phenomenon. It was actually the outcome of a natural and happy synthesis of cultural elements from the entire Asian lands where Persianate culture played a lively and dominant role. To put it another way, "The boundaries of this considerable part of the world were actually defined not politically but socially and culturally and thus covered a much larger terrain than any empire could lay claim to." Mīrzā 'Abdul Qādir-e Bīdel, perhaps is the most significant literary figure born in India in the 18th century, who played a vital role in further strengthening and integrating this cultural empire.

Mīrzā 'Abdul Qādir-e Bīdel's lifetime spanned as long as the reign of Aurangzīb 'Ālamgīr (1068/1658-1118/1707) and saw the beginning of the decline of the once- mighty Mughal empire after the demise of this Mughal ruler.

Abul Ma'ānī (creator of meaningful discourse) Mīrzā 'Abdul Qādir who first opted *Ramzī* «رمزی» as his penname and later coming across these couplets of Sa'dī-e Shīrāzī in the preface of his *Golistān*:

گر کسی وصفِ او ز من پرسد   بی‌دل از بی‌نشان چه گوید باز

عاشــقان کشــتگانِ معشــوقند   برنیایــــد ز کشــــتگان آواز

changed it to *Bīdel* (love-sick), has left a detailed account of his life in one of his monumental works namely *Chahār 'Onṣor*. But a complete picture of his career cannot be drawn only on the basis of it. He has not still clearly recorded his place of birth in it.

Contemporary biographers, among whom some were his pupils and companions, come to our rescue in reconstructing of comparatively a complete picture of his life.

It should be stated here that what Bīdel has written about his life in *Chahār 'Onṣur* is not chronologically arranged. It is, therefore, a bit risky and also difficult to draw information about his life in a historic perspective. As a result, the statements of modern biographers of Bīdel differ to an extent with each other.

One of the indispensable source for Bīdel's biography, apart from his *Chahār 'Onṣor*, is *Safīna-e Khushgū* a *Tazkirah* (biography) of poets by Bindrā Ban Dāss Khushgū[1]. He was a pupil of *Bīdel* and claims to have met his teacher more than thousand times. Khushgū has indeed given a detailed life account of Bīdel and his works. It is naturally considered authentic. Besides, Shāh Moḥammad Shafī' Tehrani pen-named *Wārid*, son of Moḥammad Sharīf, informs in his *Mer'at-e Wāridāt*[2] that *Bīdel* stayed at his residence for one

1. Bindrā Ban Dāss Khushgū (d. 1170/1756) belonged to Mathura and lived most of his life in Delhi. He passed the concluding part of his life in Allāhābād choosing the confluence of two sacred rivers – Gangā and Jamunā – as an appropriate place for spiritual retirement. His contacts with all the important literary men of his time in Delhi were intimate. Noteworthy among them were Mīrzā Afẓal Sarkhūsh (d. 1127/1715), Mīrzā 'Abdul Qādir-e Bīdel and Khān-e Ārzū (d. 1169/1756). All his life, he acknowledged his indebtedness to them and took much care in leaving pleasant descriptions of their personalities in his biographical work, *Safīna-e Khushgū* in three sections completed in 1147/1734. (For his detailed biography see his *Tazkirah Safīna-e Khushgū*)

2. Moḥammad Shafī' Wārid Tehrānī, son of Syed Moḥammad Sharīf, was born in 1087/1676-77 probably in Nagīna where his father was serving Prince Shāh 'Ālam Bahādur Shāh, the governor of this region. After coming from Iran, his father entered first the service of 'Abdullāh Quṭb Shāh of the Deccan and subsequently that of the said prince. After the death of his father in 1117/1705-6, *Wārid* served under Prince Moḥammad 'Aẓīm. He soon withdrew himself from this service to devote his energies to literature under

and a half years on his first arrival from Azimabad in Delhi. *Wārid* thus had the opportunity to know *Bīdel* closely. On the basis of his interviews with *Bīdel*, *Wārid* has given some such information about Bīdel not found in other sources. On the authority of these two, and other contemporary and later sources, an attempt has been made here to compile Bīdel's biography:

Bīdel in his *Chahār 'Onṣor*, as mentioned earlier, does not refer to his place of birth. The contemporary and later biographers consequently differ on this issue. Some of them have named Akbarābād (Āgrā), Lahore or 'Aẓīmābād as his birth place. Bindrā Ban Dāss Khushgū identifies Akbarābād as his birth place.[1] After the publication of *Shām-e Gharībān* by Lachhmī Nārain Shafīq,[2] a

the patronage of Bairam Khān (d. at Delhi in 1145/1732-33), the son of Aurangzīb's general Rūḥullāh Khān. Apart from a *Dīwān* and four *Mathnavīs*, he wrote *Mer'at-e Wāridāt*, a history of the Ṣafavīds and Mughals upto Moḥammad Shāh's 16th regnal year (1146/1733) in four *Ṭabaqāt* (sections). The third *Ṭabaqa* deals with biographies of poets and authors. (See Storey, Vol. I, p.611). I have come across two Mss. of *Mer'at-e Wāridāt*, one in Khodā Bakhsh Oriental Public Library (Cat. Vol. VII, No. 580), and the other in M.A. Arabic and Persian Research Institute, Tonk, Rajasthan, but none of them is the third Ṭabqa dealing with the biographies of poets. A part of *Mer'at-e Wāridāt* dealing with the history of the Ṣafavīds of Iran has been critically edited by Dr. Manṣūr Ṣefatgol and published by *Mīrāth-e Maktūb*, Tehrān, 1383 H.S.

1. It can reasonably be inferred that Khushgū had most probably named Akbar Nagar as Bīdel's birth place. But the ignorant scribe changed it wrongly to Akbarābād, a more popular and known city.
2. Lachhmī Nārain Shafīq (d. 1224/1809), a pupil of Mīr Gholām 'Alī Āzād of Bilgrām (d. 1200/1785) and a poet of Persian and Urdu belonged to Lahore and settled at Daulatābād. He was a prolific writer. Apart from a number of works, he is chiefly famous for his anthologies of poets – *Chamanistān-e Sho'arā* (Urdu poets), *Gol-e Ra'na* (Indian Persian poets) and *Shām-e Gharībān* completed in 1182/1768 a biography of Persian poets who migrated to India from the Persian speaking world. (See preface to published *Shām-e Gharībān* for his detailed life account)

Tazkirah of migrant Persian poets in India, this long-drawn controversy should now be settled. Shafīq's source of information about Bīdel is *Mer'at-e Wāridāt* by Shāh Moḥammad Shafī' Tehrānī pen-named *Wārid* who, as referred to earlier, was the host of Bīdel for more than one year in Delhi. *Wārid* states that Bīdel was born at Akbar Nagar (not Akbarābād as recorded in *Safīna-e Khushgū*) popularly known as Rāj Maḥal, then in Bengal.[1] It is now in Jharkhand.

It is not out of place to state with regard to Akbar Nagar or Rāj Maḥal that Akbar promoted his son Sulṭān Khusrau to Panjhazārī Manṣab and assigned him the province of Orissa in the 29th regnal year (992 A.H.). Rāja Mān Singh was appointed his Atālīq (Tutor) and Bengal was given in his Jāgīr and also the responsibility of its management was assigned to him. The Rāja annexed some of the neighbouring territories to the kingdom. He selected a place near *Āk Maḥal* in the 40th regnal year (1004 A.H.). Raja Man Singh established a centre of administration there and named it Akbar Nagar, also called Rāj Maḥal. Shīr Shāh Sūrī (1539-1545) had also liked this place.[2]

Bīdel was born in 1054/1644. This date is conveyed by these two chronograms: «انتخاب» and «فیض قدس», contained in this *Qiṭ'a* by Bīdel himself:

به‌سالی کـه بیـدل بـه‌ملـک ظهـور   ز فـیض ازل تافـت چـون آفتـاب

بزرگـــی خبـــر داد از مولـــدش   که «فیض قدس» است و هم «انتخاب»

«۱۰۵٤»

1. Bīdel refers to Bengal probably as his homeland in a verse, where the people, out of helplessness, only boast of water, rivers and ponds:

   ما سیه‌بختان حباب گریهٔ نومیـدی‌ایـم   ناز بر آب است یکسر مردم بنگالـه را

   (*Dīwān-e Bīdel*, Iran Publication, p.9)

2. *Ma'āthir-ul Omerā*, Vol. II, Calcutta, 1890, p.166.

Both these chronograms were composed by Mīrzā Abul Qāsim,[1] spiritual guide of Bīdel's father. Bīdel's father Mīrzā 'Abdul Khāliq (d. 1059/1649) belonged to the Chaghtā'ī tribe of Arlās,[2] one of the four branches of Mongols (مغول). He was attached to the Qādirī School of Ṣūfīs founded by Shaikh Moḥīuddīn 'Abdul Qādir-e Jīlānī (d. 561/1165). He was initiated in this *Silsela* by the same Mīrzā Abul Qāsim and so named his son as 'Abdul Qādir. Moreover, Bīdel as narrated by Bīdel to Wārith, had family connections with Shāh Manṣūr, son of Možaffar, the ruler of Fārs and a patron of the famous poet Ḥāfiż-e Shīrāzī (d. 791/1389). Shāh Manṣūr was killed in 1393 A.D., while fighting Amir Tīmūr (1370-1405). Now left with no option, his family members left Fārs and reached Bukhara. They lived in Transoxiana for some years. Later Bīdel's father Mīrzā 'Abdul Khāliq left that region and migrated to Bengal and entered the military service of the ruling Mughals. The family lived at Akbar Nagar, Rāj Maḥal, where Bīdel was born. Bīdel was hardly five years old when, unfortunately, his father passed away in 1059/1649. Bīdel mourns his father's death in this verse:

آن سایه گذشت از اثر دست‌نوازش　　این نقشِ قدم داغ شد و خاک به‌سر آمد[3]

After the death of his father, Bīdel was now left to the care of his God-fearing mother who taught him the Qurān[4]. Unfortunately Bīdel's mother also passed away a year later. Now his uncle Mīrzā Qalandar took charge of his upbringing[5]. He was admitted in a school where he studied upto the age of ten. Mīrzā Qalandar was a serious guardian who once visited the school and saw two scholars

---

1. *Chahār 'Onṣur*, Kabul, p.400.
2. It has been spelt differently in some sources. Barlās in *Mer'at-ul Khayāl*, Arlāt in *Majma'-un Nafā'is*. But Arlās is the correct pronunciation.
3. *Āwāzhāy-e Bīdel*, p.348.
4. *Ibid.*, p.300.
5. *Khushgū*, p.105.

deliberating some academic issue furiously. He did not approve it and then withdrew Bīdel from the school[1]. Bīdel now devoted himself to continue his studies privately. Mīrzā Qalandar also himself guided him in his education and composing poetry[2].

Interestingly it was here in this school that Bīdel came in close contact with a handsome classmate. The boy used to keep clove in his mouth and so while talking, a sweat fragrance of clove flawed out of his mouth, Bīdel composed the under noted quatrain appreciating this situation. It is the first poetic creation of Bīdel at the age of ten and also a testimony to his being a born poet:

یارم هرگه در سخن می‌آید بوی عجبش از دهن می‌آید

این بوی قرنفل است یا نگهت گل یا رایحهٔ مشک ختن می‌آید[۳]

Apart from it, Bīdel afterwards attached himself to Maulānā 'Abdul 'Azīz pen-named 'Izzat (d. 1089/1678 at the age of forty-eight years) for guidance in poetry.[4] 'Izzat was a son of 'Abdur Rashīd Akbarābādī. Bīdel has composed a chronogram on his death conveying 1089 A.H.:

عمر عزیز او چهل و هشت سال بود

شد سال رحلتش «چهل و هشت‌ساله مرد»

There are also some letters of Bīdel to 'Izzat highlighting his close and respectful association with him.

Mīrzā Qalandar and Mīrzā Żarīf, Bīdel's maternal uncle, were men of Ṣūfī tendencies and used to meet the Ṣūfīs around them. Bīdel accompanied them to benefit from the presence of these Ṣūfīs. Ultimately Bīdel emerged as one of the acclaimed scholars of his time. He was well versed in mathematics and natural sciences. He was also conversant with occult sciences like *Jafar* (جفر, the art of

1, *Ibid.*, p.105; *Āwāzhāy-e Bīdel*, p.341.

2. *Āwāzhāy-e Bīdel*, p.307.

3. *Āwāzhāy-e Bīdel*, pp.451-2.

4. Khushgū, p.108.

making amulets and charms) and *Ramal* (رمل, geomancy). Bīdel even edited *Tālīf-ul Aḥkām* (تأليف‌الاحكام) by 'Ibādullāh on this subject and wrote a *Dībācha* on it for he found many mistakes in this work because of the ignorant scribes.[1] He had also acquired a good knowledge of music, *Ṭib* and Indian mythology. He was well acquainted with Mahābhārata[2] and Yogavasishtha.[3] Apart from Persian, he learnt Turkish,[4] probably the language of his family from his father side, and Hindavī and composed verses in these languages.[5] Besides he had also studied many books on esoteric science in possession of Shāh Qāsim Howallāhī in Delhi. Of special interest was a book about incantation with strange figures and curious drawings presented to him by Shaikh Kamāl.[6] Bīdel also studied *Taẓkirāt-ul Auliā* of 'Aṭṭār.[7]

Bīdel met a number of Ṣūfīs during his lifetime. He names the following from whom he had learnt something or the other: Maulānā Shaikh Kamāl Qādirī was the spiritual guide of Bīdel's father Mīrzā 'Abdul Khāliq and uncle Mīrzā Qalandar. He was a resident of Rānī Sāgar,[8] now in district Bhojpūr in Bihar. Shāh Molūk lived under a tree in Sarāi Banaras,[9] a village in Bīhār near Rānī Sāgar. He was a Persian poet who largely composed verses in Indian language (*Hindavī*, مصطلحاتِ هند).[10] He was an ascetic saint

1. *Roqqa'āt*, Kabul, p.180.
2. Khushgū, p.138.
3. A story from Yogavasishtha has been versified by Bīdel in his *Mathnavī-e 'Irfān* as detailed latter in this preface.
4. *Catalogue of Persian Mss. in Bānkīpūr*, Vol. III, pp.124-5.
5. Mīr Taqī Mīr has quoted two of Bīdel's verses in Hindavī in his *Nekāt-ush Sho'arā*, p.2.
6. *Āwāzhāy-e Bīdel*, p.365.
7 *Ibid.*, p.508.
8. *Chahār 'Onṣur*, Kabul, p.301.
9. *Ibid.*, p.307.
10. *Ibid.*, p.318.

accustomed to nudity. Once, as per advice of the Shāh, Bīdel took notes of his conversations and collected some forty couplets out of it during his three-day stay with him. Bīdel admits that he, for his inflamed style of description in poetry as well as in prose, is indebted to the warm utterances of the Shāh Molūk.[1] Shāh Yakkeh Āzād, a wandering dervish, was in Ārrā, a district in Bihar.[2] Shāh Fāẓil is among those other Ṣūfīs who came in contact with Bīdel and with whom, he chanced to deliberate on a number of Ṣūfī subjects.[3] Shāh Qāsim Howallāhī, a poet in Orissa, was also among his acquaintances. Bīdel was in the presence of Shāh Qāsim for three years in Orissa. Bīdel has composed these verses in praise of this Ṣūfī acknowledging his high Ṣūfī stature and his indebtedness to him:

قبله خوانم یا پیمبر یا خدا یا کعبه‌ات   اصطلاح عشق بسیار است و من دیوانه‌ام
در عالمی که رنگی از خود نمود ما را   بودیم آنچه بودیم او وانمود ما را

Bīdel has also copied this quatrain of Shāh Qāsim:

در کوی دلارام گذر باید کرد   فعل بد خویش را به‌در باید کرد
آیینهٔ شوق با صفا باید داشت   دروی رُخِ یار را نظر باید کرد[٤]

The news of his demise was conveyed to Bīdel in Agra in 1083 A.H. by someone coming from Orissa.[5]

Bīdel also met Shāh Kābulī, a wandering *Derwīsh*, in Delhi and Mathura and discussed some Ṣūfī subjects with him. Shāh Kābulī lived in deserted places. Though not inclined, he took some food with Bīdel.[6]

---

1. *Safīna-e Khushgū*, p.102.
2. *Chahār 'Onṣur*, Kabul, p.319.
3. *Ibid.*, p.394.
4. *Āwāzhāy-e Bīdel*, pp.401, 406, 409.
5. *Ibid.*, p.515.
6. *Ibid.*, p.503.

It is interesting to note that there is hardly any Ṣūfī or saint among those visited by Bīdel celebrated outside the place he lived. One rarely finds any reference of these Ṣūfīs in biographical works of Ṣūfīs compiled in India. Bīdel has, thus, introduced these Ṣūfīs for the first time in his works.

Before coming to Delhi, Bīdel visited the following places with his paternal and maternal uncles: Mīrzā Qalandar and Mīrzā Żarīf, respectively. He states that his boyhood passed in Bihar.[1] He used to visit Rānī Sāgar, a place near Ārrā with his uncle Mīrzā Qalandar.[2] Apart from Ārrā, he was in Tīrhut (Możaffarpūr) for a short time in 1069/1659 with another uncle, Mīrzā 'Abdul Laṭīf, an officer in the establishment of Shāh Shujā'. At the age of 14, Bīdel entered the ancestral profession of a soldier in the army of Prince Shāh Shujā', the second son of Shāhjahān in about 1068 A.H., and also successfully took part in a military action in Tīrhut under the command of Mīrzā 'Abdul Laṭīf. This regiment scattered after the rumour of Shāh Shujā's defeat by Aurangzīb.[3] There is a *Qaṣīda* of Bīdel comprising twenty-seven couplets in praise of Shāh Shujā' indicating his attachment to the establishment of this prince.[4] After the defeat of this Prince in the war of succession at Khajua on 9th Rabī'I, 1069 A.H./25th November, 1658 A.D., Mīrzā 'Abdul Laṭīf had fled along with Bīdel to Chand Chur near Patna.[5] Shortly afterwards in 1070/1660, Bīdel is found in Mehsī, a town near Patna[6] (or district

1. There is a letter of Bīdel in which he revives his memory of his sojourn in Bihar. (*Āwāzhāy-e Bīdel*, p.215)
2. *Āwāzhāy-e Bīdel*, p.469.
3. *Gol-e Ra'na*, p.217; *Chahār 'Onṣur*, p.554.
4. *Kolliyāt*, Kabul, Vol. II, p.104.
5. *Kolliyāt*, Kabul, pp.551-54.
6. *Ibid.*, p.562.

Champaran). In 1070/1660, Mīrzā Qalandar took him to Bengal[1] which is referred to by Bīdel as his own land where people are proud of rivulets:

ما سیه‌بختان حباب گریهٔ نومیدی‌ایم   ناز بر آب است یکسر مردم بنگاله را

Afterwards Bīdel accompanied Mīrzā Żarīf, his maternal uncle and a scholar of Islamic sciences like *Tafsīr* and *Fiqh*, to Orissa in 1070/ 1660. Mīrzā Żarīf also taught him *Tafsīr*.[2] Bīdel stayed at Cuttack, the capital of Orissa[3] and other places of Orissa for three years.[4] It was in Orissa that Bīdel came in contact with Shāh Qāsim, a great Ṣūfī of his time. His mystic and literary discussions with Shāh Qāsim enlightened Bīdel.[5] After these travels, Bīdel returned to Biharin 1075/1665 and then proceeded to Delhi the same year because of lack of any support there. Bīdel has portrayed his helpless and hopeless condition in these verses also conveying the year of his departure from Bīhār to Delhi:

از ملک بهار سوی دهلی   چون اشک روان شدم بیکس
سال تاریخ این عزیمت   دریاب که «راهبر خدا بس»
(۱۰۷۵ ه)

Bīdel reached Delhi in 1076/1666 where he was received with open arms by Moḥammad Shafī' Wārid. He stayed for almost one and a half year at his residence. During this span of time, Bīdel narrated some aspects of his biography to his host who recorded it in his *Mer'at-e Wāridāt*. Wārid writes: Bīdel reaching Delhi in his prime youth, was initially attached to the establishment of Mīrzā Solaimān, the real maternal uncle of Sulṭān Moḥammad

1. *Ibid.*, p.562.
2. *Ibid.*, p.347.
3. *Āwāzhāy-e Bīdel*, p.432.
4. *Ibid.*, p.406.
5. *Āwāzhāy-e Bīdel*, p.347.

Mo'izzuddīn Jahāndār Shāh[1] (10th April, 1712-January 1713), son of Shāh 'Ālam (1707-1712), son of 'Ālamgīr (1658-1707) and earned his confidence. In the meantime, someone in the court read out some verses of Bīdel to the king. The king asked the name of the poet. "These are by Bīdel," replied the reciter. The king retorted in light vein, "My army is packed with brave (پردل) soldiers, and so there is no place for a heartless (بی‌دل) fellow." Feeling ill of it, Bīdel immediately gave up his service never to resume in spite of the persuasion of the Prince. He then left for Mathura on the bank of river Jamunā. Lāl Moḥammad, a sincere friend of Bīdel, was an administrator and the deputy of Ḥasan 'Alī Khān Bahādur Allāhwardī Khān[2] at Mathura. He warmly welcomed him. Bīdel also enjoyed his company. Suddenly Aurangzīb 'Ālamgīr summoned Lāl Moḥammad Khān to the Deccan in his presence. Lāl Moḥammad Khān reluctantly left for the Deccan but died on the way. Bīdel stayed at Mathura for three months.[3] Afterwards Bīdel left Mathura with a heavy heart[4] and came back to Delhi on 27th of Jumāda'II, 1096 A.H./21st May, 1685 A.D. Here a messenger from Shokrullāh Khān Khwāfī[5] pen-named *Khāksār*, the governor of Narnol, one of the dependencies

1. Abul Fatḥ Mo'izzuddīn Moḥammad Jahāndār Shāh, son of Shāh 'Ālam, was killed at the instance of Moḥammad Farrukh Sīyar on Sunday, the 16th Muharram, 1125 A.H./1st February, 1713 A.D. (*Tārīkh-e Moḥammadī*, p.31)
2. He was appointed *Faujdār* of Mathura on 30th Rajab, 1080 A.H./14th December, 1669 A.D. and Mathura was named Islāmābād in Sha'bān, 1080 A.H./December, 1669 A.D. (*Ma'āthir-e 'Ālamgīrī*, pp.92-6)
3. *Āwāzhāy-e Bīdel*, p.613.
4. In this regard Bīdel's words are «هنگام وداع گشتن داغی است سیاهی». (*Āwāzhāy-e Bīdel*, p.482)
5. Shokrullāh Khān Khwāfī pen-named Khāksār, son of Khwājegī Sulṭān Meḥmūd, served 'Ālamgīr's court and enjoyed a *Manṣab* of 1,500. He was the military commander of Narnol and died in the month of Rabī'I, 1108 A.H./September, 1696 A.D. at the age of sixty-two. (*Tārīkh-e Moḥammadī*, p.8; *Shām-e Gharībān*, p.57)

of Mewat, approached him with a message and some money inviting him to contact the Khān. Hence, Bīdel took leave of Wārid's father and left for Mewat. This interaction between Bīdel and Shokrullāh Khān continued till the death of the Khān in 1108 A.H. After the Khān passed away, his three sons continued to look after Bīdel. These three sons were: the eldest son, who like his father got Shokrullāh as his title; the second Shākir Khān[1] and the third Mīr Karamullāh (pen-named 'Āshiq). He was later bestowed the title of 'Āqil Khān enjoyed by his maternal grandfather 'Āqil Khān Rāzī (d. 1108 A.H./1696 A.D.).

Bīdel requested Shokrullāh Khān to arrange for his dwelling in Delhi somewhere near the bank of river[2] (i.e. Jamunā).The actual request of Bīdel in this regard is:

اگر درین سواد موضعی کنارِ دریا یا لبِ نهر به‌سهولت در اتّفاق کشاید تا تکیه‌ای اختیار نماید، مابقی مدّتِ مهلتی که از نظر یقین مختفی است، بی‌تشویش تغییرِ مکان بسربرد.

Shokrullāh Khān responded to his request favourably and bought for him a *Ḥavelī* (a big house) for Rs. 5,000/- in Mohallah-e Khākheriyān[3] by the side of Loṭf 'Alī avenue on the bank of Jamunā outside Delhi Gate and also granted a stipend of two rupees daily.[4] Thus, Bīdel ultimately settled down in Delhi.

---

1. Mīr 'Ināyatullāh entitled 'Shākir Khān' was Faujdār of the area neighbouring Delhi. He was killed by Yakkehtāz Khān Kābulī in 1130 A.H./1718 A.D. Kābulī was also latter killed in the same year by the people of Shokrullāh Khān. (*Tārīkh-e Moḥammadī*, p.38)
2. *Āwāzhāy-e Bīdel*, p.114.
3. Khākheriyān was probably situated somewhere by the side of Old Fort Delhi in the area now in exhibition ground. The author of *Moraqqa'-e Dehlī* had visited Bīdel's house between 1737 and 1741 A.D. As Sangīn Beg in his *Sair-ul Manāzil* in 1827 A.D. and, later, Sir Syed in his *Āthār-us Sanādīd* did not refer to it, the *Mohallah* obviously, was raised to ground sometimes after 1741 A.D.
4. *Safīna-e Khushgū*, p.100; *Gol-e Ra'na*, p.217.

Bīdel was, as per his will, buried in the courtyard of this house on a raised platform built by Bīdel himself for his grave ten years before his death. Bīdel's demise was mourned by the men of letters and his acquaintances. Khushgū composed this chronogram یوم پنجشنبه، چهارم صفر recording the day (Thursday) and the date (4th Ṣafar) and also the year (1133 A.H.) of the death of Bīdel. Moreover, he also composed the following *Qiṭ'a* containing the chronogram (مادّهٔ تاریخ), which conveys 1133 the year of his teacher's demise:

افسوس که بیدل ز جهان روی نهفت   وان جوهر پاک در تـه خـاک نهفـت
خوشگو چو ز عقل کرد تاریخ سوال   «از عالم رفـت میـرزا بیـدل» گفـت[1]
(۱۱۳۳ هـ)

Bīdel married four times.[2] A son was born in Delhi on Friday night, 7th Rajab, 1120/11th September, 1708, at the age of sixty-five years. He was named 'Abdul Khāliq after the name of Bīdel's father. To commemorate this event, Bīdel composed this chronogram:[3]

عبـدالخالق بعـالم کسـب ادب   در لیل ز غایب آمد از قدرتِ رب
اقبال ازل شامل این تاریخ اسـت   آدینـه اوّل شـب شـهر رجـب

The son did not survive and passed away at the tender age of four in the morning of 9th Rabī'II, 1123 A.H./16th May, 1711 A.D. It naturally shattered Bīdel who composed the following chronogram

1. *Sarv-e Āzād*, p.150; *Khazāneh-e 'Āmereh*, p.153, give 3rd Ṣafar as the date of Bīdel's demise. But in *Gol-e Ra'na* (p.220) it is 4th of Ṣafar. Moreover, the same 4th Ṣafar has been recorded as the date of death of Bīdel in a manuscript of Bīdel's Robā'īs transcribed on 8th Rabī'I, 1133 A.H., Rieu, *Supplement*, p.212. Similarly, Khushgū, who was present at the time of Bīdel's death, has provided a detailed account of his passing away and Wārid also give Thursday, 4th Ṣafar as the date of Bīdel's demise. This date, therefore, be preferred to 3rd of Ṣafar.
2. *Safīna-e Khushgū*, p.109.
3. *Kolliyāt*, Kabul, Vol. II, p.169.

recording the date and year of this unfortunate mishap:[1]

عبدالخالق آه بدیر فانی   دیر آمد و زود کرد بال افشانی
زین مصرع تاریخ وداعش دریاب   صبح نهم از ماه ربیع‌الثّانی

Bīdel has also composed a touching elegy in *Mukhammas* form beginning with this stanza:

هیهات چه برق پرفشان رفت   کاشوب قیامتم بجان رفت
گرتابی بود در توان رفت   طفلم زین کهنه خاکدان رفت
بازی بازی بر آسمان رفت

Khushgū reports that Bīdel was a man of extraordinary physical strength. He was not tall statured but had broad shoulders. He consumed seven or eight Shāhjahānī seer of food in his youth and took two or three seer in his old age. He carried a short iron staff in his hand weighing thirty-six seers. It was not easy for others to lift it. Bīdel named this staff as Naulasi meaning a thin branch in Hindī. It was usually placed by the side of his grave on his *'Ors-Day.*

A painter Anup Chand made a portrait of Bīdel. Preserved in a book, it remained with Bīdel for ten years. He fell ill in 1100 A.H. and was under its spell for seven months. Incidentally someone opened this book and found the picture losing its glow. Bīdel and others present observed this phenomenon. Bīdel got worried, but he eventually recovered, and the picture also revived to its original glow.[2]

Bīdel, as referred to earlier, had close contacts with a number of Ṣūfīs like Shāh Kamāl, Shāh Molūk, Shāh Qāsim, and Shāh Kābulī from an early age. Moreover, because of his dedication to their system of life and thought, and also his excellent interpretation of the mysticism of Ibn-e 'Arabī, he was regarded as a great Ṣūfī of his time, comparable to the reputed Junaid of Baghdad (830-910 A.D.)

---

1. *Kolliyāt*, Kabul, p.169.
2. *Āwāzhāy-e Bīdel*, pp.616-617.

and Shiblī.[1] A treatise by Shiblī provided by Shāh Qāsim to Bīdel solved some problems in Ṣūfism faced by him.[2] It has rightly been said that in the long list of the Ṣūfī poets, nobody except Bīdel could expand his thought panorama since none of them could access those sources, particularly the Indian religious and philosophical storehouse, with the needed intellectual power or the required artistic talent. It, however, appears from his biography that he was not a practicing Ṣūfī. He neither established any Khāneqāh nor made any one his *Morīd* as usually is the case with Ṣūfīs.

As a great number of Bīdel's letters exhibit, he was a man of wide contacts. People from different walks of life were among his acquaintances. Rulers, nobles and men of different arts and crafts felt it an honour to be in the circle of his intimates. They used to come to his residence and Bīdel also seldom visited their houses. He wished to contact Aurangzīb 'Ālamgīr (1658-1707) but failed. Shokrullāh Khān, his three sons and also 'Āqil Khān Rāzī, Shokrullāh Khān's father-in-law once governor of Delhi, enjoyed the most cordial relations with Bīdel. Shākir Khān, a son of Shokrullāh Khān got some Jāgīr for him from the court of Aurangzīb from the Deccan, which was declined by Bīdel.[3] Niẓāmul Molk Āṣafjāh, the founder of Āṣafjāhī[4] dynasty in the Deccan, was proud of calling himself a pupil of Bīdel.[5] He even invited him to his court in the Deccan in 1720 A.D. but Bīdel declined the offer citing the reason:

---

1. Khushgū, p.115.
2. *Āwāzhāy-e Bīdel*, p.477.
3. *Roqqa'āt*, Kabul, p.139.
4. Mīr Qamruddīn (d. 1161/1748) received the title of Chīn Qalīch Khān from Aurangzīb, *Niẓām-ul Molk* from Farrukh Sīyar and Āṣafjāh from Moḥammad Shāh. He was one of the most important nobles of the later Mughals and a great patron of men of letters, and also a good poet himself with Āṣaf as his *Takhalluṣ*. (*Khazāneh-e 'Āmereh*, pp.35-38)
5. *Gol-e Ra'na*, p.219.

دنیا اگر دهند نخیزم ز جای خویش   من بسته‌ام حِنای قناعت به‌پای خویش

[I have applied *Ḥenā* (حِنا) of contentment on my feet, so I will not move out of my place even if the whole world is given to me.]

Bīdel also enjoyed good relations with the Syed brothers; Syed 'Abdullāh Khān and Syed Ḥusain 'Alī Khān (killed in 1132/1719), called the king makers. He was also in correspondence with them. When Farrukh Sīyar (1713-1719), the Mughal ruler with whom Bīdel had good relations and who once sent for him two thousand rupees and an elephant[1], was mercilessly killed by them in 1131/1719, Bīdel was disturbed. He could not refrain himself from criticizing them in this quatrain also reporting the year of this incident:[2]

دیدی که چه با شاه گرامی کردند   صد جور و جفا از رهِ خامی کردند
تاریخ چو از خرد بجستم، فرمود   «سادات بوی نمک‌حرامی کردند»

Bīdel, consequently, fearing some harsh response from these brothers, immediately left Delhi for Lahore where he was well received by Nawwāb Saifuddaulah 'Abduṣ Ṣamad Khān, the governor of that province from 1712 to 1726 A.D. After the elimination of these brothers by Moḥammad Shāh, Bīdel returned to Delhi after one and a half years in 1720 A.D. He was almost seventy-nine years old at this time. The same year he suffered from fever for four or five days and died on Thursday, the 4th of Ṣafar, 1133 A.H./24th November, 1720 A.D.

Later an *'Ors* ceremony was held regularly at his grave on his death anniversary and it turned out to be a great literary gathering

---

1. Khushgū, p.115.
2. Contrary to Bīdel, Mīr 'Aẓmatullāh Bīkhabar Bilgrāmī supports the Syed brother's action in this quatrain:

با شاه سقیم آنچه شاید کردند   از دست حکیم آنچه آید کردند
بقراط خرد نسخهٔ تاریخ نوشت   «سادات دواش آنچه باید کردند»

(*Sarv-e Āzād*, p.169)

in Delhi. This event was organized by Moḥammad Sa'īd, a son of Mīrzā 'Ibādullāh, the maternal uncle of Bīdel, who also used to herald the proceedings by reading out a *Ghazal* of Bīdel followed by the recitation of their poems by other poets of the capital. The poets regarded it a privilege to participate and read out their compositions in this annual *'Ors*.[1]

Dargāh Qulī Khān, an officer in the principality of Hyderabad, was in Delhi for almost four years from 1737 to 1741 A.D. He most probably visited the grave of Bīdel and found it in a well-adorned enclosure.[2] As he does not refer to the *Ḥavelī*, it means that after eight years of the demise of Bīdel, his *Ḥavelī* had probably disappeared. Dargāh Qulī Khān also details the 'Ors proceedings and confirms what Khushgū has recorded in this regard.[3] But he further adds:

Moḥammad Sa'īd, a nephew of Bīdel, is ignorant of the spiritual enlightenment of the Mīrzā. He keeps himself engaged in the arrangements for the hospitality of those who attend the *'Ors* as well as with the task of lighting the lamps. He sells alchemy like herbal concoctions the Mīrzā used to make. He also, thus, manages to eke out a livelihood for himself. The couplets of Bīdel are recited from a *Kolliyāt* transcribed by Bīdel. On the title page of this copy of *Kolliyāt* is transcribed the following quatrain:

ای آیینهٔ طبع تو ارشاد پذیر   در کسب فواید ننمایی تقصیر

مجموعهٔ فکرِ ما صلای عام است   سیری کن و قسمتِ تسلّی برگیر[٤]

[In spite of the overflowing virtues and piety of nature reflected on your face, you never fail to acquire more. Everyone is welcome to sift through the collection of

---

1. *Safīna-e Khushgū*, p.121-23; *Khazāneh-e 'Āmereh*, p.153.
2. *Moraqqa'-e Dehlī*, p.57.
3. *Safīna-e Khushgū*, pp.121-23.
4. *Moraqqa'-e Dehlī*, p.57.

thoughts (contained in Bīdel's works) and derive contentment from them.]

Sangīn Beg wrote *Sair-ul Manāzil*, a detailed topography of Delhi sometime in 1827 A.D. The *Ḥavelī* and the grave of Bīdel did not exist at that time. Still he was informed that the following inscription was inscribed on the grave of Bīdel outside Delhi Gate:

پیش از این گفت سعدیِ شیراز   بیدل از بی‌نشان چگوید باز[1]

From the above statement of Sangīn Beg it appears that both the *Ḥavelī* and the grave of Bīdel disappeared before 1827 A.D.

Khwāja Ḥasan Niżāmī, Sajjāda-Nashīn of Dargāh Khwāja Niżāmuddīn Aulia and a renowned Ṣūfī and writer of his time wrongly identified a grave in a graveyard in front of Exhibition Ground, New Delhi, as belonging to Bīdel. It was not in good shape. He, so, wrote to the fourth Niżām of Hyderabad for financial assistance to repair the grave of Bīdel who was the teacher of the Niżām-ul Molk Āṣafjāh[2], the founder of Āṣafjāhī dynasty of Hyderabad. The Niżām provided two thousand rupees for the repair work in 1359/1940. The following inscription in Urdu was also installed at the grave:[3]

"اس کی ضروری تعمیر و ترمیم اعلیٰ حضرت پرنور آصف جاہ رابع دکن کی توجہات شاہانہ سے ۱۳۵۹/۱۹۴۰ میں کرائی گئی"۔

---

1. *Sair-ul Manāzil*, p.119, the second hemistich of the couplet is from this verse of Sa'dī-e Shīrāzī:

   گر کسی وصفِ او ز من پرسد   بی‌دل از بی‌نشان چه گوید باز

   It was this verse of Sa'dī after reading of which Bīdel changed his nom-de-plume from «رمزی» (*Ramzī*) to "Bīdel".
2. Bīdel was in correspondence with the Niżām. Letters of Bīdel in response of this Niżām's correspondence are included in *Roqqa'āt-e Bīdel*. These letters loudly speak of the close and sincere relations between them.
3. A detailed and interesting note about this grave of Bīdel and its repair before the Independence of India is found in "Mīrzā 'Abdul Qādir-e Bīdel: Ḥayāt-o-Kārnāmey," Vol. II, pp.464-70.

[The required repairs were carried out with the royal assistance by the fourth Nižām of Deccan in 1359/1940.]

This inscription does not exist now.

The Ministry of Foreign Affairs, government of India, has a file on the construction of the current Bīdel tomb. Dr. T.C.A. Raghawan, the then-director general of the Indian Council for World Affairs in New Delhi, graciously furnished me with some declassified papers from this file. According to the archives, the central public works department constructed a canopy on the grave of Bīdel in 1955 for Rs. 6,000/- deposited by the Afghanistan Embassy in Delhi in June 1954. Later, a platform around the canopy and an approach road were built at the cost of Rs. 1,360/- furnished by the government of India.

With this historical narration of Bīdel's house and grave, it is interesting to note that a tomb of Bīdel has been built in the enclosure of an old graveyard having the grave of Malikyār Parrān[1] in front of Dargāh Matkey Shāh and Exhibition Ground on Mathura Road. It can simply be called a memorial of Bīdel.

Bīdel was a prolific writer. The constellation of his works has been accurately preserved. He has left voluminous works both in prose and verse now preserved in almost all the important collections around the world and which have been catalogued in this work. In view of his voluminous output and his original contribution especially to mystical thought, Bīdel may be reckoned as one of the greatest poets of Indo-Persian tradition. All his works are available in manuscripts and also published editions,

1. Shaikh Nūruddīn Malikyār Parrān, a disciple of Shaikh Dāneyāl, came to Delhi from Lar in the vicinity of Bukhara and settled down at a place in front of Khāneqāh-e Abu Bakr-e Ṭusī, now near Exhibition Ground, Mathura Road, New Delhi. He died on 18thJumāda'II, 680 (or 695 A.H.). (See *Ẕikr-e Jamī'-e Auliā-e Dehlī*, pp.19, 175.

demonstrating his popularity. It is worth noting that only fourteen years after the death of Bīdel in 1133 A.H., his pupil Bindrā Ban Dāss Khushgū, himself a celebrated poet and biographer, took the trouble of counting the lines in the works of his teacher and mentor in his *Safīna-e Khushgū* (completed in 1147 A.H./ 1734 A.D.) as under:

1. *Mathnavī-e 'Irfān*	:	11,000 couplets.
2. *Mathnavī-e Ṭelesm-e Ḥairat*	:	4,000 couplets.
3. *Mathnavī-e Ṭūr-e Ma'refat*	:	2,000 couplets.
4. *Mathnavī-e Moḥīṭ-e A'żam*	:	2,000 couplets.
5. *Tanbīh-ul Mohawwesīn*	:	1,000 couplets.
6. *Tarjī'-Band* following 'Irāqī's style	:	1,000 couplets.
7. *Qaṣīdas, Tarkīb-Bands* etc.	:	7,000 couplets.
8. *Robā'īs*	:	8,000 couplets.
9. *Hazliyāt* (pleasantries)	:	3,000 couplets.
10. *Ghazals*	:	50,000 couplets.
11. *Chahār 'Onṣor*[1]	:	18,000 couplets.

Nekāt and *Ruqqa'āt* are other works of Bīdel documented in this catalogue.

It is, however, a point to be noted that the number of couplets in different manuscripts and published editions of Bīdel's works differ with each other. This variation is more discernable in his *Dīwān* of *Ghazaliyāt* for the obvious reason that he continued to compose *Ghazals* till the last phase of his life and included them in the copy of the *Dīwān* in his possession. Thus, the copies of the

1. Lāla Shiv Ram Dāss Ḥayā (d. 1144/1731-32) wrote *Golgasht-e Bahār-e Eram* imitating *Chahār 'Onṣur* of his teacher. *Safīna-e Khushgū*, p.183. It is lost to posterity.

Dīwān prepared at different points of time and stages earlier, naturally remained devoid of these new additions. All these works have adequately been described and evaluated in this catalogue at their proper places. Therefore, such an attempt is not being undertaken here.

Bīdel's popularity in his own lifetime and afterwards can be gauged from the glowing tributes of his contemporaries and later critics to his literary achievements. Even Aurangzīb 'Ālamgīr, who was not as interested in poetry as his predecessors, had quoted Bīdel's couplets in his letters to Prince Mo'ażżam and Prince A'żam:

من نمی‌گویم زیان‌کن یا به‌فکر سود باش

ای ز فرصت بیخبر، در هرچه باشی زود باش

بترس از آهِ مظلومان که هنگام دعا کـردن

اجابت از در حق بهـر اسـتقبال مـی‌آیـد

Moreover, someone requested him for an increase in his emoluments. He rejected it quoting Bīdel's following verse:

حرص قانع نیست بیدل ورنه اسـباب جهـان

آنچه ما در کار داریم، اکثری در کار نیست[1]

A great number of research books and articles on his life and works in English, Persian, Russian and Urdu are again a convincing testimony to this effect. His thought content is particularly the focus of men of letters. The Tajik scholars regard his language as Central Asian Tajik and consider Bīdel as an innovator of Persian Tajik literature.

The actual extent of Bīdel's influence on Indo-Persian, Urdu, Afghan (Dari) and Tajik literature, however, is beyond measure and it seems to have increased with each succeeding generation of poets. Imitation of Bīdel in poetry in 18th century had become commonplace. Bīdel's influence continued to exert itself

1. *Safīna-e Khushgū*, p.115.

throughout the 19th and into the early 20th century. Ṣadruddīn 'Ainī, a celebrated Tajik poet, admired the classical Khorāsānian style. He wrote *Ghazals* in the style of Bīdel at the beginning of his literary career.

Apart from it, in Afghanistan Bīdel is still more appreciated than any other Persian poet. His influence persists as a vital pervasive force in village as well as urban literary circles. Branches of a cultic group each meet weekly to recite and discuss the verses and enjoy the philosophical and mystic discourses of Bīdel. In recognition of Bīdel's importance and relevance, the Islamic Republic of Iran has established Bīdel Foundation (بنیادِ بیدل). It holds international conferences(عرسِ بیدل) on Bīdel almost every year in Tehrān.

Mīrzā Asadullāh Khān Ghālib of Delhi, the most celebrated Indian poet of 19th century, began his poetic career imitating Bīdel and could not come out of Bīdel's charm and influence. He actually owed his literary career more to Bīdel than any other poet of the Indo-Persian tradition. Bīdel's influence on 'Allāma Moḥammad Iqbāl (1877-1937), another notable poet of India, and perhaps the last great Persian poet of our continent, is more intellectual than literary. It is mainly discernible in his philosophy of Ego (خودی) with its polar qualities, at once dynamic and traditional, assertive and contemplative.

'Allāma Iqbāl in his Stray References proudly admits his indebtedness to Bīdel along with Hegel, Goethe, Ghālib and Wordsworth. He elaborates: "The first two lead me into the 'inside' of things. The third and fourth taught me how to remain oriental in spirit and expression after having assimilated foreign ideals of poetry and the last saved from atheism in my student days."[1]

While making comparison between the concept of wonder (حیرت) of Plato and that of Bīdel, Iqbāl asserts:

---

1. *Stray References*, p.61.

Wonder, says Plato, is mother of all sciences. Bīdel looks at the emotion of wonder from a different stand point, says he:

نزاکت‌هاست در آغوش میناخانهٔ حیرت

مژه برهم مزن تا نشکنی رنگِ تماشـا را

To Plato wonder is valuable because it leads to our questioning of value, to Bīdel it has a value of its own irrespective of its intellectual consequences. It is impossible to express the idea more beautifully than Bīdel.[1]

This interest in Bīdel's works has not waned. It still continues unabated in the Persian speaking world. His own voluminous works are being critically edited, and research and critical works on them are being regularly published showing the interest of men of letters in his literary achievements. Apart from it, modern poets of Iran, Afghanistan and Tajikistan are still fondly following the style of Bīdel, and thus he serves as a model for them. The lingering popularity of Bīdel rests on the fact that he refined classical Persian and Indo-Persian poetry to suit the circumstances. One finds in him the culmination of various tendencies in Indo-Persian poetry.

His poetry is characterized by a restless effort to comprehend the enigma of existence. This quality lends it a dynamism as well as universalism. Bīdel turned his attention to the basic problems of human existence and channeled his poetic genius in the direction of discovering truth through inward contemplation.

Furthermore, Bīdel is widely adorned for various reasons. Not only because he stands out head and shoulders above the Persian poets, or for being very popular in the Persian-speaking world, but also for the simple reason that he had personalized Indian ethos. To some Bīdel's critics: "The philosophy of Bīdel is an intricate

---

1. *Ibid.*, p.66.

fusion of *Vedanta* and *Waḥdat-ul Wujūd*. The flow of ideas from the perennial rivers of *Avestha*, *Veda* and the *Qur'an* is clearly visible in the works of Bīdel." He has no dearth of vocabulary or even of ideas. He has his own diction and style of expression that certain critics consider to be sometimes so obscure that it is difficult to understand the meaning of verses. This is more noticeable and felt in his lyrical poetry, which necessitates a smooth flow. His unique ideas forced him to even coin new expressions that ultimately enriched Persian language and literature to a great extent. However, Bīdel's prominence as a composer of chronograms has so far not attracted the attention of those working critically on Bīdel's contribution to Persian literature. There are innumerable chronograms composed by Bīdel recording various events – historical, social, etc. These chronograms also throw light on his close contacts with a large number of people of his time. Some of them are not known personalities, although they were likely eminent in their spheres then and came in contact with Bīdel.

Bīdel's message of universal fraternity absorbs his readers. It was his conviction that there is no difference among the human beings. It is only in appearance, otherwise their blood (DNA) is the same. In truth it speaks loudly of Bīdel's compassionate humanism:

اختلافِ وضع بیدل در لباس افتاده است

ورنه یک رنگ است خون در پیکر طاؤس و زاغ

[Difference is in attire, otherwise blood is the same in the body of a peacock and a crow.]

Bīdel was able to build bridges of understanding between the followers of particularly the two religions – Hindu and Islam. Following the footsteps of their teacher, a large number of his non-Muslim disciples endeavoured to spread the same message.

The history of Persian language and literature constitutes an important and integral segment of the composite culture in India. Persian language, literature and culture have profoundly influenced the Indian life, and letters, art and architecture, religion and philosophy, etiquette and society as a whole. Similarly, modern scholars have traced and identified the influence of Indian religious, cultural and philosophical traditions on the Persian works of Indian scholars and poets. The same is the case with Mīrzā 'Abdul Qādir-e Bīdel. He actually demonstrated in his works the vigour exceptionally possessed by great intellects. "His poetry embraced all the ideas which human imagination has been able to grasp ever since the earliest reciters of the Vedas chanted their pious lines in praise of the Transcendental Reality."[1] He studied Mahabharata, a copy of which was in his collection. It was obviously in Persian. He also went through Yogavasishtha. Bīdel has drawn some of his material in his *Mathnavī* entitled *'Irfān* from this great Hindu philosophical work and so "the global plan of the narrative in *'Irfān* follows the Aindavopakhyana, comprising the chapters 85 to 103 in Utpattipra Karama, the third section of the Yogavasishtha. Briefly, the Aindavopakhyana starts with the story of ten children of a Brahman who become creators of ten different worlds. Each one of these worlds, of course, has a Sun and one Sun narrates the story. Bīdel also has this story of ten children of a Brahman, ten worlds and the Sun. Furthermore, a Sanskrit play Malatimadhava by Bhavabhuti of eighth century has been very popular in the vernacular literature. Its folk version as the story of Madhavanal and Kamakandla has been written a dozen times in medieval Hindi. Nāṣir 'Alī Sirhindi, a Bīdel's senior contemporary also wrote a *Mathnavī* describing this story. Bīdel also integrates it into *'Irfān* as the story of Kamadi and Madan, but

1. *Dictionary of Indo-Persian Literature*; Nabi Hadi, Indira Gandhi National Centre for the Arts, New Delhi, 1995, pp.129-30.

Bīdel has transformed it into a philosophical opus that cannot be matched by anybody except perhaps the original writer.[1] Bīdel was so immersed in the Indian cultural traditions that as Khushgū narrates, he got all his works transcribed in his life time in four columns on every page. Its weight was fourteen seers of the time. He distributed metals (coins) and ornaments studded with jewels of the same weight among the poor and remarked that Indians weigh their children and give away the proceeds in alms, "I do not have any child and so my works are my creations (progeny) I have done so for the survival of them."

A close assessment of all that Bīdel wrote not only in the *Mathnavī-e 'Irfān*, reveals that whatever novelty or difficulty is found in him, all that makes him so attractive and at the same time so incomprehensible, can be sourced to his direct familiarity with the facts and deep knowledge of the classical Indian thought. In *'Irfān* he has summed up:

خـط ترسـا و اختـراع هنـود همچنان تاب گیسوی مقصـود

[The left to right script and the creativity of the Hindus constitute complex systems just like the curls of the intended.]

Again he says:

همـه اشـکال راز سـربر هنـد همه مشـتاق جنبش نگـه‌انـد

[All the letters of the alphabets are altitudes of the history of India. They all demand a movement (upwards) of the eye.]

Similarly, in a couplet he refers to his traversing all the paths of intellectual domains:

خواب بیداریی که مـا داریـم بر همان جـاده سـیرها داریـم

---

1. Mīrzā Bīdel's 'Irfān and Yogavasishtha; an article by Wagish Shukla included in 'Mīrzā 'Abdul Qādir-e Bīdel,' edited by Prof. Qamar Ghaffar, Jāmia Millia Islāmīa, New Delhi, 2017, pp.115-24.

[The sleep of awakening that I have got, it is because I have toured on all the path ways.]

Intelligent and scholarly attempts, as stated above, have been made to establish the influence of Indian religions and philosophy or classical Indian knowledge on Bīdel. Besides, he himself refers to his roaming around the Brindraban region, taking a dip in the river Jamunā and sometimes being awestricken to the point of fever.[1] His quest for truth led him to hold discussions with people of different faiths, especially Brahmans. He chanced to meet Ṣūfīs, saints, Yogis and Sadhus in the course of his wide travels.

A Brahman accompanies Bīdel on his way to Ḥasan Abdāl. Bīdel had discussions with him on various issues related to mysticism and philosophy.[2] He had even attempted to compare non-Muslim ideologies with Islamic thinking,[3] thus trying to evolve a compromise particularly between Hindu and Muslim ways of life.

Today, the study of Persian language and literature is indispensable for researches in and understanding of India's past, its life and society. Furthermore, it serves as a basis for us to maintain long-standing contacts with our friendly neighbours – Afghanistan and Iran, and also the rest of Persian world – Tajikistan, Uzbekistan, Azerbaijan, and Turkmenistan. In this case, Bīdel is the epitome of Indo-Persian, Indo-Afghan and Indo-Tajik literature.

For various reasons, I have not been able to visit numerous personal collections spread throughout India to collect the relevant data. Similarly, despite my best attempts, it should also be honestly stated here that I could not consult all published catalogues of the libraries abroad most probably because of their non-availability in India. Hence this "A Master Catalogue of the

1. *Kolliyāt*, Vol. IV, p.41; *Āwāzhāy-e Bīdel*, pp.379-80.
2. *Chahār 'Onṣur* in *Kolliyāt*, Kabul, p.377.
3. *Kolliyāt*, Vol. IV, p.280.

Manuscripts and Published Editions of Bīdel's Works" is not an exhaustive work of its kind. However, the numbers of all the works of Bīdel in manuscript form and published editions in different Indian and foreign collections traced in this catalogue are as follows:

Kolliyāt: 18, *Dīwān*: 323, *Intekhāb-e Dīwān* (Selection of *Dīwān*): 18, *Bayāẓ* in which selections from Bīdel's poetry have been made: 105, *Robā'īs*: 20, *Mathnavī-e Moḥīṭ-e A'żam*: 41, *Mathnavī-e Ṭelesm-e Ḥairat*: 25, *Mathnavī-e Ṭūr-e Ma'refat*: 14, *Mathnavī-e 'Irfān*: 28, *Chahār 'Onṣur*: 65, *Roqqa'āt*: 85, *Nekāt*: 52.

Apart from these manuscripts of Bīdel's works, their published editions recorded in this catalogue are as follows:

Kolliyāt: 8, *Dīwān*: 73, *Roqqa'āt*: 7, *Robā'īyāt*: 5, *Nekāt*: 4, *Chahār 'Onṣur*: 2, *Moḥīṭ-e A'żam*: 2, *'Irfān*: 1.

Additionally, 67 published books in Persian, English and Urdu written on the life and works of Bīdel have been recorded in this catalogue. Similarly, I was able to trace 61 important research articles written on various aspects of Bīdel's life and works. In the light of this documentation, it can humbly be claimed that it is not an insignificant achievement.

On the basis of this detail, it can be concluded that *Dīwān* of Bīdel (*Ghazaliyāt*) had been more popular and celebrated. Similarly, 105 Bayāẓ (Selection from different poets by the interested men of letters for their personal use) having selections from Bīdel's poetry further corroborate the above statement. Moreover, this catalogue also leads us to realize that the *Dīwān* of Bīdel and its selections were repeatedly published more from Tajikistan, indicating its widespread appeal and popularity in that region more than anywhere else.

The method adopted in this master catalogue for documenting the works of Bīdel is similar to that devised by the reputed cataloguers like Hermann Ethe in his Catalogue of the Persian Manuscripts in the India Office Library, Charles Rieu in his Catalogue of the Persian Manuscripts in the British Museum and Maulavī 'Abdul Muqtadir in his Catalogue of the Persian and Arabic Manuscripts in the Khodā Bakhsh Oriental Public Library, Patna. Following these authorities, the information about the manuscripts has been arranged in the following manner:

> Name of the Manuscript, script, number of folio/pages, name of the scribe, date and place of transcription if recorded, any other important information about the manuscript.

Dr. T.C.A. Raghawan has distinctly served as an Indian envoy to Singapore and Pakistan. His works: Attendant Lords Bairam Khān and 'Abdur Raḥīm Khān, Courtiers and Poets in Mughal India and also The People Next Door: The Curious History of India's Relations with Pakistan have been well received. He was the Director of Indian Council of World Affairs, New Delhi. His scholarly instinct urged and encouraged me to undertake this project. He had the opportunity to interact with the delegations particularly from Persian speaking world while serving in our ministry of foreign affairs. As he once told me, a number of the high ranking members from these delegations enquired about the location of the Tomb of Mīrzā 'Abdul Qādir-e Bīdel in Delhi. Moreover, he came across a file in the archives of the said ministry regarding the construction of the existing structure called *Mazār-e Bīdel* in *Bāgh-e Bīdel* in front of Exhibition Ground on Mathura Road, New Delhi. Some declassified documents from this file, were kindly provided to me by Dr. Raghawan for reference. Consequently, he realized the fact that Bīdel had been a delineator of Indo-Central Asian, Afghanistan and Iran cultural and historical relations, as well as the importance and relevance of Bīdel in the present-day Persian speaking world and also the everlasting role this son of India can still play in further strengthening our cultural bonds with this significant part of the globe. The present catalogue, as Dr. Raghawan has envisaged, may accomplish this noble task. I am sincerely grateful to Dr. Raghawan for the wholehearted support he extended to me in getting this project approved by the Indian Council of World Affairs. I wish to express my deep sense of gratitude to Janab Ambassador Vijay Thakur Singh, director general ICWA for his unwavering assistance to get this catalogue accepted and published by ICWA. My thanks are also due to Dr. Nivedita Ray, an experienced Director of Research, for guidance and help in accomplishing this project.

I am thankful to all the librarians and directors of the collections who had extended facilities to me to consult their repositories to collect the required data.

Mr. Abdur Rehman Qureshi, Arsons Computer Text, Delhi, deserves my gratitude for his dedicated endeavours in page-setting this catalogue.

Presently, when we are trying to build, expand and consolidate our relations with Afghanistan, Iran and Central Asia, jewels of our common cultural heritage, like Bīdel, require in-depth study. This catalogue will inspire the academic community in India andbeyondto collaborate to shed light on our common past and evolve a shared understanding of its different aspects.

Prof. Sharif Husain Qasemi
D-23, Hzt. Nizamuddin East
New Delhi-110013
Mobile: 9871702648.

Chapter I

Manuscripts of Kolliyāt-e Bīdel (Dated)

Bindrā Ban Dāss Khushgū, a pupil of Bīdel, has given the total number of the verses in the *Kolliyāt* as ninety nine thousand (excluding those he certainly would have composed later that were not included in the edition with Khushgū). It includes all the works of Bīdel in poetry and prose. Bīdel has got it transcribed in his lifetime in four columns on every page. Its weight was fourteen sears of the time. He also distributed metals and ornaments studded with jewels of the same weight among the poor. In this regard he remarked that Indians weigh their children and give away the proceeds in alms. "I do not have any child and my works are my creations. I have done so for the survival of them (Khushgū)." It should be stated here that his prayer was answered, as all of his works have survived till date, both in manuscript form and in printed editions.

*

«1»

Khodā Bakhsh, No. 381

Nasta'līq, fol.515, Moḥammad Wārith b. Moḥammad Bāqer Ṣiddīqī, 7th Moḥarram, 1136 A.H./[26th September, 1723 A.D.].
Complete prose and poetical works of Bīdel. Moḥammad Wārith has copied a number of works of Bīdel and so he was probably the personal copyist of Bīdel.

It contains:

1) *Chahār 'Onṣor*:
   Beginning:

   خداوندا زبان معذور هرصرفه‌سرایی است عذر هرزه درایان بپذیر...

   Ending: Two chronograms for its completion:

   نخست افسونی از اعجاز پرداخت   که از افراد هـر عنصـر فنـا رفـت
   دوّم در اجتمـــاع چـــار عنصـــر   نحوست بود چون زنگ از صفا رفت

   Its transcription was completed on 9th Ẕilḥijja, 1134 A.H./[9th September, 1722 A.D.] by Moḥammad Wārith b. Moḥammad Bāqer Ṣiddīqī, the personal scribe of Bīdel.
   Colophon:

   نهم شهرِ ذیحجّه سنهٔ ۱۱۳۴ یکهزار و یکصد و سی و چهار هجری بخطِّ اعجزالعباد محمّد وارث بن محمّد باقر الصدّیقی به‌اتمام رسید.

2) *Roqqa'āt-e Bīdel*(رقّعاتِ بیدل):
   Beginning:

   عجز مراتب حمد و ثنا تسلیم بارگاهِ صمدی...

3) *Dīwān*(دیوان):
   Preface to the old or the first *Dīwān*:
   Beginning:

   حمد مبدعی که تردّد انفاس هستی موجودات تحریکی است...

   This copy contains *Qaṣīdas*, *Qiṭ'as*, *Robā'īs* etc. without any alphabetical order:
   First *Qaṣīda* begins thus:

بنـــام آن صـــمد بیچگونـــهٔ یکتـــا   که کردکون و مکان را بحرف کن پیـدا

Mathnavī-e Tanbīh-ul Mohawwesīn (تنبیه‌المهوّسین):
Beginning:

ای مهوّس در هوای کیمیا...

Robā'īyāt-e Hazl (رباعیّاتِ هزل):
Beginning:

یاران در زندگی ز هرچیز رسا...

Ghazaliyāt (غزلیات) in alphabetical order:
Beginning:

به‌اوج کبریا کز پهلوی عجز است راه آنجا...

«2»

Khodā Bakhsh, No. 382

This copy is the continuation of the copy of the Ms. (No. 381) recorded above.

Fair *Nasta'līq*, fol.337, Moḥammad Wārith b. Moḥammad Bāqer Ṣiddīqī, 1136 A.H./[1724 A.D.].

It consists:

1) *Robā'īyāt* (رباعیّات) in alphabetical order:
   Beginning:

   آنکس که منزه است از آب و گل ما...

   Its transcription was completed in Sha'bān, 1136 A.H./[April, 1724 A.D.].
2) *Ṭūr-e Ma'refat* (طور معرفت):

   طپش فرسوده شوق ناله تمثال   ز تحریک نفس وا می‌کند بـال

   This *Mathnavī* was transcribed in Ẕilḥijja, 1136 A.H./[August, 1724 A.D.].
3) *Moḥīṭ-e A'żam*(محیطِ اعظم):
   Beginning with a prose preface:

   حمد نشاء آفرینی که میخانهٔ حقیقت انسانی را از نشاء کرمنا بنی‌آدم علوّ مفاخرت ظهور بخشید...

It is dated Shawwāl, 1136 A.H./[June, 1724 A.D.].

4) *Ṭelesm-e Ḥairat*(طلسمِ حیرت):

Beginning:

بهنام آن که دل کاشانهٔ اوست   نفس کرده متاعِ خانـهٔ اوسـت

5) 'Irfān (عرفان):

Beginning:

عشق از مشت خاک آدم ریخت   آنقدر خون که رنگ عالم ریخـت

Dated Jumāda'II, 1136 A.H./[February, 1724 A.D.].

«3»

N. Archives, Afghanistan, No. 7/132.

Nasta'līq, fol.108, Moḥammad Yūnos, 1147 A.H./[1734 A.D.].

«4»

N. Archives, Afghanistan, No. 35/123.

Nasta'līq, fol.522, 1222 A.H./[1807 A.D.].

«5»

N. Archives, Afghanistan, No. 4/113.

Nasta'līq, fol.560, 'Abdur Reḥmān, 1234 A.H./[1819 A.D.].

«6»

N. Archives, Afghanistan, No. 14/39.

Nasta'līq, fol.418, A'żam, 1236 A.H./[1821 A.D.].

«7»

N. Archives, Afghanistan, No. 10/148.

Nasta'līq, fol.237, Mīr Moḥammad, 1248 A.H./[1832 A.D.].

«8»

N. Archives, Afghanistan, No. 22/52.

Nasta'līq, fol.1058, Moḥammad Qāsim, 1252 A.H./[1836 A.D.].

«9»

N. Archives, Afghanistan, No. 16/94.

Nasta'līq, fol.1140, Moḥammad 'Azīz, 1267 A.H./[1851 A.D.].

«10»

N. Archives, Afghanistan, No. 10/149.

Nasta'līq, fol.985, Mīr Moḥammad, 1270 A.H./[1854 A.D.].

«11»

N. Archives, Afghanistan, No. 12/66.

Nasta'līq, fol.562, Mīr Moḥammad, 1272 A.H./[1856 A.D.].

«12»

N. Archives, Afghanistan, No. 4/127.

Nasta'līq, fol.98, Ṣafdar 'Alī, 1283 A.H./[1866 A.D.].

«13»

N. Archives, Afghanistan, No. 11/147.

Nasta'līq, fol.555, Gholām Ḥusain, 1309 A.H./[1891 A.D.].

«14»

N. Archives, Afghanistan, No. 1200

Nasta'līq, 1330 A.H./[1912 A.D.].

«15»

N. Archives, Afghanistan, No. 22/44.

Nasta'līq, fol.745, Amīn Moḥammad, 1392 A.H./[1972 A.D.].

Manuscripts of Kolliyāt-e Bīdel (Undated)

«1»

Majlis-e Shorā-e Millī, Tehran, No.1355.

Contains: *Ghazaliyāt*, *Robā'īyāt*, *Chahār 'Onṣor* in 2675 *Bait* «بيت» and *Nekāt*.

Nasta'līq, fol.526, Moḥammad 'Ālam b. Ākhund Mollā Moḥammad Yousof Nawgānvī.

«2»

Tonk, Rajasthan No.4693.

Majmū'a-e Dīwān-e Bīdel

Nasta'līq, p.742.

«3»

Research Library, Kashmīr University, Srinagar, No. 2494.

No details about it are provided by the cataloguer.

Chapter II

Manuscripts of Dīwān-e Bīdel (Dated)

Bīdel is primarily a *Ghazal*-writer. His *Dīwān*, mostly containing *Ghazals*, was published from Inteshārāt-e Sanā'ī, Tehran, Iran, in 1386 H.S./[2008 A.D.] and edited by Moḥsin Āthārjūi in two volumes with 2,870 *Ghazals*. Manuscripts and printed editions of Bīdel's *Ghazals*, in the libraries around the world, particularly Tajikistan, are more in number than the manuscripts of his other works. It indicates the popularity of his *Ghazals* in the literary circles. Similarly, a good number of available selections of Bīdel's *Ghazals* also confirm the above statement.

Bīdel had himself transcribed his *Dīwān*, Ms. of which is in possession of the librarian of Karachi University Library, Pakistan (*Dānishnāmeh-e Adab-e Fārsī*, Dr. Ḥassan Anūsheh, *Sāzmān-e Chāp-o-Inteshārāt-e Wizārat-e Farhang-o-Irshādāt-e Islāmī*, Tehran, Iran, 1378 H.S./[1999 A.D.], entry on Bīdel). I contacted Prof. 'Arif Naushāhī, a prominent Persian scholar of Pakistan, who has prepared a number of catalogues of Persian manuscripts in Pakistan, to confirm this statement in the said *Dānishnāma*. He termed it as incorrect.

Some of the selections of *Ghazals* were made by Bīdel himself at the request of his friends. A number of such selections have feature additions in Bīdel's hand that add to their authenticity.

*

«1»

Sālār, No. A.N./161
Mukhammas

It is included in a *Majmū'a* on one page.

Excellent *Shafī'ā*, fol.1, Moḥammad Mehdī Iṣfahānī, 14th Ramaẓān, 1086 A.H./22nd November, 1675 A.D., gold-sprinkled paper, gold-ruled borders. It was transcribed nearly forty-seven years before the death of Bīdel (1133 A.H./1720 A.D.).

«2»

Ḥabībganj, M.A. Library, AMU, Aligarh, No. 5513/2:1
***Guzīda'ī Az Dīwān* (Selection from the *Dīwān*)**

Shafī'ā, p.180, Wednesday, 4th Shawwāl, 1098 A.H./[3rd August, 1687 A.D.], Narnol, beautiful gold-ruled borders.

Beginning:

نفس آشفته می‌دارد چو گـل جمعیـت مـا را

پریشان می‌نویسد کلک موجِ احـوالِ دریـا را

This is an important Ms. as it was presented to Bīdel by his pupil Ānand Rām Mukhliṣ for his comments. Its date of transcription, i.e. 1098 A.H., indicates that it was completed thirty-five years before his death (1133 A.H./1720 A.D.) and was seen by him as recorded in the following notes in the Ms:

روزِ چهارشنبه، چهارم شوّال سنهٔ یکهزار و نود و هشت، در مقام نارنول به‌تحریر رسید. این اشعار از دیوانِ قدیم و جدید به‌طریق اختصار نوشت تا برای نسخه برداشتنِ دوستان را عذر کاهلی نباشد، والسّلام.

It has the following note indicating that Bīdel had seen it:

دستخط حضرت بیدل علیه‌الرحمه فقیر آنند رام مخلص از نظر میرزا صاحب گذرانده، این معنی به‌صحت رسانیده.

It has the following seal of *Mukhliṣ*:

آنند رام فدوی محمّد شاه عالم غازی.

«3»

Sālār, No. A./Nm.270

Ordinary *Nasta'līq*, fol.226, Moḥammad Zāhid, 9th Ramaẓān,

1106 A.H./13th March, 1695 A.D., 30th Jolūs which appears incorrect, worm holes.
Containing *Ghazals* and a few *Mukhammasāt* after the *Robā'īs*.
Beginning: as usual.
Ending:

اینجا کل جمعیت خلق است فشـردن ......

هرقطره کزین بحـر گهـردار برآمـد دل گشـت وکـران شـد

«4»

Ethe, No. 1676

Distinct *Nasta'līq*, fol.338, Khwāja Bāber Qalandar Qādirī, Shahjahanabad, at the request of Mīrzā Sa'īd, 15th Ẕilḥijja, 1106 A.H./ [17th July, 1695 A.D], i.e. twenty-seven years before the poet's death in 1133 A.H./[1720 A.D.]. In the colophon it is named as *Dīwān-e Qādir Mīrzā Bīdel*. The copy has a preface in prose.
Beginning:

حمد مبدعی که تردد انفاس هستی موجودات تحریکی است...

Ghazals are in alphabetical order.
Beginning:

نفس آشفته می‌دارد چو گل جمعیت ما را

پریشان می‌نویسد کلک موج احوال دریا را

Some *Qaṣīdas*:
Beginning:

در حریم خاک ما را موی پیری رهبر است...

Robā'īs in alphabetical order.
Beginning:

حمد دو جهان سزاست سبحانی را...

«5»

Ganj Bakhsh, Islamabad, No. 1497, Monzavī 8, 1024

Shikesta-Nasta'līq, p.852, Ramaẓān, 1108 A.H./[March, 1697 A.D.], Shahjahanabad, preface in prose:

حمد مبدعی که تردّد انفاس اعیان کیف...

«6»

Sālār, No. A./Nm.731

Good *Nasta'līq*, fol.159, 1109 A.H./1698 A.D., transcribed during poet's lifetime, contains part of his *Dīwān*.

1) *Terkībāt*:
Beginning:
بنـــام آن صـــمد بیچگونـــه و یکتـــا   که کرد کون و مکان را بحرف کن پیـدا

2) *Terjī'āt*:
Beginning:
مـــا حریفـــان بـــزم اســـراریم   مست جـام شـهود و دیـداریم

This *Tarjī'* has been transcribed separately several times under the title of *Mā Ḥarīfān* (ما حریفان).

3) *Qaṣa'īd*:
Beginning:
در حریم خاک ما را موی پیری رهبر اسـت
جامۀ احرام مرگ شعله با خاکسـتر اسـت

4) *Ghazals* in alphabetical order:
Beginning:
ای بهارسـتان اقبـال ای چمـن سـیما بیـا
فصل سیرِ دل گذشت اکنون بچشم مـا بیـا

5) *Qiṭ'āt*:
Beginning:
تو آن رفیع جنابی که مرغ ناطقـه را   باوج مدحت تو بال و پر فروریـزد

6) *Robā'īyāt*:
Beginning:
ای خلق ز جام کرمت مست دعـا   انفاس جهانی ز تو پا بسـت دعـا

7) *Mathnavī Tanbīh-ul Mohawwesīn* (تنبیه‌المهوّسین):
ای مهـــوس در هـــوای کیمیـــا   می‌طپد فیضِ تو چو زنبیـق چـرا

Ending:
ز طرفـــه نگـــاه کـــه داری پیـــام   کز آب تو خون می‌چکد والسّلام

«7»

Punjab University, Lahore, No. 1525 pp/VI 46A, Monzavī 8, 1024

Containing *Qaṣīdas*.

Nasta'līq, fol.65, 1109 A.H./[1698 A.D.].

Beginning:

بنـــام آن صـــمد بیچگونـــه و یکتـــا که کرد کون و مکان را بحرف کن پیدا

«8»

Chawk Naṣīr Khān, Peshawar, Monzavī 8, 1024

Containing *Ghazals*, *Robā'īs* and *Qiṭ'āt*.

Nasta'līq, p.144, Thursday, 1st Ṣafar, 1117 A.H./[14th May, 1705 A.D.].

«9»

University, No. 25 Fārsiya 1

Naskh, fol.721, Moḥammad Wārith Ṣiddīqī, 1126 A.H./[1714 A.D.].

Moḥammad Wārith Ṣiddīqī, as stated earlier, was probably the personal scribe of Bīdel. He has transcribed a number of works of Bīdel as would be observed in this catalogue. It is an important Ms. with the following note on the first page indicating that it was given to the owner (probably to Ānand Rām Mukhliṣ) by Bīdel in 1132 A.H./1720 A.D. (a year before his death).

دیوان میرزا بیدل، دیوان، مسوده‌های غزلیّات قدیم و جدید تا دوازدهم شهر صفر ۱۱۳۰ سنهٔ یکهزار و یکصد و سی هجری [چهارم ژانویهٔ ۱۷۱۸] بتحریر رسید العاقبه التوفیه.

این دیوان را از راه فضلی میرزا صاحب و قبله در سنهٔ یکهزار و یکصد و سی و دو هجری [۱۱۳۲ هـ/۱۷۲۰ م] به‌بنده عنایت فرمودند.

There is also a seal not readable on the margin; Bīdel has written some *Ghazals* with his own hand with«الراقمه».

Ending with a *Tarjī'*:

تو ز خود نرفته آنقدر که ترا تصوّر او کنی.

Colophon:

چهاردهم شهر رمضان‌المبارک ۱۱۲۶ هجری [دوازدهم سپتامبر ۱۷۱۴ م] مبارک بخط اقل‌العباد محمّد وارث الصدّیقی به‌اتمام رسید احمدلله علی ذالک.

This note is again important recording the date of Bīdel's death:

در سنهٔ یکهزار و یکصد و سی و سه هجری [۱۱۳۲ ه/۱۷۲۰ م] مرزا صاحب و قبله مرزا عبدالقادر بیدل از سرای فانی به‌دارالبقا شتافت.

«10»

Rampur, No. 3066M

Nasta'līq, fol.124, Raḥīmollāh, 1127 A.H./[1715 A.D.].

«11»

Rampur, No. 1207 (3656)

Nasta'līq, fol.845, 1131 A.H./[1719 A.D.].

This beautiful copy was presented by Bīdel to his pupil Bindrā Ban Dāss Khushgū. It was reproduced in facsimile from *Kār Āfrīnān-e Farhang-o-Honar* (کار آفرینانِ فرهنگ و هنر), Tehran, Iran in 1388 H.S. (2009 .A.D.). (See "Published Works of Bīdel for detail)

«12»

Khodā Bakhsh, No. 381

***Dīwān Included in the Kolliyāt* (No. 381)**

Nasta'līq, fol.515, Moḥammad Wārith b. Moḥammad Bāqer Ṣiddīqī, 7th Moḥarram, 1136 A.H./[26th September, 1723 A.D.].

Beginning:

حمد مبدعی که تردّد انفاس هستی موجودات تحریکی است...

This *Dīwān* contains:

Qaṣīdas, *Qiṭ'āt* and *Robā'īs*, etc., without any alphabetical order.

1) First *Qaṣīda* begins thus:

بنـــام آن صـــمد بیچگونـــه و یکتـــا   که کرد کون و مکان را بحرف کن پیدا

2) *Mathnavī Tanbīh-ul Mohawwesīn* (تنبیه‌المهوّسین):

Beginning:

ای مهوّس در هوای کیمیا...

3) *Robā'īyāt-e Hazl* (رباعیاتِ هزل):
   Beginning:

یاران در زندگی ز هرچیز رسا...

4) *Ghazals*(غزلیّات) in alphabetical order:
   Beginning:

به‌اوج کبریا کز پهلوی عجز است راه آنجا...

«13»

ASB, No. 836

Shikesta-Nasta'līq, fol.123, 'Abdul Mū'min b. Moḥammad Taqī b. Moḥammad Fāẓil, 1141 A.H./[1728 A.D.].

Containing chiefly *Ghazals* in alphabetical order and a number of *Robā'īs* at the end.

Beginning:

نفس آشفته می‌دارد چو گـل جمعیـت مـا را

پریشان می‌نویسد کلک موج احـوال دریـا را

Quatrains beginning:

آندم که حقیقت عدم پیدا شد...

«14»

Maktaba Ḥabībīya, Dera Isma'il Khan, Monzavī 8, 1024

Nasta'līq, p.468, 1142 A.H./[1729 A.D.].

Beginning:

به‌اوج کبریا کز پهلوی عجزست راه آنجا...

«15»

Bahlwal, 'Abdul Laṭīf, Sargodha, Monzavī 8, 1024

Nasta'līq, Amīn Afghān Samarqandī, Khushab, Sha'bān, 1149 A.H./[December, 1736 A.D.].

Beginning:

به‌اوج کبریا کز پهلوی عجزست راه آنجا...

«16»

Madras, No. 10.

Shikesta-Nasta'līq, fol.184, Moḥammad Ismā'īl, 14th Rabī'I, 1151 A.H./

21st June, 1738 A.D., worm eaten.
Robā'īyāt in the end.
Beginning:

گداز گوهردل بادهٔ ناب است نسیم را　　نم خم تحیّر عالم آب است شـبنم را

Ending:

کـــه بـــود بـــزم خیـــال　　بـــی‌طـــاقتی آه نمایـــد پامـــال

جوشش هرحبابـدر جنـبشِ مـوج　　پیداســت شکســت بیضـــه از...

This couplet of Bīdel is written on a flyleaf:

در راهِ توهرچــه از غبــارم　　برداشت فلک کفِ دعا بود

«17»

Public Library, Khairpur, Monzavī 8, 1024
Nasta'līq, p.56, Daulat Rāi, 1151 A.H./[1738 A.D.].
Beginning:

بخیال چشم که می‌زند قدح جنـون دلتنـگِ مـا

که هزار میکده می‌دهد برکاب گردش رنگِ مـا

«18»

Kitābkhāna-e Majlis-e Shorā, Tehran, No. 8725
Contains *Mathnavī-e Moḥīṭ-e A'żam*, *Ghazals* and *Robā'īyāt*.
Nasta'līq, fol.208, Mīr Muqīm, 1152 A.H./[1739 A.D.].

«19»

Rāja Meḥmūdābād Library, Lucknow, No. 147
Shikesta-Nasta'līq, p.118, Moḥammad Kamāl, 1161 A.H./[1748 A.D.], worm eaten.
Beginning:

حمد مبدعی که تردّد انفاس هستی موجوداتِ تحریکیست از سر انگشت ارادتِ او...
(از دیباچه بر کلیّات).

Ending:

صبحی که بهار ساز گل خواهد بـود　　بلبل همه حرف بار گل خواهد بـود

«20»

Kitābkhāna-e Āstān-e Quds-e Reẓavī, Mashhad, No. 24539

Shikesta-Nasta'līq, Moḥammad Kamāl, 1162 A.H./[1749 A.D.].

Beginning:

حمد مبدعی که تردد انفاس هستی...

Ending from colophon:

... رازِ دل کاتب به‌زبان قلم است... محمّد کمال...

«21»

Anjuman Taraqqī-e Urdū, Karachi, Monzavī 8, 1024

Contains 4218 couplets.

Nasta'līq, p.216, 12th Ramaẓān, 1165 A.H./[June, 1752 A.D.].

«22»

Punjab Public Library, Lahore, Monzavī 8, 1024

Containing *Ghazals*.

Shikesta, p.37, 1179 A.H./[1765 A.D.], an incomplete from the end.

Beginning:

نفس آشفته می‌دارد چو گل جمعیت ما را...

«23»

Khodā Bakhsh, No. 384

Fair *Nasta'līq*, fol.125, Jān Moḥammad, Ẕīqa'da 1180 A.H./[April, 1767 A.D.], coloured borders.

Beginning:

غیر وحدت برنتابد همّت عرفانِ ما...

Robā'īyāt beginning:

بیدل چشمت بشور امکان مکشا...

This copy is signed by Sir Gore Ousley.

«24»

Punjab University, Lahore, No. 3700 Spi/VI 103A, Monzavī 8, 1024

Nasta'līq, Moḥammad Ashraf resident of Thatta, 18th Jumāda'II, 1182 A.H./[30th October, 1768 A.D.].

«25»

Punjab University Library, Lahore, No. 170, Spi/VI 103A, Monzavī 8, 1024

Containing *Ghazals* and *Robā'īs*.
Nasta'līq, fol.148, Moḥammad Ashraf, 1184 A.H./[1770 A.D.].
Beginning:

نفس آشفته می‌دارد چو گـل جمعیـت مـا را

پریشان می‌نویسد کلک موجِ احـوالِ دریـا را

«26»

University, No. 118(1)

Beautiful *Nasta'līq*, fol.83, 7th Ṣafar, 1190 A.H./[28th March, 1776 A.D.].
Beginning:

غمخوار دل سوختگان گرمی شوقی اسـت

جز شـعله نسـوزد جگـر کـس بسـر داغ

In *Dīwān-e Bīdel* published from Tehran by Moḥsin Āthārjūi, this verse is like this:

غمخواری ما سوخته جانان چه خیال است

جز شعله نسوزد جگـر کـس بـه‌سـر داغ

Ending:

ای آن که به‌عیبِ زندگی متهمـی   از خود اگر آگاه نـه‌ای مغتنمـی

یا بیخبری ساز که مانـنـد حبـاب   تا چشم کشوده بخـواب عـدمی

«27»

ASB, No. 838

Shikesta-Nasta'līq, fol.170, two columns in the centre and one on the margins, 1191 A.H./[1777 A.D.], in the 18th regnal year of Shāh 'Ālam, Mohammadabad (Banaras).
Considerably abbreviated *Dīwān*.
Contains *Ghazals* with a few *Terjī'-Bands* at the end.

«28»

Ethe, No. 1678

Careless *Nasta'līq*, fol.210, Gholām Moḥīoddīn b. Moḥammad 'Abdollāh b. Moḥammad Wajīhoddīn, 7th Ẕilḥijja, 1192 A.H./ [27th December, 1778 A.D.].

Beginning:

به‌اوج کبریـا کـز پهلـوی عجزسـت راه آنجـا

سرمویی گر اینجا خم شوی بشکن کـلاه آنجـا

«29»

Kitābkhāna-e Shaikh 'Alī Ḥaider, Mashhad, No. 1211

Nasta'līq, fol.323, 323, 1197 A.H./[1783 A.D.].

Ghazaliyāt including *Ṭūr-e Ma'refat* and *Ṭelesm-e Ḥairat*.

Beginning:

آغــازِ بیــانِ ســیر بیــرات　　　تحقیق سواد قـدرت آیـات

Ending of *Mathnavī-e 'Irfān*:

بتاریخش زبـان کلـک خلقـت　　　رقم می‌زد یکی عرفـان نوشـتم

«30»

Ganj Bakhsh, Islamabad, No. 8591, Monzavī 8, 1024

Nasta'līq, p.500, Moḥammad Fāẓil b. Mollā Faiẓ, 1199 A.H./ [1785 A.D.].

Beginning:

به‌اوج کبریا کز پهلوی عجزست راه آنجا...

«31»

National Museum, Karachi, No. N.M.-1972-110/A-B, Monzavī 8, 1024

Nasta'līq, (1201 A.H.)/[1787 A.D.], worm eaten.

«32»

National Museum, Karachi, No. N.M.-1972-109, Monzavī 8, 1024

Nasta'līq, p.382, 1203 A.H./[1789 A.D.].

Beginning:

به‌اوج کبریا کز پهلوی عجزست راه آنجا...

«33»

N. Archives, Afghanistan, No. 30/201
Dīwān Volume I
Nasta'līq, fol.58, 1205 A.H./[1791 A.D.].

«34»

Ganj Bakhsh, Islamabad, No. 1394, Monzavī 8, 1024
Shikesta-Nasta'līq, p.388, Mollā 'Azīz Moḥammad b. , Mollā Moḥammad, Moḥarram, 1208 A.H./[August, 1793 A.D.].
Beginning:

به‌اوج کبریـا کـز پهلـوی عجزسـت راه آنجـا
سرمویی گر اینجا خم شوی بشکن کـلاه آنجـا

«35»

Kitābkhāna-e Millī, Tehran, No. 2112
Transcribed in 1209 A.H./[1794 A.D.], bought from Reẓā Shaikhān.

«36»

N. Archives, Afghanistan, No. 32/44
Nasta'līq, fol.164, Maulā Beg, 1210 A.H./[1795 A.D.].

«37»

Tajikistan, No. 1622
Beautiful *Nasta'līq*, fol.654, 1215 A.H./[1800 A.D.], scribed in two columns, gold work.

«38»

Tajikistan, No. 1449
Shikesta-Nasta'līq, fol.233, Mollā 'Abdur Razzāq b. Mollā Āghā Murād Nūr Āghāī, Rabī'I, 1216 A.H./[July, 1801 A.D.].

«39»

Tajikistan, No. 2696
Only Ghazaliyāt
Shikesta-Nasta'līq, fol.191, Tursun Moḥammad b. 'Awaẓ Moḥammad, 1217 A.D./1802 A.D., incomplete in the end.

«40»

Tajikistan, No. 2694
Shikesta-Nasta'līq, fol.380, Mīrzā Moḥammad Nāṣir Bukhārī, 1220 A.H./1805 A.D.

«41»

N. Archives, Afghanistan, No. 1/58
Dīwān Volume I
Nasta'līq, fol.278, 1220 A.H./[1805 A.D.].

«42»

Punjab University, Lahore, No. 37 Pi/VI 167, Monzavī 8, 1024
Containing *Ghazals* and *Robā'īs*.
Shikesta, fol.153, Moḥammad Faiẓollāh Moḥammad Hāshim, 21st Moḥarram, 1222 A.H./[11th March, 1807 A.D.].
Beginning:

به‌اوج کبریا کز پهلوی عجزست راه آنجا...

«43»

Jhāwaryān, Sargodha, Monzavī 8, 1024
Shikesta-Nasta'līq, p.574, 1225 A.H./[1810 A.D.], gold borders.
Beginning:

به‌اوج کبریا کز پهلوی عجزست راه آنجا...

«44»

Museum, Peshawar, No. 6, Monzavī 8, 1024
Shikesta-Nasta'līq, p.144, Mīrzā 'Abdul Mū'min at the instance of 'Uthmān Shāh Qarāwal, Friday, 1225 A.H./[1810 A.D.].
Beginning:

به‌اوج کبریا کز پهلوی عجزست راه آنجا...

«45»

N. Archives, Afghanistan, No. 22/128
Dīwān Volume I

Nasta'līq, fol.118, Moḥammad Ḥusain, 1225 A.H./[1810 A.D.].

«46»

Majlis-e Shorā-e Millī, Tehran, No. 58

Contains *Ghazals, Qaṣā'īd* and *Robā'īyāt.*

Nasta'līq, fol.328, 'Abdul Qādir b. Mīrzā Moḥammad Nāṣir, Moḥarram, 1226 A.H./[January, 1811 A.D.], a seal of Syed Aḥmad, dated 1230 A.H.

«47»

Mīr Collection, Sadiqabad, Rahimyar Khan, No. 276, Monzavī 8, 1024.

Shikesta-Nasta'līq, p.376, Amīr Mużaffarus Sulṭān b. Amīr Ḥaider, Madrasa Khāksar, 1227 A.H./[1812 A.D.].

Beginning:

به‌اوج کبریا کز پهلوی عجزست راه آنجا...

«48»

Mīr Collection, Sadiqabad, Rahimyar Khan, No. 248, Monzavī 8, 1024

Only *Ghazals.*

Nasta'līq, p.304, [1228 A.H.]/1813 A.D.

Beginning:

به‌اوج کبریا کز پهلوی عجزست راه آنجا

سرمویی گر اینجا خم شوی بشکن کلاه آنجا

«49»

Kitābkhāna-e Molavī, Tehran, No. 2111

Nasta'līq, 1230 A.H./[1815 A.D.], bought from Reẓā Shaikhān.

«50»

Tajikistan, No. 1839

Shikesta-Nasta'līq, fol.236, Mīr 'Aẓīm b. Khwāja Mīr Fāẓil,

1232 A.H./1816 A.D. It was bound by Mollā 'Aṣmatollāh, incomplete copy.

«51»

Majlis-e Shorā-e Millī, Tehran, No. 13406

Ghazals and *Robā'īs*.

Nasta'līq, fol.402, Mīrzā Moḥammad Nāṣir b. Mīrzā Moḥammad Mīrak Bukhārī, 1232 A.H./[1817 A.D.].

Beginning:

به‌اوج کبریا کز پهلوی عجزست راه آنجا...

Ending:

بیدل چه نمود شخصیت از پیدایی جز شهرت حرص و حسد و خودرایی

ای ننگ ظهور هیچ شرمت نامد خود را دیدن باز به‌این رسوایی

There is a *Ghazal* in the end with this *Maṭla'*:

هرکجا نقّاش نقشِ آن پری‌رو می‌کشد

چون به‌ریحان خطّ او می‌رسد بومی‌کند

«52»

Tajikistan, No. 1615

Shikesta-Nasta'līq, fol.238, Khwāja b. Reḥmatollāh Khwāja, 1233 A.H./1818 A.D.

«53»

N. Archives, Afghanistan, No. 14/115

Dīwān Volume II

Nasta'līq, fol.620, Naṣrollāh, 1234-36 A.H./[1819-21 A.D.].

Beginning:

به‌اوج کبریا کز پهلوی عجزست راه آنجا...

Ending:

من باشم و من باشم، من باشم و من

On some folios, *Mathnavīs* like *Miratollāh* (مثنوی مرآت الله) (from fol.251 to 301), some *Qaṣīdas* (from fol.542 to 555) and *Qaṣā'īd-e Foyūẓ* (قصایدِ فیوض) on fol.571 to 592 are transcribed.

«54»

N. Archives, Afghanistan, No. 14/75

Dīwān Volume II

Nasta'līq, fol.140, Naṣrollāh, 1235 A.H./[1820 A.D.].

«55»

Ganj Bakhsh, Islamabad, No. 5779, Monzavī 8, 1024

Nekāt on margins.

Nasta'līq, 'Abdur Rusūl, (1235 A.H.)/[1820 A.D.].

«56»

Ganj Bakhsh, Islamabad, No. 8441, Monzavī 8, 1024

Only *Ghazals*.

Shikesta-Nasta'līq, p.6-301, 'Abdul Wahhāb, 4th Shawwāl, 1236 A.H./[5th July, 1821 A.D.].

Beginning:

به‌اوج کبریا کز پهلوی عجزست راه آنجا

سرمویی گر اینجا خم شوی بشکن کلاه آنجا

«57»

Tajikistan, No. 2964/1

Shikesta, fol.241, Mollā 'Abdur Reḥmān b. Mollā Yādgār, Ẕīqa'da, 1236 A.H./August, 1821 A.D. Bound by Moḥammad Syed Khwāja.

«58»

N. Archives, Afghanistan, No. 15/121

Dīwān Volume II

Nasta'līq, fol.525, Sa'doddīn 'Alī Khwāja Tāshkendī, 1236 A.H./ [1821 A.D.].

It is a part of a *Kolliyāt*. *Dīwān-e Bīdel* up to *Radīf* (ردیف) *Dāl* «د» published from Kabul at the instance of Sardār Naṣrollāh Nā'ib-us Salṭanat, was probably copied from this manuscript.

Beginning after preface:

بـه‌نـام آن صـمد یگانـه و یکتـا   که کرد کون و مکان را بحرف کن پیدا

Ending:

به‌خویش آمدن جز تصنّع کجاست   درینجا میا هرکه گوید خطاست

«59»

Malik Library, Tehran, No. 4669

Nasta'līq, fol.480, 1236 A.H./[1821 A.D.].

«60»

Tajikistan, No. 3033

Shikesta, fol.256, Mīr 'Ażīm b. Khwāja Mīr Fāẓil, 1236 A.H./ [1821 A.D.].

«61»

Tajikistan, No. 2533

Shikesta-Nasta'līq, fol.179, 1237 A.H./[1822 A.D.].

«62»

Kitābkhāna-e Āstān-e Quds-e Reẓavī, Mashhad, No. 4613

Shikesta-Nasta'līq, fol.238, Mollā Faiẓ b. Mollā Faiṣal, 1239 A.H./ [1824 A.D.], Bukhara and Samarqand, presented by Ḥājī Qā'īm Maqām.

Beginning:

به‌اوج کبریا کز پهلوی عجزست راه آنجا...

Ending:

کنم جرعهٔ جامِ وحدت بکام   همه نشأء چون می‌شوم والسّلام

«63»

Gulzār Aḥmad Library, Khushab, Monzavī 8, 1024

There is a note by Munshī Rām Chand Rām.

Nasta'līq, p.586, 'Abdollāh Ṣeḥatī, Pichabad, 1240 A.H./ [1824 A.D.].

Beginning:

به‌اوج کبریا کز پهلوی عجزست راه آنجا...

«64»

Āyātollāh-e Golpāyeganī Library, Qom, No. 38/26-76.6

Ghazals from *Radīf* ذ to ی.

Nasta'līq, fol.287, Murād Ḥusain b. Mollā Yatīm Ḥusain, 1241 A.H./ [1825 A.D.].

Beginning:

ای شعله نهال از قلمت گلشنِ کاغذ   دود از خطّ مشکین تو در خرمنِ کاغذ
بیدل دل عاشق به‌هوس بند نگردد   اخگر نشود تکمه به‌پیراهنِ کاغذ

Ending:

دنیا که پراکندگی‌اش اسباب است   آرام در او هم سبق سیماب است
بحریست که موج او پریشانی‌هاست   روی دل جمع گوهر نایاب است

تمام شد دیوانِ شریف میمون لطیف میرزا عبدالقادر بیدل.

«65»

N. Archives, Afghanistan, No. 14/117

Complete *Dīwān*.

Nasta'līq, fol.640, Moḥammad Laṭīf b. Moḥammad Sharīf Shahr Sabzī, 1241 A.H./[1825 A.D.].

Beginning:

به‌اوج کبریا کز پهلوی عجزست راه آنجا...

Ending:

عبث چند رنج بیانش کشی   کتاب قصاید عنانش کشی

«66»

Āyātollāh-e Golpāyegānī Library, Qom, No. 1/54-54

Nasta'līq, fol.372, 1241 A.H./[1825 A.D.], number of *Ghazals* in this Ms. is 155, incomplete from the beginning, gold work.

Beginning:

ز بس فیض سحر می‌خورد از گردِ سواد شب
همه گر شب شوی روزت نمی‌گردد سیاه آنجا
به‌کنعان هوس گردی ندارد مطلبِ یوسف
مگر در خود فرورفتن کند ایجاد چاه آنجا

Ending:

ز سوزدل تجلّی منظر برقیست هـر عضـوم

چو مجمر دارم از یک شعله سامان چراغانی

اگر بیدل چو گل پـایم بـدامن برنمـی‌آیـد

نـدارد کـوتهی دسـتِ مـن از سـرِگریبانی

«67»

N. Archives, Afghanistan, No. 13/24

Nasta'līq, fol.425, Amīr Moḥammad, 1242 A.H./[1826 A.D.].
Beginning:

به‌اوج کبریا کز پهلوی عجزست راه آنجا...

Ending:

ور سهو و خطایی شده باشد واقع   ربّ اغفرلی انّک انـت الوهـاب

«68»

N. Archives, Afghanistan, No. 11/24

Scribed on 13th Jumāda'II, 1242 A.H./[12th January, 1827 A.D.].
Beginning:

به‌اوج کبریا کز پهلوی عجز است راه آنجا...

Ending:

... ور سهو و خطایی شده باشد واقع...

«69»

Ganj Bakhsh, Islamabad, No. 1454, Monzavī 8, 1024

Nasta'līq, p.1236, Murād Ḥusain b. Mollā Yatīm Ḥusain town Darvaz, Ẕīqa'da, 1242 A.H./[June, 1827 A.D.].
Beginning:

به‌اوج کبریا کز پهلوی عجزست راه آنجا...

«70»

Maktaba Ḥabībīya, Dera Isma'il Khan, Monzavī 8, 1039

Mā Ḥarīfān* (ما حریفان) *(Tarjī'-Band)

A *Tarjī'* with 30 Bands (720 verses) included in *Kolliyāt* published

from Kabul. In some Mss. the number of Bands is 34 and that of verses 714. It has a mystic bend. Bīdel imitated the famous Ṣūfī poet Fakhroddīn 'Irāqī's *Mā Muqīmā* (ما مقیما).
Nasta'līq, p.42, 1242 A.H./[1827 A.D.].
Beginning:

ما حریفان بزم اسراریم مست جام شهود و دیداریم
خوش بحر محیط لاهوتیم فیض صبح جهانِ انواریم

«71»

Aḥmad Khān, Bahlwal, Sargodha, Monzavī 8, 1024
Shikesta-Nasta'līq, p.386, Radhan b. Gol Moḥammad Ḥasan, 1244 A.H./[1828 A.D.].
Beginning:

به‌اوج کبریا کز پهلوی عجزست راه آنجا...

«72»

Tajikistan, No. 836/1
Shikesta, fol.234, 1245 A.H./[1829 A.D.], Bukhara.

«73»

N. Archives, Afghanistan, No. 22/43
It has gold work and its transcription was carried out in 1246, 1247 and 1292 A.H./[1830, 1831, 1875 A.D.] by Moḥammad Laṭīf Kīshī and Gholām Āghā Jān Abul Ḥasan.

«74»

N. Archives, Afghanistan, No. 11/60
Nasta'līq, fol.310, Mīr Moḥammad, 1248 A.H./[1832 A.D.].

«75»

Tajikistan, No. 2870
Shikesta-Nasta'līq, fol.258, 'Abdur Reḥmān Khatlānī, Ramaẓān, 1249 A.H./[January, 1834 A.D.], Sultanabad, Bukhara.
Some seals are also affixed.

«76»

Chishtī Solaimān Library, Faizabad, Monzavī 8, 1039

Mā Ḥarīfān* (ما حریفان) *(Tarjī'-Band)

Nasta'līq, p.981-1043, 'Alī Aṣghar, 1250 A.H./[1834 A.D.].

Beginning:

ما حریفان بزم اسراریم   مست جام شهود و دیداریم

«77»

Ganj Bakhsh, Islamabad, No. 3607, Monzavī 8, 1039

Mā Ḥarīfān* (ما حریفان) *(Tarjī'-Band)

It is introduced as *Sāqī Nāma* in the catalogue.

Shikesta-Nasta'līq, p.320-323, 1250 A.H./[1834 A.D.].

Beginning:

ما حریفان بزم اسراریم   مست جام شهود و دیداریم

«78»

Ganj Bakhsh, Islamabad, No. 8438, Monzavī 8, 1024

Nasta'līq, p.368, Hedāyatollāh b. Ḥāfiẓ 'Ināyatollāh, Saturday, 1251 A.H./[1835 A.D.].

Beginning:

به‌اوج کبریا کز پهلوی عجزست راه آنجا...

«79»

Tajikistan, No. 1841

Shikesta, fol.178, Moḥammad Sharīf b. Dāmollā Kinjiyā Bai Yāghnabī, Shawwāl, 1251 A.H./[January, 1836 A.D.].

«80»

N. Archives, Afghanistan, No. 20/96

Nasta'līq, fol.222, Moḥammad Ṣābir, 1252 A.H./[1836 A.D.].

«81»

N. Archives, Afghanistan, No. 40/96

Scribed by Moḥammad Ṣābir b. 'Uthmān Moḥammad in Sha'bān, 1253 A.H./[November, 1837 A.D.].

Beginning:

به‌اوج کبریا کز پهلوی عجز است راه آنجا...

Ending:

این فرقه که باوجود اسباب عجز و غرور سازند به‌عجز یعنی که چون ما به‌خاک یکسان باشیم... رانند.

«82»

Kitābkhāna-e Āstān-e Quds-e Reẓavī, Mashhad, No. 22521

Nasta'līq, 1253 A.H./[1837 A.D.].

Beginning:

ای خدا خـــواهم ســرِ ســـودایی　　در میـــان عشـــق زان رســـوایی

«83»

N. Archives, Afghanistan, No. 23/114

Dīwān Volume I

Nasta'līq, fol.230, Ne'matollāh, 1254 A.H./[1838 A.D.].

«84»

Ganj Bakhsh, Islamabad, No. 1384, Monzavī 8, 1024

Shikesta-Nasta'līq, p.357, Moḥammad Jān, 21st Jumāda'I, 1255 A.H./[2nd August, 1839 A.D.].

Beginning:

به‌اوج کبریا کز پهلوی عجزست راه آنجا...

«85»

Ganjīna-e Khaṭṭī-o-Hunarī-e Talpūrān, No. 70

Nasta'līq, Baqā Faqīr, 1255 A.H./[1839 A.D.], gold borders, incomplete in the beginning.

«86»

Tajikistan, No. 806

Shikesta-Nasta'līq, fol.408, Qorbān Moḥammad pen-named Kharāmī, 1256 A.H./[1840 A.D.].

«87»

Tajikistan, No. 2833

Shikesta, fol.619, Mīrzā 'Umar b. Mīrzā Ḥakīm, Shawwāl, 1258 A.H./[November, 1842 A.D.].

«88»

N. Archives, Afghanistan, No. 35/246

Nasta'līq, fol.462, 1258 A.H./[1842 A.D.].

«89»

Ganj Bakhsh, Islamabad, No. 11112, Monzavī 8, 1024

Containing *Ghazals, Mukhammas* and *Robā'īs*.
Shikesta-Nasta'līq, p.503, 1258 A.H./[1842 A.D.].
Beginning:

به‌اوج کبریا کز پهلوی عجزست راه آنجا

سرمویی گر اینجا خم شوی بشکن کلاه آنجا

«90»

Tajikistan, No. 1217

Shikesta-Nasta'līq, fol.234, Mīrzā 'Abdur Raḥīm, Moḥarram, 1258 A.H./[February, 1842 A.D.].

«91»

Tajikistan, No. 1838

Shikesta-Nasta'līq, fol.297, Mīr Khartan b. Ākhund Mollā 'Āshūr Moḥammad Modarris, 7th Rajab, 1259 A.H./[3rd August, 1843 A.D.].

«92»

N. Archives, Afghanistan, No. 15/182

Dīwān Volume II

Nasta'līq, fol.270, Sa'doddīn, 1259 A.H./[1843 A.D.].

«93»

Tajikistan, No. 220

Shikesta-Nasta'līq, fol.328, 1260 A.H./[1844 A.D.].

«94»

Tajikistan, No. 902
Shikesta-Nasta'līq, fol.328, 1260 A.H./[1844 A.D.].

«95»

Tajikistan, No. 903
Shikesta-Nasta'līq, fol.190, 1261 A.H./[1845 A.D.].

«96»

Tajikistan, No. 184
Shikesta-Nasta'līq, 1261 A.H./[1845 A.D.].

«97»

Ganj Bakhsh, Islamabad, No. 3763, Monzavī 8, 1024
Shikesta-Nasta'līq, p.420, Mollā Ādīna Moḥammad b. Ḥāfiż Moḥammad Shahābī Badakhshī, 1263 A.H./[1847 A.D.].
Beginning:

به‌اوج کبریـا کــز پهلـوی عجزسـت راه آنجـا

سرمویی گر اینجا خم شوی بشکن کـلاه آنجـا

«98»

N. Archives, Afghanistan, No. 15/115
Dīwān Volume II
Nasta'līq, fol.215, Laṭīf, 1263 A.H./[1847 A.D.].

«99»

N. Archives, Afghanistan, No. 19/6
Dīwān Volume II
Nasta'līq, fol.210, 1263 A.H./[1847 A.D.].

«100»

N. Archives, Afghanistan, No. 7/122
Dīwān Volume I
Nasta'līq, fol.136, 1265 A.H./[1849 A.D.].

«101»

Ganj Bakhsh, Islamabad, No. 3347, Monzavī 8, 1024
Shikesta-Nasta'līq, p.450, 1269 A.H./[1853 A.D.].

Beginning:

به‌اوج کبریا کز پهلوی عجزست راه آنجا...

«102»

Tajikistan, No. 112

Shikesta-Nasta'līq, fol.216, Mollā Mīrzā, Jumāda'II, 1270 A.H./[March, 1854 A.D.].

«103»

Tajikistan, No. 3072

Shikesta-Nasta'līq, fol.181, 'Abdul Ghanī b. Asadollāh Ghajdawānī, 1270 A.H./[1853-4 A.D.].

«104»

Ganj Bakhsh, Islamabad, No. 4062, Monzavī 8, 1039

Mā Ḥarīfān* (ما حریفان) *(Tarjī'-Band)

Nasta'līq, p.100-171, 1270 A.H./[1854 A.D.].

Beginning:

مـــا حریفـــان بـــزم اســـراریم   مست جـــام شـــهود و دیـــداریم

«105»

Ganj Bakhsh, Islamabad, No. 4062, Monzavī 8, 1033

***Tarkīb-Band* (ترکیب‌بند)**

Nasta'līq, 1270 A.H./[1854 A.D.].

Beginning:

بنـــام آن صـــمد بیچگونـــه و یکتـــا

که کرد کون و مکان را به‌حرف کن پیدا

«106»

Ganj Bakhsh, Islamabad, No. 3711, Monzavī 8, 1024

Shikesta-Nasta'līq, p.139, Syed Kamāl b. 'Abdur Raḥmān, Jumāda'I, 1271 A.H./[February, 1855 A.D.].

Beginning:

به‌اوج کبریا کز پهلوی عجزست راه آنجا...

«107»

Tajikistan, No. 1846

Shikesta-Nasta'līq, fol.225, 1271 A.H./[1855 A.D.].

«108»

N. Archives, Afghanistan, No. 16/135

Nasta'līq, fol.265, Ibrāhīm, 1272 A.H./[1856 A.D.].

«109»

Faqīr Syed Mughīthoddīn, Lahore, Monzavī 8, 1024

Containing *Ghazals* and *Robā'īs*.

Shikesta, fol.170, Moḥammad Sharīf, 1272 A.H./[1856 A.D.].

Beginning:

به‌اوج کبریـا کـز پهلـوی عجزسـت راه آنجـا

سرمویی گر اینجا خم شوی بشکن کـلاه آنجـا

«110»

National Museum, Karachi, No. N.M.-1972-111, Monzavī 8, 1024

Nasta'līq, p.352, Moḥammad b. Mollā Moḥammad Amīn, Ramaẓān, 1273 A.H./[May, 1857 A.D.].

Beginning:

به‌اوج کبریا کز پهلوی عجزست راه آنجا...

«111»

Tajikistan, No. 2422

Shikesta-Nasta'līq, fol.193, Mollā Moḥammad Sharīf b. Khwāja Moḥammad Raḥīm, 14th Ramaẓān, 1274 A.H./[28th April, 1858 A.D.].

«112»

Tajikistan, No. 217/2

Shikesta-Nasta'līq, fol.141, 1275 A.H./[1859 A.D.].

«113»

Āyātollāh-e Mar'ashī Library, Qom, No. 780

Nasta'līq, fol.356, Syed 'Umar Maulavī, 1277 A.H./[1860 A.D.]. Qūniyā in the vicinity of Maulānā's (i.e. Maulānā Rūmī's) Tomb. In the end a *Qaṣīda*, probably by the scribe, has been transcribed.

Beginning:

به‌اوج کبریا کز پهلوی عجزست راه آنجا...

Ending:

ای نقـــد امـــل مایهاســـتغنا کـــو   جنس و همی که کرده ما انشا کو

پیداست ز حال قـدر اسـتقبالت   امروز که هست هستی فـردا کـو

«114»

Nūr Bakhsh Library, Tehran, No. 306

Contains *Qaṣīdas*, *Ghazals* and *Robā'īs*.

Nasta'līq, p.472, 1277 A.H./[1860 A.D.].

Beginning:

به‌اوج کبریا کز پهلوی عجزست راه آنجا...

Ending:

اکنون چکـنـم اگـر نـنـالم بیـدل   منقار شود کسیکه گردید دونـیـم

دل خوش شـود..............   بپـــای تـــو رســـد ســـبحان الله

Name of the author has wrongly been given as Moḥammad Ẓīā'oddīn Naqshbandī Mujaddedī Khāledī pen-named Bīdel-e Bukhārī.

«115»

N. Archives, Afghanistan, No. 25/20

Contains *Ghazaliyāt* and *Robā'īyāt*.

Nasta'līq, fol.230, 1277 A.H./[1860 A.D.].

Beginning:

به‌اوج کبریا کز پهلوی عجز است راه آنجا...

Ending:

خلق آیینه است نور احمد دریاب   حق فهم اگـر علـی مـی‌خـواهی

«116»

N. Archives, Afghanistan, No. 26/56

Nasta'līq, fol.402, 1277 A.H./[1860 A.D.].

«117»

Malik Library, Tehran, No. 5449

Shikesta-Nasta'līq, fol.176, Shawwāl 1277 A.H./[April, 1861 A.D.].

Beginning:

به‌اوج کبریا کز پهلوی عجزست راه آنجا...

Ending:

... چون موج که در طبع گهر محو شود...

تمام یافت دیوان... میرزا عبدالقادر بیدل در شهر شوال سنهٔ ۱۲۷۷ (هـ).

It is a complete *Dīwān* of *Ghazals*, but in *Robā'īs* section only *Radīf* الف، ب، ت and ر have been copied.

«118»

Tajikistan, No. 829

Shikesta-Nasta'līq, fol.227, Mīr Burhān Bukhārī, 1278 A.H./[1861 A.D.].

«119»

Tajikistan, No. 597

Shikesta-Nasta'līq, fol.242, 1278 A.H./[1861 A.D.].

«120»

Ganj Bakhsh, Islamabad, No. 6000, Monzavī 8, 1024

Shikesta-Nasta'līq, p.457, Moḥammad Qāsim b. Nād Moḥammad Bai, 11 Mīzān, 1278 A.H./[1862 A.D.].

Beginning:

به‌اوج کبریا کز پهلوی عجزست راه آنجا...

«121»

Ganj Bakhsh, Islamabad, No. 8673, Monzavī 8, 1024

Nasta'līq, p.460, 1278 A.H./[1862 A.D.].

Beginning:

به‌اوج کبریا کز پهلوی عجزست راه آنجا...

Bought for 85 Afghānīs in Qandahar in 1354 Khorshīdī/(1976 A.D.).

«122»

Tajikistan, No. 1848

Shikesta-Nasta'līq, fol.212, Mīrzā 'Abdul Qādir, Ṣafar, 1279 A.H./ [August 1862 A.D.].

«123»

Record Office, Peshawar, No. 64, Monzavī 8, 1024

Nasta'līq, p.358, 12th Ẕīqa'da, 1279 A.H./[1st May, 1863 A.D.], at Bāgh-e Dasht, Herat.

Beginning:

به‌اوج کبریـا کـز پهلـوی عجزسـت راه آنجـا

سرمویی گر اینجا خم شوی بشکن کـلاه آنجـا

«124»

Ganj Bakhsh, Islamabad, No. 8500, Monzavī 8, 1024

Nasta'līq, p.6-524, Mollā Moḥammad Faiẓ Bārakza'ī Bahlolrānī, resident of district Mohassas, in the vicinity of Ashraful Belād-e Aḥmad Shāhī (Qandahar), 1280 A.H./[1863 A.D.].

Beginning:

به‌اوج کبریا کز پهلوی عجزست راه آنجا...

«125»

Tajikistan, No. 1397

Shikesta, fol.172, Yaldesh Khwāja, 18th Rabī'I, 1281 A.H./[21st August, 1864 A.D.].

«126»

Tajikistan, No. 901

Shikesta-Nasta'līq, fol.189, Moḥammad Sharīf b. Dāmollā Kinjiyā Bai Yāghnabī, Jumāda'I, 1281 A.H./[October, 1864 A.D.], Ghajdawan, Bukhara.

«127»

Tajikistan, No. 2872

Shikesta-Nasta'līq, fol.220, 1281 A.H./[1864 A.D.].

«128»

N. Archives, Afghanistan, No. 41/11

Containing only *Ghazals*.

Nasta'līq, fol.500, Mollā Ḥusain, 1282 A.H./[1865 A.D.].

«129»

N. Archives, Afghanistan, No. 35/121

Dīwān Volume I

Contains only *Ghazals*.

Nasta'līq, fol.413, 1282 A.H./[1865 A.D.].

«130»

N. Archives, Afghanistan, No. 30/176

Dīwān Volume II

Nasta'līq, fol.240, 1282 A.H./[1865 A.D.].

«131»

Tajikistan, No. 1691

Shikesta-Nasta'līq, fol.201, 1282 A.H./[1865 A.D.].

«132»

Ganj Bakhsh, Islamabad, No. 2188, Monzavī 8, 1024

Shikesta, p.158-242, 1282 A.H./[1865 A.D.].

Beginning:

به‌اوج کبریا کز پهلوی عجزست راه آنجا...

«133»

Pushtū Academy, Peshawar, No. 590, Monzavī 8, 1024

Nasta'līq, p.121, Shīr Moḥammad, 1282 A.H./[1865 A.D.], first page damaged.

Beginning:

ز طرز مشرب (عشّاق سیر بی‌نـوایی کـن)

شکست آن که آبی نـدارد زیـر کـاه آنجـا

In Iranian edition of published *Ghazals*:

شکست رنگ کس آبی...

«134»

Tajikistan, No. 2836

Shikesta-Nasta'līq, fol.257, Rabī'II, 1284 A.H./[August 1867 A.D.].

«135»

Ganj Bakhsh, Islamabad, No. 538, Monzavī 8, 1024

Shikesta-Nasta'līq, p.450, Gol Moḥammad b. Niyāz Arbāb Dozābī, 1284 A.H./[1867 A.D.].

Beginning:

به‌اوج کبریا کز پهلوی عجزست راه آنجا...

«136»

National Museum, Karachi, No. N.M.1957-928/19, Monzavī 8, 1024

Nasta'līq, p.397, Ẕilḥijja, 1284 A.H./[April, 1868 A.D.].

«137»

Tajikistan, No. 1773

Fair *Nasta'līq*, fol.208, Mollā 'Abdul Khāliq b. Mollā Pīrmoḥammad Khuqandī, 1285 A.H./[1868 A.D.].

«138»

Tajikistan, No. 1373

Shikesta-Nasta'līq, fol.159, Mollā 'Ewaẓ Moḥammad, 1285 A.H./ [1868 A.D.].

«139»

Ganj Bakhsh, Islamabad, No. 8837, Monzavī 8, 1024

Nasta'līq, p.608, Gol Moḥammad b. 'Alī Moḥammad, Jumāda'II, 1287 A.H./[September, 1870 A.D.], Andkhu'i.

Beginning:

به‌اوج کبریا کز پهلوی عجزست راه آنجا...

«140»

N. Archives, Afghanistan, No. 1/147

Dīwān Volume I

Nasta'līq, fol.191, 'Abdul Ḥafīẓ, 1287 A.H./[1870 A.D.].

«141»

Ganj Bakhsh, Islamabad, No. 8476, Monzavī 8, 1024

Nasta'līq, p.36, 1288 A.H./[1871 A.D.].

Beginning:

به‌اوج کبریا کز پهلوی عجزست راه آنجا...

«142»

Allāh Dattā Library, Bahlwal, Sargodha, Monzavī 8, 1024

Nasta'līq, p.400, Wazīr 'Alī Qāẓī, Alipur, Khushab, 1289 A.H./[1872 A.D.], gold sprinkled pages.

Beginning:

به‌اوج کبریا کز پهلوی عجزست راه آنجا...

«143»

Tajikistan, No. 742

Shikesta, fol.301, 1289 A.H./[1872 A.D.].

«144»

Tajikistan, No. 900

Shikesta-Nasta'līq, fol.219, Qorbān Moḥammad b. Mollā Ẕākir, Ṣafar, 1290 A.H./[April, 1873 A.D.], Sultanabad, Bukhara.

«145»

Mo'aẓẓam Khān Book-Seller, Dera Isma'il Khan, Monzavī 8, 1024

Shikesta-Nasta'līq, p.258, 'Atīqollāh Samarqandī, 8th Sha'bān, 1290 A.H./[29th November, 1873 A.D.], Kabul.

Beginning:

به‌اوج کبریا کز پهلوی عجزست راه آنجا...

«146»

Tajikistan, No. 2513

Beautiful *Shikesta-Nasta'līq*, fol.223, Syed 'Abdur Reḥmān Khwāja, Rajab, 1292 A.H./[August, 1875 A.D.].

«147»

Ganj Bakhsh, Islamabad, No. 5878, Monzavī 8, 1035
Shahr Āshūb* (شهرآشوب) *(Mukhammas)

Not found in his published *Kolliyāt*, still may be the work of the same Bīdel. It is different from that *Shahr Āshūb* included in "*Shahr Āshūb Dar She'r-e Fārsī* (شهرآشوب در شعر فارسی)" by Golchīn-e Ma'ānī, p.81-2.

In this Ms. there are few *Mukhammas*, each having 12 bands.

Nasta'līq, p.22-29, Ḥāj Mīrzā, Samangān, 1292 A.H./[1875 A.D.].

Beginning:

آن خیره‌سرانی که نه حالند و نه قالند   وز جهل رسا منکر ارباب خیالند

حیزند و سفیه‌اند و ضلالند   حمال نگون سار تلاش زر و مالند

His *Takhalluṣ* Bīdel is found in this couplet:

بیدل تو از اینها مبراندوه، کم و بیش   زین ریش و بروت جعلی، هیچ میندیش

خوش باشکه این شیرنران، ماده شغالند

The second one begins:

نگویمت که بیکباره ز اشتعال برآ

His *Takhalluṣ* is also found in this couplet:

نه سجده یافت حضور و نه توبه شد مقبل   ز سرنوشت تو توفیق داغ شد بیدل

به‌این چنین عرق گل کن، ز انفعال برآ

«148»

Ganj Bakhsh, Islamabad, No. 1177, Monzavī 8, 1024

Shikesta-Nasta'līq, p.564, Mollā Mīrzā Nūr b. Qāẓī Beg Hazārā'ī, Ramaẓān, 1294 A.H./[September, 1877 A.D.].

Beginning:

به‌اوج کبریا کز پهلوی عجزست راه آنجا

سرمویی گر اینجا خم شوی بشکن کلاه آنجا

«149»

Tajikistan, No. 3007

Shikesta-Nasta'līq, fol.176, 1295 A.H./[1878 A.D.].

«150»

Upsala, No. 465

Nasta'līq, fol.462, 1296 A.H./[1879 A.D.].

Beginning:

خیال جلوه زار نیستی هم عالمی دارد   مگر در خود فرورفتن کند ایجاد جاه آنجا

«151»

Lahore Museum, Lahore, Monzavī 8, 1024

Nasta'līq, fol.157, Moḥammad 'Azīz b. Moḥammad Ṣāleḥ, 1296 A.H./[1879 A.D.], golden work on opening page.

Beginning:

به‌اوج کبریا کز پهلوی عجزست راه آنجا...

«152»

Tajikistan, No. 1207

Shikesta-Nasta'līq, fol.187, Moḥammad Rajab, 1297 A.H./[1880 A.D.].

«153»

Tehran University Library, Tehran, No. 7892

Nasta'līq, fol.403, Sulṭān Moḥammad Dīwān, 1297 A.H./[1880 A.D.]. Presented by Amir Syed 'Ālam Khān Manāghītī Amīr-e Bukhara to Raḥīm Khān son of Mīrzā 'Abdur Razzāq Khān with his signature and seal. A biographical note of the same Amīr in the hand of 'Abdur Raḥmān Afghān Kābulī who presented it to 'Alī Tabātabā'ī.

«154»

Tajikistan, No. 1178

Shikesta, fol.301, 1298 A.H./[1881 A.D.].

«155»

Upsala, No. 463

Ghazals and *Robā'īs*.

Nasta'līq, fol.181, Mollā Nižām Bai, Jumāda'I, 1300 A.H./[February, 1883 A.D.].

«156»

Tajikistan, No. 2409

Shikesta-Nasta'līq, fol.184, Mollā Ẕākir b. Ḥājī Bai, Jumāda'II, 1300 A.H./[April, 1883 A.D.].

«157»

Dayāl Singh Trust, Lahore, No. 602, Monzavī 8, 1024

Nasta'līq, fol.156, 1300 A.H./[1883 A.D.].

Beginning:

به‌اوج کبریا کز پهلوی عجزست راه آنجا...

«158»

Tajikistan, No. 1851

Nasta'līq, fol.662, Moḥammad Qorbān b. Moḥammad Yūsuf Yazqandī, 26th Ṣafar, 1301 A.H./27th December, 1883 A.D.

«159»

Maẕhabī Kotobkhāna, Wardak, Peshawar, Monzavī 8, 1039

Mā Ḥarīfān* (ما حریفان) *(Tarjī'-Band)

Nasta'līq, Gholām Ḥusain Mahmand, 1302 A.H./[1885 A.D.].

Beginning:

ما حریفان بزم اسراریم   مست جام شهود و دیداریم

«160»

N. Archives, Afghanistan, No. 2/46

Dīwān Volume I

Nasta'līq, fol.249, 'Abdul Qādir, 1303 A.H./[1886 A.D.].

Beginning:

به‌اوج کبریا کز پهلوی عجز است راه آنجا...

Ending:

حرف نامش اگر کنی تکرار   ... کند لا اله الا الله...

«161»

N. Archives, Afghanistan, No. 4/179

Dīwān Volume I

Nasta'līq, fol.173, Mollā Niżāmoddīn, 9th Shawwāl, 1304 A.H./ [1st July, 1887 A.D.].

Beginning:

ستم است اگر هوست کشد که به‌گشت سرو و چمن درآ...

Ending:

گر از واجب ممکن علما با خبرنـد   درویـــش نیســت فضــول الله

«162»

Āyātollāh-e Golpāyeganī Library, Qom, No. 2/29-209

Nasta'līq, fol.195, 1304 A.H./[1887 A.D.].

Beginning:

به‌اوج کبریـا کـز پهلـوی عجزسـت راه آنجـا

سرمویی گر اینجا خم شوی بشکن کـلاه آنجـا

Ending:

ای آنکه بـه‌عرصـهٔ تـوهم گـردی   هرگاه بـه‌تحقیـق رسـیدی فـردی

با این کسوت که باطلش می‌نـامی   گر غیرحق از جیب بـراری مـردی

اللّهمّ اغفرلی ولوالدین و لاستاذی و لجمیع المؤمنین... تمّت.

«163»

Markaz-e Motāle'āt, Qom, No. 427

Shikesta-Nasta'līq, fol.205, Mīr Moḥammad Fāẓil, b. Mollā Mīr 'Abdul Muqīm Bukhārī, Ṣafar, 1305 A.H./[November, 1887 A.D.].

Beginning:

به‌اوج کبریـا کـز پهلـوی عجزسـت راه آنجـا

سرمویی گر اینجا خم شوی بشکن کـلاه آنجـا

Ending:

ادب گــاه محبّــت نــاز شــوخی برنمــی‌دارد

چو شبنم سر به‌مهر اشک مـی‌بالـد نگـاهِ آنجـا

«164»

National Museum, Karachi, No. N.M.-1972-183, Monzavī 8, 1024

Shikesta, p.358, Mollā Nūrgol b. Mollā Mīr Afghān, 19th Rajab, 1305 A.H./[1st April, 1888 A.D.], at Maimana.

«165»

N. Archives, Afghanistan, No. 20/83
Dīwān Volume II

Nasta'līq, fol.185, Faṣīḥoddīn, 1305 A.H./[1888 A.D.].

«166»

Tajikistan, No. 3095

Shikesta-Nasta'līq, fol.180, 1305 A.H./[1888 A.D.].

«167»

Tajikistan, No. 3130

Shikesta-Nasta'līq, fol.116, 1305 A.H./[1888 A.D.].

«168»

N. Archives, Afghanistan, No. 13/132

Nasta'līq, fol.182, Gholām Ḥusain, 1309 A.H./[1892 A.D.].

Beginning:

به‌اوج کبریا کز پهلوی عجزست راه آنجا

سرمویی گر اینجا خم شوی بشکن کلاه آنجا

Ending:

ای ننگ ظهور هیچ شرمت ناید خود را دیدن باز باین رسوایی

«169»

'Abdur Rashīd Fārūqī, Gujrānwālā, Monzavī 8, 1024

Containing *Ghazals* and *Robā'īs*.

Nasta'līq, p.370, 1310 A.H./[1892 A.D.].

Beginning:

به‌اوج کبریا کز پهلوی عجزست راه آنجا...

«170»

Tajikistan, No. 1845

Shikesta-Nasta'līq, fol.145, 1311 A.H./[1894 A.D.].

«171»

N. Archives, Afghanistan, No. 13/118

Selection (انتخاب دیوان)

Shikesta-Nasta'līq, fol.29, Qārī Moḥammad Ismā'īl b. Qāẓī Shamsoddīn b. Qāẓī Mīrzā, end of Jumāda'II, 1317 A.H./[October, 1899 A.D.]. It has gold work.

«172»

Pīr Ḥusāmoddīn Rāshidī, Karachi, Monzavī 8, 1024

Containing Ghazals in alphabetical order, *Qaṣīda*, *Mokhammas*, *Mosaddas*, *Mathnavī*, *Robā'ī* and some Urdū *Ghazals*.

Nasta'līq, p.277, 'Alī Bakhsh b. La'l Moḥammad Lāherī, District Hazrat Laheri, 5th Ṣafar, 1321 A.H./[3rd May, 1903 A.D.].

Beginning:

الهی مطلع‌الانوار وحدت ساز جانم را...

«173»

Ganj Bakhsh, Islamabad, No. 10527, Monzavī 8, 1024

Ordinary *Nasta'līq*, p.364, Syed Hādī Khān b. Īshān Syed Khān, 1332 A.H./[1914 A.D.].

Beginning:

به‌اوج کبریا کز پهلوی عجزست راه آنجا...

«174»

Ganj Bakhsh, Islamabad, No. 10608, Monzavī 8, 1038

Qaṣīda-e Sawād-e A'ẓam

Nasta'līq, p.428-535, 1332 A.H./[1914 A.D.].

This *Qaṣīda* was composed in 1082 A.H. as revealed in this couplet with the chronogram:

نیست از فطرت نهان کیفیت تاریخ او

سالِ تاریخش همان در حرف نامش مضمر است

It also contains *Mathnavī Dar Kīmīa Garī* and other poems.
Beginning:

در حریم خاک ما را موی پیری رهبـر اسـت
جامۀ احرام مرگِ شـعله بـا خاکسـتر اسـت

«175»

Maulānā Moḥammad Ibrāhīm Nāżim, Gadhī Yāsīn, Shikarpur, Monzavī 8, 1024

Shikesta-Nasta'līq, p.160, Moḥammad Ḥusain, 17th Rajab, 1339 A.H./[27th March 1921 A.D.].
Beginning:

الهی مطلع‌الانوار وحدت ساز جانم را...

«176»

N. Archives, Afghanistan, No. 2/152
Dīwān Volume I

Nasta'līq, fol.237, Mīrzā Moḥammad Kabīr b. Daulat Moḥammad, 1352 A.H./[1933 A.D.].
Beginning:

به‌اوج کبریا کز پهلوی عجز است راه آنجا...

Ending:

از تعظیم ملک چی(چه)ها می‌انگیخت　　آدم کرده است این‌قـدر شـیطانش

«177»

Tajikistan, No. 1840

Fair *Shikesta-Nasta'līq*, fol.223, scribed in [1353 A.H.]/ 1934 A.D., gold work.
An oval shape seal of 'Abdohu Moḥammad Raḥīm and a note by Yaḥyā Khān Solaimān.

«178»

Tajikistan, No. 1450

Shikesta, fol.144, 'Āṣim, 1371 A.H./[1951 A.D.].

Manuscripts of Dīwān-e Bīdel (Undated)

«1»

Kitābkhāna-e Sipehsālār, Tehran, No. 403

Fair *Shikesta-Nasta'līq*, p.407.

This is an important copy that was most likely transcribed for the author. Additions made on the margins are in Bīdel's handwriting. *Nekāt* have been transcribed on folios 235-87. There are one or two letters written by Bīdel at the end of the manuscript, and some other notes obviously in Bīdel's hand. It has been compared with other manuscripts.

Beginning:

به‌اوج کبریا کز پهلوی عجز است راه جـا

سرمویی گر اینجا خم شوی بشکن کلاه آنجا

«2»

A Ms copy of the *Dīwān* said to be transcribed by Bīdel himself. It is a personal copy of the librarian of the Karachi University Library, see *Adab-e Fārsī*: Anūsheh, *Sāzmān-e Chāp-o-Inteshārāt-e Wizārat-e Farhang-o-Irshād-e Islāmī*, Tehran, Iran, 1378 (entry on Bīdel). Date of its transcription is not given. This information is probably baseless.

«3»

Sālār, No. 2056 (A.N.19)
Selection (انتخاب دیوان)

Naskh, fol.133, gold and coloured ruled borders.

It is an important selection of 782 *Ghazals* and 235 *Robā'īs*.

Bīdel has added some *Ghazals* in his own hand in *Shafī'ā* script with (لراقمه) on the margins of some of the pages.

A seal of Żahīroddīn Ḥasan Khān Bahādur, who could not be identified, is affixed on the first page of the Ms. On the same first page, four unreadable signatures are seen, together with the dates 1131, 1148, 1151 A.H. It means that this Ms. was prepared two years earlier before the death of Bīdel in 1131 A.H./[1719 A.D.]. This selection of *Dīwān* of Bīdel edited by me, has been published twice in Tehran, Iran, and once in India. See the list of Bīdel's published works in this catalogue.

«4»

Majlis-e Shorā-e Millī, Tehran, No. 18259

Transcribed in 11th or 12th century.

«5»

Punjab University, Lahore, No. 371.Spi/VI 103, Monzavī 8, 1024

Containing *Ghazals*, *Robā'īs*, *Mathnavīs*, *Mukhammas*, *Qiṭ'as*.
Nasta'līq, fol.488, 12th century A.H.
Beginning:

به‌اوج کبریا کز پهلوی عجزست راه آنجا...

«6»

ASB, No. 837

Nasta'līq, fol.479, 12th century A.H., good.
This oldest of all the copies of the *Dīwān* in this library contains only *Ghazals* in alphabetical order.
Beginning:

به‌اوج کبریا کز پهلوی عجزســت راه آنجــا
سرمویی گر اینجا خم شوی بشکنی کلاه آنجــا

«7»

Sālār, No. A./Nm.730

Nasta'līq, fol.447, late 12th century A.H., a few folios damaged, seal of Ḥaider Yār Khān Bahādur Shīr Jung, 1171 A.H. and Syed Ḥazāqat Khān, 1168 A.H.
Contains *Ghazals* and *Robā'īs*:

1) *Ghazals* in central columns:
   Beginning:

   به‌اوج کبریا کز پهلوی عجز است راه آنجـا
   سرمویی گر اینجا خم شوی بشکنی کلاه آنجـا

   Ending:

   پی استعاره مدد عبث چو خیال بیدل بیخبـر
   تو ز خود برفته آن‌قدر که مرا تصوّر او کنی

2) *Robā'īs* on outer margins:

   بیرنگی ما رنگِ نگار است اینجـا   از آدمی بندگی شعار است اینجـا

   Ending:

   بر خلق ببخشا که منِ نـاکس هـم   آیـم بشـمار گـردِ دامـانِ کسـی

«8»

Sālār, No. A./Nm.271

Good *Naskh*, fol.271, 20th Ramaẓān, late 12th century A.H., coloured ruled borders, good condition, seal of Gholām Moḥīoddīn, an autograph dated 1163 A.H./1750 A.D.
Beginning: as usual.
Ending:

افسون پری رهِ خیالـت زده اسـت   در شیشه همان گیر که بیرون دیدی

«9»

Ganj Bakhsh, Islamabad, No. 12536, Monzavī 8, 1024

Nasta'līq, p.518, 12th century A.H.
Incomplete *Ghazals* in *Radīf* الف and *Robā'īs* in the end.

«10»

Idāreh-e Adabiyāt-e Urdū, Hyderabad, No. 268 (*Taẕkireh-e Makhṭūṭāt*, Vol. II)

Beautiful *Nasta'līq*, fol.240, late 12th century A.H., coloured ruled, additions on margins, a small seal of Moḥammad Akram (1191 A.H.) on the first page. This manuscript also contains *Seh Nathr* of Żohūrī Tarshīzī.

«11»

Madrasa Ẓiāul 'Ulūm, Quetta, Monzavī 8, 1024

Shikesta-Nasta'līq, p.450, 12th century A.H.

Beginning:

به‌اوج کبریا کز پهلوی عجزست راه آنجا...

Ending:

بیدل از زخمِ دل غمگین چراغان مـی‌کنـد

دیده گل، نظاره گل، آن سرو خوش رفتار گل

(This *Maqṭa'* could not be traced in the Iranian edition).

«12»

Ganj Bakhsh, Islamabad, No. 336, Monzavī 8, 1024

Nasta'līq, p.411, 12th century A.H.

Beginning:

به‌اوج کبریا کز پهلوی عجزست راه آنجا...

«13»

Bahlwāl, Nasirabad, Maulabad, Sargodha, Monzavī 8, 1024

Nasta'līq, p.400, Ḥasan Shāh b. Maṭlūb Ḥusain Shāh, Jhang Syedan, 12th century A.H.

Beginning:

به‌اوج کبریا کز پهلوی عجزست راه آنجا...

«14»

Ganj Bakhsh, Islamabad, No. 491, Monzavī 8, 1024

Nasta'līq, p.396, 12th century A.H.

Beginning:

به‌اوج کبریا کز پهلوی عجزست راه آنجا...

«15»

Khodā Bakhsh, No. 383

Fair *Nasta'līq*, fol.192, within gold ruled borders, 18th century A.D.

Only *Ghazals* in alphabetical order.
Beginning:

به‌اوج کبریا کز پهلوی عجز است راه آنجا...

«16»

Central Library, Bhawalpur, Monzavī 8, 1024
Begins with *Radīf* د and ends with *Radīf* ن.
Nasta'līq, p.370, 12th century A.H.
Beginning:

مگر دل از غم و صبر از جفا خبر دارد   سر بریده ز تن خویش جدا خبر دارد

«17»

Ganj Bakhsh, Islamabad, No. 3391, Monzavī 8, 1024
Shikesta-Nasta'līq, p.366, 12th century A.H.

«18»

Ganj Bakhsh, Islamabad, No. 6246, Monzavī 8, 1024
Shikesta-Nasta'līq, p.366, 12th century A.H.
Beginning:

به‌اوج کبریا کز پهلوی عجزست راه آنجا...

«19»

Handlist of Persian Mss, British Museum, London, No. Or.12987
Fol.181, written in Khoqand, 18th century A.D.
Containing only *Ghazals*.

«20»

Ganj Bakhsh, Islamabad, No. 8749, Monzavī 8, 1024
Containing *Ghazals* from *Radīf* الف to ت.
Shikesta-Nasta'līq, p.349, 12th century A.H.
Beginning:

به‌اوج کبریا کز پهلوی عجزست راه آنجا...

«21»

Ganj Bakhsh, Islamabad, No. 8148, Monzavī 8, 1024

Nasta'līq, p.340, 12th century A.H.

Beginning:

به‌اوج کبریا کز پهلوی عجزست راه آنجا...

«22»

Jahānzīb Library, Jhelum, Monzavī 8, 1024

Nasta'līq, p.316, 12th century A.H.

Beginning:

به‌اوج کبریا کز پهلوی عجزست راه آنجا...

«23»

Ganj Bakhsh, Islamabad, No. 1591, Monzavī 8, 1024

Shikesta-Nasta'līq, p.251, 12th century A.H.

Beginning:

به‌اوج کبریا کز پهلوی عجزست راه آنجا...

«24»

Ganj Bakhsh, Islamabad, No. 706, Monzavī 8, 1024

Nasta'līq, p.200, 12th century A.H.

Beginning:

به‌اوج کبریا کز پهلوی عجزست راه آنجا...

«25»

Dayāl Singh Trust, Lahore, No. 448, Monzavī 8, 1024

Nasta'līq, fol.140, 12th century A.H.

Beginning:

نفس آشفته می‌دارد چو گل جمعیتِ ما را...

«26»

Ganj Bakhsh, Islamabad, No. 8464, Monzavī 8, 1024

Dīwān Volume I

Ghazals from *Radīf* الف upto س.

Nasta'līq, fol.136, 12th century A.H.

Beginning:

به‌اوج کبریا کز پهلوی عجزست راه آنجا...

«27»

Ganj Bakhsh, Islamabad, No. 4506, Monzavī 8, 1024

Shikesta-Nasta'līq, p.130, 12th century A.H.

Beginning:

به‌اوج کبریا کز پهلوی عجزست راه آنجا...

«28»

ASB, No. 840

Shikesta-Nasta'līq, 12th century A.H., good, stray notes and quatrains on fly-leaves and margins.

Contains *Ghazals* in alphabetical order.

Beginning:

دریای خیالیم و نمی‌نیست در اینجا جز وهم وجود و عدمی نیست در اینجا

The *Ghazal* that is placed first in most of the copies is the second one in this copy.

«29»

Ganj Bakhsh, Islamabad, No. 9988, Monzavī 8, 1024

Ghazals from *Radīf* الف to د, *Mukhammas*.

Nasta'līq, fol.518, 12th/13th century A.H., 18 folios in the beginning are missing.

«30»

ASB, No. 839

Shikesta-Nasta'līq, 12th or 13th century A.H., good condition.

Contains *Ghazals* in alphabetical order with a few quatrains and *Fards* (stray couplets) at the end.

«31»

Ganj Bakhsh, Islamabad, No. 404, Monzavī 8, 1033

***Tarkīb-Band* (ترکیب‌بند)**

There are 30 bands having 470 couplets. In some other Mss. of *Dīwān* there are 31 bands and nearly 650 verses.

Shikesta-Nasta'līq, 13th century A.H.

«32»

Ganj Bakhsh, Islamabad, No. 9832, Monzavī 8, 1024

Containing *Ghazals* and *Robā'īs*.

Ordinary script, p.482, 13th century A.H.

Beginning:

به‌اوج کبریا کز پهلوی عجزست راه آنجا...

«33»

Ganj Bakhsh, Islamabad, No. 10817, Monzavī 8, 1024

Containing *Ghazals*, *Mukhammas* and *Robā'īs*.

Nasta'līq, p.480, 13th century A.H.

Beginning:

به‌اوج کبریا کز پهلوی عجزست راه آنجا...

«34»

Sa'diya Library, Kandiyān, Miyanwali, Monzavī 8, 1024

Containing *Ghazals* and *Robā'īs*.

Nasta'līq, p.384, 13th century A.H.

Beginning:

به‌اوج کبریا کز پهلوی عجزست راه آنجا...

«35»

Ganj Bakhsh, Islamabad, No. 8682, Monzavī 8, 1024

Nasta'līq, p.356, 13th century A.H.

«36»

Ḥabībollāh Khān Library, Banon, Monzavī 8, 1024

Nasta'līq, p.286, Gholām Moḥīoddīn b. Waḥīdoddīn b. Shaikh Nūroddīn Mughal, 13th century A.H.

Beginning:

به‌اوج کبریا کز پهلوی عجزست راه آنجا...

«37»

Buḥār, No. 410

Fair *Nasta'līq*, fol.117, 19th century A.D., having two seals of one

Syed 'Abdul Bāsit dated 1221 A.H./[1806 A.D.] on fol.1b and 117b respectively.
Only *Ghazals* in alphabetical order.
Beginning:

ای آینهٔ حسن تمنّای تو جان‌ها   اوراق گلستان ثنای تو زبان‌ها

«38»

Madrasa Ẓiāul 'Ulūm, Quetta, Monzavī 8, 1024
Nasta'līq, p.229, 13th century A.H.
Beginning:

به‌اوج کبریا کز پهلوی عجزست راه آنجا...

«39»

Ganj Bakhsh, Islamabad, No. 10986, Monzavī 8, 1024
Shikesta-Nasta'līq, p.186, 13th century A.H.
Ghazals in alphabetical order.
Beginning:

به‌اوج کبریا کز پهلوی عجزست راه آنجا...

Ending:

به‌ذوقِ دل نفی طوق خویش کن   تو کعبه در بغل جابجا چه می‌خواهی

«40»

Ganj Bakhsh, Islamabad, No. 2233, Monzavī 8, 1024
Nasta'līq, p.185, 13th century A.H.
Beginning:

به‌اوج کبریا کز پهلوی عجزست راه آنجا...

«41»

Dr. Khwāja Moḥammad Salīm, Peshawar, No. 1738/947, Monzavī 8, 1024
Shikesta-Nasta'līq, p.158, 13th century A.H.
Beginning:

به‌اوج کبریا کز پهلوی عجزست راه آنجا...

«42»

Maktaba Solaimān, Sargodha, Monzavī 8, 1039

Mā Ḥarīfān (ما حریفان) *(Tarjī'-Band)*

Nasta'līq, p.60, Moḥammad Nawāz Pisarwārī Nafīs-Raqam, 13th century A.H.

Beginning:

مـــا حریفـــان بـــزم اســـراریم   مست جام شـــهود و دیـــداریم

«43»

Ganj Bakhsh, Islamabad, No. 9815, Monzavī 8, 1024

Shikesta-Nasta'līq, 13th century A.H.

Ghazals in alphabetical order, *Tarjī'*, *Tarkīb*, *Robā'īs* and *Qaṣīdas*.

«44»

Ganj Bakhsh, Islamabad, No. 8468, Monzavī 8, 1024

Nasta'līq, 13th century A.H.

Beginning:

به‌اوج کبریا کز پهلوی عجزست راه آنجا...

«45»

Kitābkhāna-e Millī, Tehran, No. 21.97

Transcribed in 13th century. Bought from Reẓā Shaikhān.

«46»

Sprenger, No. 174

Only *Ghazaliyāt*.

P.231, very fine copy.

Beginning:

به‌اوج کبریا کـــز پهلـــوی عجزســـت راه آنجـــا

سرمویی گر اینجا خم شوی بشکن کلاه آنجـــا

«47»

Fort William College, (N. Archives), No. 545

Nasta'līq, p.818.

Beginning:

الهی پاره‌ای تمکین رم وحشی نگاهـان را

به‌قدر آرزوی ما شکستی کـج کلاهـان را

It is 28th *Ghazal* in the Tehran edition of *Dīwān*.

«48»

Punjab University, Lahore, No. 265.APi/VI 70, Monzavī 8, 1024

Containing *Ghazals*, *Qaṣīdas*, *Mukhammas* and *Robā'īs*.
Nasta'līq, fol.529.

«49»

Tajikistan, No. 2297

Nasta'līq, fol.498, Moḥammad Ḥakīm, bound by Amīn Moḥammad.
There are notes and also couplets by other poets on the margins.
In the catalogue of the library, the name of the author has been wrongly written as Moḥammad Zīā'oddīn Naqshbandī Mujaddedī Khāledī pen-named Bīdel-e Bukhārī.

«50»

Fort William College, No. 148 (Acc. No. 545)

Contains *Ghazals*, *Robā'īs* and short *Mathnavīs*.
Good *Nasta'līq*, p.818.
Ghazals are alphabetically arranged.
Beginning:

الهی پاره‌ای تمکین رم وحشی نگاهـان را

به‌قدر آرزوی ما شکستی کـج کلاهـان را

«51»

Āyātollāh-e Mar'ashī Library, Qom, No. 11659/1

Beautiful *Nasta'līq*, fol.366.
A beautiful copy with gold work in Kashmīrī style.
Nekāt in the end.

Beginning:

به‌اوج کبریا کز پهلوی عجزست راه آنجا...

Ending:

جان و جسد قوی و اعضای حواس این جمله برای یک نفس می‌باید.

«52»

Tajikistan, No. 1406

Selected *Ghazaliyāt* and *Robā'īyāt*.

Beautiful *Shikesta*, fol.354, gold work.

«53»

Upsala, No. 462

Ghazals in alphabetical order and *Robā'īyāt*.

Nasta'līq, fol.300.

Beginning:

به‌اوج کبریا کز پهلوی عجزست راه آنجا

سرِمویی گر اینجا خم شوی بشکن کلاه آنجا

«54»

Patiala (Public Library), No. 1574

Nasta'līq, fol.298, some pages on both sides are worm eaten.

Beginning:

به‌اوج کبریا کز پهلوی عجز است راه آنجا

سرِمویی گر اینجا خم شوی بشکن کلاه آنجا

Ending:

بلبل الم غنچهٔ کشد بیشتر از گل ظلم است به‌عاشق چه مدارا چه تغافل

«55»

Kitābkhāna-e Meghnisā (Manisa) in Turkey, No. 5162

It has wrogly been ascribed to Bīdel-e Bukhārī in the printed catalogue.

Nasta'līq, fol.288, golden *Loḥ* and gold borders. A beautiful copy. The transcription was completed on Thursday.

Beginning:

به‌اوج کبریا کز پهلوی عجز است راه آنجا

سرمویی گر اینجا خم شوی بشکن کلاه آنجا

Ending:

از پرده رنگ این نوا می‌آید کی خودبینان بجانب من نگهی

The scribe has added some couplets in the end of which the last line is:

شد بتوفیق خدای لا بنام این کتابت روز پنجشنبه تمام

«56»

Madras, No. D11

Nasta'līq, fol.273, condition good.

Robā'īyāt in the end.

Beginning:

به‌اوج کبریا کز پهلوی عجزست راه آنجا...

Ending:

ای آن که بعرصه توهم گردی هرگاه بتحقیق رسیدی فردی

با این کسوت که باطلش می‌نامی گر غیرحق از جیب بر آری مردی

«57»

Rampur, No. 329

Nasta'līq, fol.257.

«58»

N. Archives, Afghanistan, No. 29/118

Nasta'līq, fol.248.

«59»

Islāmia College, University, Peshawar, No. 1812, Monzavī 8, 1024

Nasta'līq, p.461.

Beginning:

به‌اوج کبریا کز پهلوی عجزست راه آنجا...

«60»

Islāmia College, University, Peshawar, No. 1800, Monzavī 8, 1024

Shikesta-Nasta'līq, p.462.

Beginning:

به‌اوج کبریا کز پهلوی عجزست راه آنجا...

«61»

Ghālib Institute, New Delhi, No. ف091.511

Nasta'tīq, fol.222, 19th Rajab, 4th regnal year (?).

Beginning:

به‌اوج کبریا کز پهلوی عجز است راه آنجا

سرمویی گر اینجا خم شوی بشکن کلاه آنجا

Ending:

با این کسوت که باطلش می‌نامی   گر غیرحق از جیب برآری مردی

Seal of Moḥammad 'Ażīmoddīn Khān on the first page.

«62»

Dayāl Singh Trust, Lahore, No. 56, Monzavī 8, 1024

Shikesta-Nasta'līq, p.428.

Beginning:

به‌اوج کبریا کز پهلوی عجزست راه آنجا...

«63»

University, No. 26 (1)

Ghazals, *Robā'īyāt* and *Qaṣā'īd*.

Nasta'līq, fol.184, incomplete in the end, not in good condition.

Beginning:

بنـــام آن صـــمد هیچگونـــه و یکتـــا

که کرد کون و مکان را بحرف کن پیـدا

Ending:

ار بستانید عذر تقصـیر معـاف   پیر نادانید عذر تقصیر معـاف

این فرض گرفتن و تغافل کردن   بی‌ایمانید عذر تقصـیر معـاف

«64»

Tajikistan, No. 2283

Nasta'līq, fol.184, in two columns, gold work.

«65»

Banaras, No. 0164, IK37,I

Containing *Ghazals* and some *Robā'īs*.
Nasta'līq, fol.182, defective.
Beginning:

نیست چندان رونقی در رنگ حسن عاریت

خندهٔ گل ورنه در هر مشتِ زر داریم ما

«66»

Kitābkhāna-e Millī, Tehran, No. 5453

Nasta'līq, fol.176, Mollā Moḥammad Rajab b. Narbuteh Bāshī.

«67»

Rampur, No. 3065M

Nasta'līq, fol.168, Ḥāfiż Fateḥoddīn scribed it at the instance of Gholām Ḥaider.

«68»

N. Archives, Afghanistan, No. 36/11

Shikesta-Nasta'līq, fol.160.

«69»

Tajikistan, No. 1406

Nasta'līq, fol.150, Mollā Khwāja Reḥmatollāh son of Islām Mollā 'Ażīm Mollā Khwāja, in a village named Khānqāh-e Khawlang, incomplete copy, gold work.

«70»

Jamia, No. 1524.

Containing *Ghazals*, *Qaṣīdas*, *Mathnavīs*, *Qiṭ'ās* and *Robā'īs*.
Nasta'līq, fol.144, worm eaten.

Beginning:

نفس آشفته می‌دارد چو گل جمعیتِ مـا را

بریشان می‌نویسد کلک موج احوال دریا را

«71»

Banaras, No. 0164, IK37,I

Containing *Ghazals* in alphabetical order.

Nasta'līq, fol.139, defective.

Beginning:

به‌اوج کبریا کز پهلوی عجزست راه آنجـا

سرمویی گر اینجا خم شوی بشکنی کلاه آنجا

«72»

N. Archives, Afghanistan, No. 8/149

Dīwān Volume IV

Nasta'līq, fol.129.

«73»

Upsala, No. 466

Ghazals and *Robā'īyāt*.

Nasta'līq, fol.109.

«74»

Tajikistan, No. 1842

Shikesta-Nasta'līq, fol.109.

«75»

Punjab University, Lahore, No. 1527.PPi/VI 46C, Monzavī 8, 1024

Nasta'līq, fol.104.

Beginning:

به‌اوج کبریا کز پهلوی عجزست راه آنجا...

«76»

Majlis-e Shorā-e Millī, Tehran, No. 8177/68

Nasta'līq, fol.102.

Beginning:

ای جهل پرست از چه قدح باده کشیدی   کز صاف خمستان یقین درد کشـیدی

Ending:

سوز نفسی این همه طوفان جنون ریخت   جز سهو چه بود اینکه در آفاق دمیـدی

It is a *Mukhammas*.

«77»

Kitābkhāna-e Millī, Tehran, No. 17404

Nasta'līq, fol.98.

It was bought from Muṣṭafā Ḥusainī.

«78»

Islāmia College, University, Peshawar, No. 1821, Monzavī 8, 1024

Shikesta, p.214.

Beginning:

به‌اوج کبریا کز پهلوی عجزست راه آنجا...

«79»

Ganj Bakhsh, Islamabad, No. 8465, Monzavī 8, 1024.

Dīwān Volume II

Ghazals from *Radīf* ش to the end.

Nasta'līq, p.170.

«80»

Tehran University, Tehran, No. 427

Nasta'līq, fol.84, Moḥammad Ẓīā'oddīn Naqshbandī Mujaddedī Khāledī pen-named Bīdel-e Bukhārī.

Beginning:

به‌اوج کبریا کز پهلوی عجزست راه آنجا...

Ending:

لفظ حیرت نقشم از مضمون غمّازم مپـرس

بال معذورم ز شوخی‌های پـروازم مپـرس

همچو تــار ســاز از تحقیــق آوازم مپــرس

بر تو رمزی می‌سرایم بشنو و بــازم مپــرس

بیـــدلی در پـــرده دارم ترجمـــان بیـــدلم

In the catalogue of the library, name of the author has been wrongly written as Bīdel-e Bukhārī.

«81»

Tonk, No. 4058/2
Qaṣīda-e Mīrzā Bīdel
Nasta'līq, p.78.

«82»

Rāja Meḥmūdābād Library, Lucknow, No. 2155
Nasta'līq, p.150, worm easten.
Beginning:

نفس آشفته می‌دارد چو گل جمعیتِ مـا را

بریشان می‌نویسد کلک موج احوال دریا را

Ending:

چو هر گوش این سخن را نیست محرم   ســـخن را خـــتم کـــن والله عـــالم

«83»

Kitābkhāna-e Millī, Tehran, No. 17411
Nasta'līq, fol.74.
It was bought from Muṣṭafā Ḥusainī.

«84»

Tajikistan, No. 2970/5
Nasta'līq, fol.65.

«85»

Rampur, No. 888
Only *Ghazals* of *Radīf* الف.
Nasta'līq, fol.1b-49a.

«86»

Ethe, No. 1680.
Selection from *Ghazals* and *Robā'īs*.
Nasta'līq, fol.1-31.
Beginning:

به‌خیال چشم که می‌زند قدح جنون دل تنگِ ما...

Seal of an owner: Qāsim 'Alī Mīr Khān with date 1191 A.H. (1777 A.D.).

«87»

Idāreh-e Adabiyāt-e Urdū, Hyderabad, No. 268 (*Tazkireh-e Makhṭūṭāt*, Vol. II)
Beautiful *Nasta'līq*, fol.24, bearing seal of Moḥammad Akram dated 1191 A.H./[1777 A.D.].

«88»

Upsala, No. 467
Only *Ghazals* of Bīdel alongwith *Ghazals* and *Robā'īs* of Ṣā'ib Tabrīzī.
Nasta'līq, fol.1-23.
Beginning:

ز هر نقاب خجالت برهنه رویی‌ها   خموشی تو زبان بند کامجویی‌ها

«89»

Ganj Bakhsh, Islamabad, No. 7303, Monzavī 8, 1024
Shikesta-Nasta'līq, p.754, 12th century A.H., incomplete in the end.

«90»

Hamdard Library, Nazimabad, Karachi, No. R.167, Monzavī 8, 1024
Shikesta-Nasta'līq, p.298, 12th century A.H., incomplete from the beginning and end.

«91»

Dr. Khwāja Moḥammad Salīm, Peshawar, No. 1894/110, Monzavī 8, 1024
Shikesta-Nasta'līq, p.148, 12th century A.H., incomplete from both ends.

Beginning:

اضطراب شعله ما داغ افســردگی نداشــت

چون نفس از خجلت آرام دلهــا ســوختیم

Ending:

به‌حالی می‌رسم بیدل مباش از جستجو غافــل

دری از آشیان تا واشــود یکچنــد پــروازی

«92»

National Museum, Karachi, No. N.M.1961-1312, 206FQ3, Monzavī 8, 1024.

Nasta'līq, 12th century A.H., incomplete from both ends.

«93»

Ganj Bakhsh, Islamabad, No. 3331, Monzavī 8, 1024

Shikesta-Nasta'līq, p.380, 13th century A.H., incomplete in the beginning.

«94»

'Ābid Ḥusain, Bahlwal, Sargodha, Monzavī 8, 1024

Nasta'līq, p.284, 13th century A.H., incomplete in the end.

Beginning:

به‌اوج کبریا کز پهلوی عجزست راه آنجا...

«95»

Ganj Bakhsh, Islamabad, No. 8358, Monzavī 8, 1024

Nasta'līq, p.244, 13th century A.H., incomplete from both sides.

Beginning:

عمری‌ست در طلسم کدورت نشسته‌ایم

بیــدل غبــار خــاطر مــا آشــیانِ ماســت

Opening couplet of this *Ghazal* is:

عشرت فروز انجمن هستی‌ام حیاست چون شبنم گلم عرق آیینهٔ بقاســت

«96»

Ganj Bakhsh, Islamabad, No. 828, Monzavī 8, 1024

Shikesta-Nasta'līq, p.228, 13th century A.H., incomplete from both ends. *Ghazals* not arranged.

Beginning:

سادگی نگاه رنگ جز تو چه آورد به‌عرض...

«97»

N. Archives, Afghanistan, No. 23/83

Dīwān Volume II

Nasta'līq, fol.880, incomplete in the end.

Beginning:

به‌اوج کبریا کز پهلوی عجز است راه آنجا

سرمویی گر اینجا خم شوی بشکن کلاه آنجا

Ending:

ز رمز صورت و معنی دل خود جمع کن بیدل

بهار اینجاست سامانش درون بویی برون رنگی

It is one of the finest manuscripts of *Dīwān* of Bīdel in this collection. It has a complete list of contents and additions on margins.

«98»

N. Archives, Afghanistan, No. 15/43

Dīwān Volume II

Nasta'līq, fol.545, Laṭīf, incomplete in the end.

Beginning:

به‌اوج کبریا کز پهلوی عجز است راه آنجا...

Ending:

کار من بیچاره قوی بسته شده است   بکشای خدایا که کشاینده توئی

«99»

N. Archives, Afghanistan, No. 30/49

Dīwān Volume II

Nasta'līq, fol.530, incomplete in the end.

«100»

Majlis-e Shorā-e Millī, Tehran, No. 18187

Containing *Ghazals* and *Robā'īs*.

Nasta'līq, fol.395, incomplete in the end.

Beginning:

به‌اوج کبریا کز پهلوی عجزست راه آنجا...

Ending:

... کین فیض طغیان طلسم غم فتد.

«101»

N. Archives, Afghanistan, No. 25/29

Nasta'līq, fol.390, incomplete in the end.

«102»

N. Archives, Afghanistan, No. 8/49

Dīwān Volume I

Contains *Ghazals*, *Nekāt*, *Chahār 'Onṣor* and *Robā'īyāt*.

Nasta'līq, fol.343, incomplete in the end.

Beginning:

به‌اوج کبریا کز پهلوی عجز است راه آنجا...

Ending:

نقشست در آب ترک هم کردیم قلندر گشـتیم

ما را در باب...

«103»

N. Archives, Afghanistan, No. 19/139

Nasta'līq, fol.302, Moḥammad Yūnos, incomplete in the end.

«104»

Ethe, No. 1677

Small *Nasta'līq*, fol.264, incomplete series of *Robā'īs* in the end.

Ghazals in alphabetical order.

Beginning:

نفس آشفته می‌دارد چو گل جمعیت مـا را

پریشان می‌نویسد کلک موج احوال دریا را

«105»

Tajikistan, No. 3117

Shikesta-Nasta'līq, fol.241, incomplete, *Robā'īs* are transcribed in *Shikesta* script.

«106»

N. Archives, Afghanistan, No. 6/156

Dīwān Volume I

Nasta'līq, fol.235, incomplete in the end, two gold front pieces.
Beginning:

به‌اوج کبریا کز پهلوی عجز است راه آنجا...

Ending:

جان و جسد قوی و اعضای حواس   این جمله برای یک نفس مـی‌بایـد

«107»

N. Archives, Afghanistan, No. 14/16

Nasta'līq, fol.228, Amīn Aḥmad, incomplete from both ends.
Beginning:

عیش ترک خانمان از مـردم آزاده پـرس

کس نداند جز صدا قدر شکست شیشه را

Ending:

آخر دم یاسی بی‌تکلّم گشـتن   شد محو تـاخر و تقـدّم گشـتن

«108»

N. Archives, Afghanistan, No. 32/58

Dīwān Volume II

Nasta'līq, fol.220, incomplete in the end.

«109»

Kitābkhāna-e Kāżmīnī, Yazd, No. 141

Nasta'līq, fol.219, incomplete from both ends.
Beginning:

به‌هرسو چشم واکردم نگه وقف خطا کردم

نمی‌دانم چه پیش آمد من غفلت تقاضـا را

Ending:

بیکاری وضـع بیـدلان افتادسـت   یک قطره بباران و آن همچو گهـر

«110»

ASB (First Supplement), No. 809

Shikesta-Nasta'līq, fol.199, worm eaten.

Only *Ghazals* arranged in alphabetical order.

Incomplete in the beginning. The *Ghazals* that are usually given first in other copies are missing in this manuscript.

Beginning:

ای کرد تک و پوی سراغ تو لسان‌ها   وامانده اندیشه راهِ تـو مکـان‌هـا

«111»

Tajikistan, No. 2335

Shikesta-Nasta'līq, fol.183, incomplete.

«112»

N. Archives, Afghanistan, No. 8/149

Ghazaliyāt.

Nasta'līq, fol.179, Moḥammad Yūnos, incomplete in the end, two headpieces, gold work.

Beginning:

به‌اوج کبریا کز پهلوی عجز است راه آنجا...

Ending:

گر نسبت رعایـت تحقیـق اسـت   خود را بکسی چنان که هستی منمـا

«113»

N. Archives, Afghanistan, No. 30/193

Dīwān Volume II

Nasta'līq, fol.170, Laṭīf, incomplete in the end.

«114»

N. Archives, Afghanistan, No. 18/16

Dīwān Volume I

Nasta'līq, fol.160, incomplete in the end.

Beginning:

به‌اوج کبریا کز پهلوی عجز است راه آنجا...

Ending:

بهر سو دیدیم حرص می‌رقصد و بس

کو... کاین است... سرد است و بس

«115»

N. Archives, Afghanistan, No. 30/54
Dīwān Volume II
Nasta'līq, fol.155, incomplete in the end.

«116»

N. Archives, Afghanistan, No. 32/84
Nasta'līq, fol.140, incomplete in the end.
It also contains life account of Khayyām.

«117»

Tajikistan, No. 2693
Shikesta, fol.137, incomplete. It ends with *Radīf* م (*Mīm*).

«118»

N. Archives, Afghanistan, No. 35/93
Nasta'līq, fol.120, incomplete in the end.

«119»

N. Archives, Afghanistan, No. 29/125
Dīwān Volume II
Nasta'līq, fol.120, incomplete in the end.

«120»

Tajikistan, No. 1844
Ghazals* and *Robā'īs
Nasta'līq, *Robā'īs* are scribed in *Shikesta*, fol.119, incomplete copy.

«121»

Tajikistan, No. 3117
Nasta'līq, fol.119, incomplete copy.

«122»

Tajikistan, No. 1842

Nasta'līq, fol.109, incomplete copy.

«123»

Curzon, No. 286

Nasta'līq, fol.95, incomplete at the beginning and the end.

It opens with a series of alphabetically arranged *Qaṣīdas*. Some of these contain chronograms, *Ghazals* alphabetically arranged.

Beginning:

ای آیینهٔ حسن تمنّای تو جان‌ها   اوراق گلستان ثنای تو زبان‌ها

It is the thirtieth *Ghazal* in the printed edition.

Robā'īs begin:

یارب ز می شوق اياغی بفرست   وز نشاء آرزو چراغی بفرست

«124»

N. Archives, Afghanistan, No. 23/171

Nasta'līq, fol.90, incomplete in the end.

«125»

Tajikistan, No. 1137

Nasta'līq, fol.85, incomplete copy, in two columns.

«126»

Idāreh-e Adabiyāt-e Urdū, Hyderabad, No. 383 (*Taẕkireh-e Makhṭūṭāt*, Vol. II)

Only *Ghazaliyāt*, from *Radīf* الف up to *Radīf* ع.

Shikesta-Nasta'līq, fol.8, *Ghazals* also on margins of some pages, incomplete in the end.

«127»

Majlis-e Shorā-e Millī, Library, Tehran, No. 14209/208

***Bahāriya* (بهاريه)**

Nasta'līq, probably transcribed by the poet himself.

It is a *Qaṣīda* in *Na't*.

Beginning:

بیار باده که در صیدگاه عالم هوش   بهار می‌رسد از موج گل کمند بدوش

«128»

Kitābkhāna-e Āstān-e Quds-e Reẓavī, Mashhad, No. 26954

Nasta'līq, incomplete copy in the end.

Beginning:

به‌اوج کبریا کز پهلوی عجز است راه آنجا

سرِمویی گر اینجا خم شوی بشکن کلاه آنجا

Ending:

دیدیم که دستِ ما بجایی نرسید   از سعی جنون داد که بنیان دادیم

«129»

Kitābkhāna-e Āstān-e Quds-e Reẓavī, Mashhad, No. 22814

Nasta'līq, incomplete copy from both ends.

Beginning:

بر اهلِ بیت طاهره زان زاده ز ناز...

Ending:

مترس از آتشِ دوزخ اگر گبری اگر ترسا.

«130»

N. Archives, Afghanistan, No. 25/46

Incomplete from both ends.

Beginning:

علاج زخم دل از گریه کی ممکن بود بیدل   به‌شبنم بخیه نتوان کرد چاک سینه گل را

Ending:

... دلان در حقیقت یکسر...

«131»

N. Archives, Afghanistan, No. 4/11

Transcribed by Mollā Ḥusain b. Mollā Ḥakīm.

Beginning:

به‌اوج کبریا کز پهلوی عجز است راه آنجا...

Ending:

با این کسوت که باطلش می‌نامی   گر غیرحق از جیب برآری مـردی

In the end کتابِ دوّم (II Volume) has been noted.

«132»

N. Archives, Afghanistan, No. 7/13

Transcribed by Moḥammad Yūnos Khwāja b. Bābā Khwāja Shahr Sabzī. It includes *Qaṣā'īd*, *Robā'īyāt* and *Qiṭ'āt*.

Beginning:

به‌اوج کبریا کز پهلوی عجز است راه آنجا...

Ending:

عبث چند رنجِ بیـانش کشـی   کتاب قصـاید عنـانش کشـی

«133»

N. Archives, Afghanistan, No. 7/122

Included *Ghazals* and *Robā'īs*.

Beginning:

به‌اوج کبریا کز پهلوی عجز است راه آنجا...

Ending:

کم‌ظرفی ما (ز) وصل (ما) مانع نیست   گر قطره بود (همان) محیط است محـیط

«134»

N. Archives, Afghanistan, No. 22/164

Contains *Ghazals*, *Qaṣā'īd*, *Tarkīb-Bands*, *Tarjī'-Band* and *Mathnavī*-e *Tanbīh-ul Mohawwesīn*.

Begins after preface:

به‌اوج کبریا کز پهلوی عجز است راه آنجا...

Ending:

ترک این تدبیر تدبیرت بس است   از گداز خویش اکسیرت بس اسـت

It was presented to Amīr Ḥabībollāh Khān, king of Afghanistan by Syed 'Ālam Shāh Amīr of Bukhara.

«135»

Record Office, Peshawar, No. 189, Monzavī 8, 1024

Shikesta-Nasta'līq.

«136»

Kitābkhāna-e Miftāḥ, Tehran, No. 825

Nasta'līq, Sharīf Bukhārī, Bukhara.

«137»

Tehran University, Tehran, No. 1769ف

Nasta'līq.

«138»

Kitābkhāna-e Millī, Tehran, No. 1743

It was bought from Muṣṭafā Ḥusainī.

«139»

Kitābkhāna-e Millī, Tehran, No. 17449

It was bought from Muṣṭafā Ḥusainī.

«140»

Kitābkhāna-e Millī, Tehran, No. 25727

Bought from Mīr Dād Khān.

«141»

Mīnuvī Library, Tehran, No. 74

Nasta'līq.

«142»

Punjab University, Lahore, Shīrānī Collection, No. 4610/1659, Monzavī 8, 1024.

«143»

Sharaful Mulk Library, Chenna'ī, No. 715

«144»

Sharaful Mulk Library, Chenna'ī, No. 720

«145»

N. Archives, Afghanistan, No. 23/112

Incomplete in the beginning.

Beginning:

نـدارد عبـرت احـوال دنیـا فرصـت اندیشـی
گرت چشمی است از مژگان گشودن پیشتر بگشـا

Ending:

از شوق سراغ بسملش دست به‌دست   چون سایهٔ دود سیاهی چشم غـزال

Chapter III

Manuscript of Sharḥ-e Dīwān-e Bīdel

«1»

Ganj Bakhsh, Islamabad, No. 8718, Monzavī 8, 1032

Commentator not known, commentary only on *Ghazals* of *Radīf* الف.

Nasta'līq, p.258, Friday, Rabī'I, 1327 A.H./[April, 1909 A.D.].

Beginning:

حمدت حمدالک یا ملاذالملولین و یا غیب‌الغیّوبین و یا غیب‌الغیّوبات والصّلاة... بسمله یعنی شروع می‌کنم به‌نامِ مبارک آن ذاتِ مستجمع جمیع کمالاتِ وجوبی... به‌اوج کبریا... یعنی به‌بلندی کبریای کبیر متعال که صفت کبریت در افعال او و صفاتِ او و شئوناتِ او و اعتباراتِ او و ذات...

Probably it is the only commentary on *Ghazals* of *Radīf* «ردیف الف» of Bīdel. No other manuscript of it could be traced. Similarly, no such attempt has been made so far.

Chapter IV

Manuscripts of Intekhāb-e Dīwān-e Bīdel (Dated)

A good number of the manuscripts of selections from Bīdel's *Ghazals* made by Bīdel and others are available in India and abroad. It indicates the encouraging response his *Ghazals* received from the interested people throughout the Persian world. Similarly, Bīdel was often requested to make selections of his *Dīwān* for them which he did. Consequently, some manuscripts of such selections also can be found in some libraries. In some such selections, Bīdel has added a few *Ghazals* in his own handwriting mostly *in Shafī'ā* script. Moreover, there are a great number of *Bayāẓ* in which others have selected Bīdel's verses along with the works of other poets. It again highlights the popularity of Bīdel's poetry.

*

«1»

Ethe, No. 1679

Selection of *Ghazals* and *Robā'īs.*

Nasta'līq, fol.163, 6th Rajab, 13th year of Moḥammad Shāh's reign [1144 A.H./24th December, 1731 A.D.].

Beginning:

ای مردهٔ تکلّف از کیف و کم برون آ　　گاهی برغم دانش، دیوانه هم بـرون آ

Beginning of *Robā'īs*:

گردون در خاک اگر نشاند ما را...

«2»

Rieu, No. Add.25,822.

Ghazals in alphabetical order, *Robā'ī*, *Mukhammasāt*.

Nasta'līq, fol.166, Sha'bān, 1145 A.H./[January, 1733 A.D.], from the camp of Niẓāmul Mulk Aṣefjāh, near the fort of Ausa (Owsa), Deccan.

Beginning:

بهر جبین که بود سطری از کتابِ حیا　　ز نقطـهٔ عـرقم دارد انتخـابِ حیـا

«3»

Faiẓ Library, Qāẓiyān, Bhawalpur, Monzavī 8, 1024

A selection from the *Dīwān* transcribed after 34 years of the death of the poet.

Nasta'līq, p.164, Mollā Mūsā Alwarī, 1167 A.H./[1854 A.D.]

Beginning:

چو غبار نالهٔ مستان زدیم کامی از امتحان...

«4»

Sālār, No. A./Nm.272

Shikesta-Nasta'līq, fol.68, Benī Prashād, 10th Moḥarram, 1182 A.H./ 27th May, 1768 A.D., subsequent additions by Shādī Lāl made in 1184 A.H./1770 A.D. at Bhopal (Madhya Pradesh).

Some verses of other poets on folios 69-70, a *Risāla* (رساله) on folios: 71-77, and *Bahārīya*, a specimen of ornate prose (from a letter) of Bīdel on folios 78-82.

Beginning:

نفس آشفته می‌دارد چو گل جمعیت مـا را

پریشان می‌نویسد کلک موج احوال دریا را

Ending:

غبارِ من ز شوق سـجده مـی‌آیـد بـدامانت

شکست چین دامان تو محراب است پنداری

«5»

N. Archives, Afghanistan, No. 13/142
Intekhāb-e Bīdel
Nasta'līq, fol.190, 1281 A.H./[1864 A.D.].

«6»

Austrian National Library, No. Mixt.1221 (3124)
Selection from *Ghazaliyāt*.
Nasta'līq, fol.326, Moḥammad Akram, 1301 A.H./[1884 A.D.]
Beginning:

به‌اوج کبریا کز پهلوی عجزست راه آنجا...

Ending:

شبِ بیدل نشـود روز چـه امکـان دارد

که تو خورشیدی و در کشورِ ما می‌آیی

Colophon:

اگرچه اشعارِ میرزا عبدالقادر بیدل علیه‌الرحمه همه منتخب است، آنچه به‌نظر ناقص منتخبِ‌تر آمد، بر صفحهٔ کاغذ نوشتم تا وسیلهٔ یادگار باشد اللّهمّ اغفر لکاتبه شهر شعبان‌المعظّم سنهٔ ۱۳۰۱ هجری، محمّد اکرم.

Manuscripts of Intekhāb-e Dīwān-e Bīdel (Undated)

«1»

Sālār, No. 2056

Nasta'lāq, fol.133.

It has 782 *Ghazals* and 235 *Robī 'ās*. Bīdel has written some of his *Ghazals* in the margins of some of its folios.

It has a seal of one Żahīroddīn Ḥasan Khān affixed on the first page of the Ms., and signatures of four other persons with the years 1131, 1148 and 1151 A.H. It can thus safely be said that this Ms. was scribed before 1131 A.H./1720 A.D., i.e. in the life of Bīdel.

It was first printed in Delhi in 1388 H.S./2009 A.D. and was afterwards published by Sūr-e Mehr, Tehran, in 1393 H.S./2014 A.D. It was reprinted by the same publication house in 1394 H.S./ 2015 A.D. These printed editions are named "Bīdel Be Intekhāb-e Bīdel" and edited by Prof. Sharif Husain Qasemi and Dr. Ali Reza Ghazveh.

«2»

Khāneqāh-e Reḥmānia, Monger, Bihar

Ījād-e Bīdelī

It is a selection of some verses from 340 *Ghazals* and a *Mukhammas*. It was copied from the author's copy written in his own hand as indicated in this colophon:

نقل از نسخهٔ منقولهٔ دستخطِ میرزا عبدالقادر بیدل قدّس‌سرّه نوشته شد و بی‌استعدادی کاتب معذور باد.

The following note in the beginning of the Ms. indicates that it was presented to Nawwāb Ḥusain 'Alī Khān Shahīd (one of the famous Syed brothers assassinated in 1132 A.H./1720 A.D.), a friend of Bīdel who was the governor of Deccan for some time:

نامِ این انتخاب «ایجادِ بیدلی» که طرزی که میرزا جدا از همهٔ شعرا مخصوص خود دارد، به‌همان‌طور خاص این همهٔ اشعار انتخاب کرده به‌نوّاب حسین علی شهید داده بود.

It means that this selection was made before 1132 A.H./1720 by Bīdel. It has now been edited by Prof. Sharif Qasemi and published by National Mission for Manuscripts, New Delhi, in 1438 A.H./2017 A.D.

«3»

Anjuman Taraqqī, Karachi, No. 206FQ3, Monzavī 8, 1024

Selection from the *Dāwī n*.

Nasta'lāq, p.120, Harpat Rāi, 12th century A.H.

«4»

Sālār, No. A.N.674/1

Good *Nasta'lāq*, fol.72, a late 12th century A.H. copy, gold and coloured ruled borders, fair condition, seals of Aṭhar 'Alī Khān and Monīrol Mulk, 1206 A.H., containing *Qaṣī 'āl* and *Robī 'ās* at the end.

Beginning with the first *Ghazal* in the *Dāwī n*.

Ending:

بســـیار ذرایـــع فضـــایل بـــودش   مجموع بدین غریب بسرود و برفت

«5»

Sālār, No. A./Nm.273

Shikesta-Nasta'lāq, fol.70, a late 12th century A.H. copy, defective at both ends.

Beginning:

به‌هر جبین که بود سطری از کتاب حیا   ز نقطـهٔ عـرقم دارد انتخـابِ حیـا

It is the 97th *Ghazals* in the published edition.

Ending:

غباری که از دامن صحرا بلند می‌شود چو...

«6»

Sālār, No. A./Nm.974

Shikesta-Nasta'lāq, fol.15, an early 13th century A.H. copy, seals of Mostaqīm Jung, 1204 A.H.; Mostaqīmuddaula, 1209 A.H.; Moḥammad 'Alī, 1234 A.H.; Mostaqīmuddaula, 1246 A.H.

Beginning:

ستم است اگر هوست کشد که بسیر سرو و سمن درآ

تو ز غنچه کم ندمیده‌ای در دلکشا بـه‌چمـن درآ

Ending:

گریبان عالمی دارد که در دامن نمی‌گنجد.

«7»

Hardayāl, R135

Nasta'lāq, fol.199, at the instance of Khānzādeh Kāżim Khān Bahādur, worm eaten.

Containing 73 *Ghazals*, 44 *Robī 'ās*.

Beginning:

غیـر وحـدت برنتابـد همّـتِ عرفـان مـا

دامن خویش است چون صحرا گل دامانِ مـا

«8»

Upsala, No. 460

Nasta'lāq, fol.162.

A selection of *Ghazals* and *Robī 'āyī t*.

«9»

Baldīyā Library, Turkey, No. Be.k.34

Abyī tāaz Bīdel (ابیاتی از بیدل)

It is included in a collection of treatises (مجموعةالرسایل).

Nasta'lāq, p.199.

Beginning:

دانـم از کیفیّـتِ آگـاهی و اوهـام هـم

جنس بسیار است و نقد فرصت ناکام کم

«10»

Jawāhar, No. ج ن 336

Ghazals and a few *Robī 'ās* in the end.
Nasta'lāq, fol.94, incomplete in the end.
Beginning:

نفس آشفته می‌دارد چو گل جمعیت مـا را
پریشان می‌نویسد کلک موج احوال دریا را

Ending:

آفاق همه جرعه کش جام فناست   هر زنده که هست...
در پیری صید زندگی نتوان کرد   قد خم گشته حلقه دام فناسـت

«11»

Sobḥānallāh, No. 891,5514/82

Bound with a *Mathnavā* by Bu'Alī Shāh Qalander.
Beautiful *Nasta'lāq*, fol.52, scribed in three columns on every folio.
Beginning:

تغافل تا نگاهی چشم مستش فرق نیسـت
نشئه دیگرگون نباشد دُرد و صاف جام را

Ending:

در تن خود یک هدف در استخوان دارم هنوز
نسبت دوری بـآن ابـرو کمـان دارم هنـوز

«12»

Bursā Library, No. 2402/1

Selection of the *Dāwī n*.
Nasta'lāq, fol.41-2+1.
Beginning:

به‌اوج کبریا کز پهلوی عجزست راه آنجـا
سرمویی گر اینجا خم شوی بشکن کلاه آنجا

Ending:

تا نام گرفتن گذرد وصف کشیدن   شمشـــیر و قلـــم را (تمّـــت)

It is a Ms. of the *Dāwī n* of Bīdel of Delhi and not Bukhara as wrongly stated in the catalogue.

«13»

Āyātollāh-e Mar'ashī Library, Qom, No. 4283

Containing only a selection of *Ghazals*.

Nasta'lāq, fol.34, golden headpieces.

Chapter V

Manuscripts of Bayāẓ, Including Selected Verses of Bīdel (Dated)

«1»

Tajikistan, No. 2671

Bayāẓ (انتخاب ابیاتِ شعرای مختلف)

It has a selection of poems by 36 poets including Bīdel.

A part of it was scribed in 1122 A.H./1710 A.D., and the other in Ṣafar 1187 A.H./1773 A.D.

«2»

Tajikistan, No. 786/1

Transcribed in 1246 A.H./1830 A.D.

«3»

Tajikistan, No. 1003/2

Bayāẓ (انتخاب)

Transcribed in 1251 A.H./1836 A.D.

«4»

Tajikistan, No. 2842/1

Bayāẓ (انتخاب)

Transcribed in 1252 and 1253 A.H./1836 and 1837 A.D.

«5»

Tajikistan, No. 123/4

It was transcribed in 1256 A.H./1840 A.D.

«6»

Tajikistan, No. 3024/2

It was transcribed in 1256 A.H./1840 A.D.

«7»

Tajikistan, No. 84/4

It was transcribed in Ẕīqa‘da, 1257 A.H./December, 1841 A.D.

«8»

Tajikistan, No. 2475/5

It was transcribed in 1261 A.H./1845 A.D.

«9»

Tajikistan, No. 14/1

Transcribed in 1263 A.H./1846 A.D.

«10»

Tajikistan, No. 2521/1

Transcribed in 1265 A.H./1848-49 A.D.

«11»

Ganj Bakhsh, Islamabad, 4062, Monzavī 8, 1024

Selection of verses of Bīdel are included in a *Bayī ā*.
Nasta'lẓq, p.1-36 and 234-42, 1270 A.H./[1854 A.D.].
Beginning:

به‌اوج کبریا کـز پهلـوی عجزسـت راه آنجـا

سرمویی گر اینجا خم شوی بشکن کلاه آنجـا

«12»

Idāreh-e Adabiyāt-e Urdū (Hyderabad) Volume V, No. 940

It is a *Bayī ā* by Mīrzā 'Aṭā Ẓiā Burhānpūrī prepared at Bitala in 1171 A.H./[1758 A.D.]. It contains selected verses by Bīdel.
Nasta'lẓq, fol.60. It is a beautiful copy.

«13»

Tajikistan, No. 2229/2

Transcribed in 1276 A.H./1859 A.D.

«14»

Tajikistan, No. 2245

Transcribed in 1279 A.H./1862 A.D.

«15»

Tajikistan, No. 109/2

Transcribed in 1283 A.H./1866 A.D.

«16»

Tajikistan, No. 1855
Transcribed in 1286 A.H./1869 A.D.

«17»

Tajikistan, No. 1197
Transcribed in 1287 A.H./1870 A.D.

«18»

Tajikistan, No. 2642/1
Transcribed in Moḥarram, 1289 A.H./March, 1872 A.D.

«19»

Tajikistan, No. 1135
Transcribed in 1291 A.H./1874 A.D.

«20»

Tajikistan, No. 3148/3
Transcribed in 1296 A.H./1878 A.D.

«21»

Tajikistan, No. 1862/1
Transcribed in 1297 A.H./1879 A.D.

«22»

Tajikistan, No. 2488
Transcribed in 1301 A.H./1884 A.D.

«23»

Tajikistan, No. 1075
Transcribed in 1303-1348 A.H./1885-1930 A.D.

«24»

Tajikistan, No. 1424
Transcribed in Moḥarram, 1317 A.H./May, 1899 A.D.

«25»

Tajikistan, No. 189
Transcribed in 1331 A.H./1912 A.D.

«26»

Tajikistan, No. 2293

Copied from a manuscript of Syed 'Omar Khwāja Mīr Kātibī in 1336 A.H./1917 A.D.

Manuscripts of Bayāẓ, Including Selected Verses of Bīdel (Undated)

«1»

Idāreh-e Adabiyāt-e Urdū (Hyderabad) Volume V, No. 1131

It is entitled *Bayāẓ-e Kalām* and was prepared during the period of Naṣīr Jung Shahīd at Bidar and Aurangabad. The verses of many Persian and Urdū poets are selected in it.

Nasta'līq, fol.144, Moḥammad Ḥusain resident of Mohammadabad Bidar.

«2»

Tajikistan, No. 1137

Beautiful *Shikesta-Nasta'līq*, fol.85.

«3»

Madrasa Moḥammadī Library, Madras (Chenā'ī)

There is a small *Bayāẓ* of 82 folios in this library containing stray verses from Persian poets. Selections from some of the poets in this *Bayāẓ* are transcribed by the poets themselves in their own hands. This line on page 22 indicates that it was prepared at the instance of some minister but his name and date have not been given:

حسب‌الامر بندگان وزارت پناه تحریر یافت.

It has seven complete *Ghazals* by Bīdel in his own hand, one of them has been transcribed as under:

لمحرّرهٔ عبدالقادر بیدل

نیست به‌مژگان تعلّق اشک وحشت پیشه را

دانه با دام راه خویش راند ریشه را

Prof. Mukhtāroddīn Aḥmad has introduced this *Bayāẓ* is his article in Urdū entitled *Fārsī kī Ek Nādir Bayāẓ*, published in *Risāla Safīna* (Patna), No. 8. The same article has also been reprinted in *Mo'āṣir*, Patna and *Dānish* (Islamabad), March 1989 A.D.

«4»

Persian Research Centre, Iran Culture House, New Delhi

Verses from Asadī Ṭūsī and Bīdel are copied on the last two pages.

Nasta'līq, fol.61, incomplete in the end and not in good condition.

«5»

Ganj Bakhsh, Islamabad, No. 850, Monzavī 8, 1024

Selection

Nasta'līq, p.2-94, 13th century A.H.

«6»

Aḥsan, AMU, Aligarh, No. 329

***Ash'ẓr-e Bīdel* (اشعار بیدل)**

Some verses from Bīdel included in a *Bayāẓ*.

Shikesta-Nasta'līq, fol.28.

«7»

Majlis-e Shorā-e Millī, Tehran, No. 8177/5

Selection

Nasta'līq, fol.9, only one *Ghazal*.

Beginning:

آن که از بوی بهارش رنگ امکان ریختنـد

گرد راهش جوش زد آثار اعیـان ریختنـد

Ending:

غیر رازش نیست بیدل در خیال آباد صنع

هرچه این بستند نفس هر قدر آن ریختنـد

«8»

Tajikistan, No. 122/1

13th century A.H./19th century A.D.

Only one *Ghazal* of Bīdel has been selected in it.

«9»

Tajikistan, No. 3922/3
12th century A.H./18th century A.D.

«10»

Tajikistan, No. 7
12-13th century A.H./18-19th century A.D.

«11»

Tajikistan, No. 10/1
13th century A.H./19th century A.D.

«12»

Tajikistan, No. 10/2
13th century A.H./latter half of 19th century A.D.

«13»

Tajikistan, No. 10/3
13th century A.H./19th century A.D.

«14»

Tajikistan, No. 104
13th century A.H./19th century A.D.

«15»

Tajikistan, No. 273
13th century A.H./19th century A.D.

«16»

Tajikistan, No. 286
13th century A.H./19th century A.D.

«17»

Tajikistan, No. 436/3
13th century A.H./19th century A.D.

«18»

Tajikistan, No. 490
13th century A.H./19th century A.D.

«19»

Tajikistan, No. 593

13th century A.H./19th century A.D.

«20»

Tajikistan, No. 675

13th century A.H./19th century A.D.

«21»

Tajikistan, No. 710

13th century A.H./19th century A.D.

«22»

Tajikistan, No. 740

13th century A.H./19th century A.D.

«23»

Tajikistan, No. 758/3

13th century A.H./19th century A.D.

«24»

Tajikistan, No. 865

13th century A.H./19th century A.D.

«25»

Tajikistan, No. 913/1

13th century A.H./19th century A.D.

«26»

Tajikistan, No. 973/2

13th century A.H./19th century A.D.

«27»

Tajikistan, No. 1008/1

Transcribed in 13th century A.H./19th century A.D.

«28»

Tajikistan, No. 1229

13th century A.H./19th century A.D.

«29»

Tajikistan, No. 1243/7

13th century A.H./19th century A.D.

«30»

Tajikistan, No. 1321

13th century A.H./19th century A.D.

«31»

Tajikistan, No. 1376/1

13th century A.H./19th century A.D.

«32»

Tajikistan, No. 1407/1

13th century A.H./19th century A.D.

«33»

Tajikistan, No. 1425

Transcribed in 13th century A.H./19th century A.D.

«34»

Tajikistan, No. 1441

13th century A.H./19th century A.D.

«35»

Tajikistan, No. 1469/1

13th century A.H./19th century A.D.

«36»

Tajikistan, No. 1482

13th century A.H./19th century A.D.

«37»

Tajikistan, No. 1535/1

13th century A.H./19th century A.D.

«38»

Tajikistan, No. 1581

13th century A.H./19th century A.D.

«39»

Tajikistan, No. 1756
13th century A.H./19th century A.D.

«40»

Tajikistan, No. 1757
13th century A.H./19th century A.D.

«41»

Tajikistan, No. 1796
13th century A.H./19th century A.D.

«42»

Tajikistan, No. 1853/2
13th century A.H./19th century A.D.

«43»

Tajikistan, No. 1859
13th century A.H./19th century A.D.

«44»

Tajikistan, No. 2242/1
Late 13th century A.H./19th century A.D.

«45»

Tajikistan, No. 2357/2
13th century A.H./19th century A.D.

«46»

Tajikistan, No. 2387
13th century A.H./19th century A.D.

«47»

Tajikistan, No. 2394/1
13th century A.H./19th century A.D.

«48»

Tajikistan, No. 2490/2
13th century A.H./19th century A.D.

«49»

Tajikistan, No. 2503/20

13th century A.H./19th century A.D.

«50»

Tajikistan, No. 2550

13th century A.H./19th century A.D.

«51»

Tajikistan, No. 2585

13th century A.H./19th century A.D.

«52»

Tajikistan, No. 2595

13th century A.H./19th century A.D.

«53»

Tajikistan, No. 2610

13th century A.H./19th century A.D.

«54»

Tajikistan, No. 2692/3

13th century A.H./19th century A.D.

«55»

Tajikistan, No. 2933

13th century A.H./19th century A.D.

«56»

Tajikistan, No. 2969

13th century A.H./19th century A.D.

«57»

Tajikistan, No. 3034/1

13th century A.H./19th century A.D.

«58»

Tajikistan, No. 5222

13th century A.H./19th century A.D.

«59»

Tajikistan, No. 81/2

Transcribed in 19th century A.D.

«60»

Tajikistan, No. 227/2

Transcribed in 19th century A.D.

«61»

Tajikistan, No. 474/2

14th century A.H./20th century A.D.

«62»

Tajikistan, No. 657

Though date of transcription not given but a beautifully scribed copy.

«63»

Rieu, Vol. II, p.737.

It is in two volumes.

«64»

Tajikistan, No. 150/3

«65»

Tajikistan, No. 209/2

«66»

Tajikistan, No. 243/1

«67»

Tajikistan, No. 285

«68»

Tajikistan, No. 705/2

«69»

Tajikistan, No. 1005.

«70»

Tajikistan, No. 1132

«71»

Tajikistan, No. 1228.

«72»

Tajikistan, No. 1315/3

«73»

Tajikistan, No. 1445/2

«74»

Tajikistan, No. 1453

«75»

Tajikistan, No. 1460

«76»

Tajikistan, No. 1636

«77»

Tajikistan, No. 2228

«78»

Tajikistan, No. 2646

«79»

Tajikistan, No. 4963/3

«80»

Tajikistan, No. 49641/1.

Chapter VI

Manuscripts of Robā'īyāt-e Bīdel (Dated)

Bīdel is regarded as one of the best *Robā'ī*-writers of his time. His *Robā'īs* included in the *Kolliyāt* published from Kabul are 2,949 in number but are said to amount to four thousand (Khushgū), far more than the *Robā'īs* of any other *Robā'ī*-writer. Their contents are varied and vide, and they make Bīdel worthy of the tributes paid to him as a master of this genre of poetry.

Shaikh Sa'dollāh popularly called Shāh Golshan (d.1140 A.H./ 1727 A.D.), one of the last great Ṣūfīs of Delhi who was also famous for his piety, used to say «رباعی گویی حقّ اوست» (He has every right to compose quatrains[1]).

Bīdel compiled a separate selection of his *Robā'īs* in his own hand in as early as 1115 A.H./1703 A.D.,[2] to which he would have certainly added later during his remaining life of eighteen years. The chief characteristic of Bīdel's *Robā'īs* is its aphoristic style and comprehensive expression. It helps to understand his philosophy in a nutshell. Bīdel himself defines his *Dīwān* of *Robā'īs* as a collection of *Robā'īs* on varied subjects «رنگینی»:

در مکتب شوق کم کسی دارد یاد   دیوان رباعی به‌این رنگینی[3]

*

---

1. *Safīna-e Khushgū*, p.125.
2. Bānkīpūr, Vol. III, p.202.
3. *Āwāzhāy-e Bīdel*, p.44.

«1»

Khodā Bakhsh, No. 386

This copy contains a smaller number of Bīdel's *Robā'īs*.
It is supposed to be in the author's own handwriting.
Shikesta, fol.161, 19th Moḥarram, 1115 A.H./[24th May, 1703 A.D.].
This note on fol.1a in a different hand, suggests that it is an autographed copy of the author:

به‌خطِّ مرزا بیدل مرحوم.

«2»

Khodā Bakhsh, No. 385

It is a valuable copy of the *Robā'īs* written eleven years before the death of Bīdel. *Robā'īs* are arranged in alphabetical order.
Nasta'līq, fol.230, Wednesday, 18th Jumāda'I, 1122 A.H./[4th July, 1710 A.D.], within gold-ruled borders.
Beginning:

آنکس که منزّه است از آب و گِلِ ما   بی‌او عدم است خلوت و محفلِ ما

Colophon:

روز چهارشنبه هژدهم ماه جمادی‌الاولی سنهٔ یکهزار و یکصد و بیست و دو هجرت.

«3»

Ethe, No. 1681

It is probably the most complete extant collection of Bīdel's *Robā'īs*. It contains nearly 3,500 epigrams in a strictly alphabetical order.
Distinct *Naskh*, fol.288, Moḥammad Wārith b. Moḥammad Bāqer Al-Ṣiddīqī, 17th Moḥarram, 1126 A.H./[2nd February, 1714 A.D.].
Transcribed in the lifetime of the poet.
Beginning:

آنکس که منزّه است از آب و گِلِ ما   بی‌او عدم است خلوت و محفلِ ما

«4»

Rieu (Supplement), No. 338

Cursive Indian character, fol.135, 9th Rabī'I, 1133 A.H./(28th December, 1720 A.D.).

Beginning:

آنکس که منزّه است از آب و گِلِ مـا   بی‌او عدم است خلوت و محفلِ ما

At the end of the alphabetical series fol.126, is a colophon stating that while the scribe was engaged in transcribing these verses, Bīdel died on Thursday, the 4th of Ṣafar 1133 A.H./[24th November, 1720 A.D.].

The latter part of the Ms. fol.126b-135 is occupied by a selection of mixed contents, consisting of satires in *Qaṣīda* form, *Mukhammas* and *Robā'īs* by the same Bīdel. It is imperfect at the end.

Beginning:

این دورِ دور حیز است وضع متین کـه دارد

باد بروت مردی غیـر از سـرین کـه دارد

It is a *Maṭla'* of a *Ghazal* of Bīdel.

«5»

Sprenger, No. 175

Only *Robā'īyāt* are alphabetically arranged. Eight *Robā'īs* on a page.

Nasta'līq, p.500, 1133 A.H./1721 A.D.].

Beginning:

اوّل ترکیب وضع و نسبت دریـاب   آن گه ربط معنی و صورت دریاب

عالم گاوی به‌پشت ماهی است سـوار   آن ماهی بر هـوا حقیقـت دریـاب

«6»

Punjab University, Lahore, No. 4671, Spi/VI 103C, Monzavī 8, 1024

Containing only *Robā'īs*.

Nasta'līq, 11th Moḥarram, 1135 A.H./[11th October, 1722 A.D.], 4th regnal year (Naṣīroddīn Moḥammad Shāh), copied from the poet's copy with a seal of Mahārāja Nekhat (Teket) Rai, 1193 A.H./[1779 A.D.], from Meḥmūd Shīrānī's collection.

«7»

Banaras, No. 0164,1

One of the most complete collection of *Robā'īs* of Bīdel arranged in alphabetical order.

Nasta'līq, fol.233, 1230 A.H./(1814 A.D.).

Beginning:

آنکس که منزّه است ز آب و گِل ما   بی‌او عدم است خلوت و محفلِ ما

«8»

Idāreh-e Adabiyāt-e Urdū, Hyderabad, *Tazkireh-e Makhṭūṭāt*, Vol. IV No. 772

There are some *Robā'īyāt* of Bīdel in a Ms. entitled «کلامِ آصفجاه و میرزا بیدل استادِ آصفجاه».

Nasta'līq, fol.10.

It was donated by Nawwāb 'Ināyat Jung Bahādur. As recorded in a note, it was copied on 27th Moḥarram, 1238 A.H./[14th October, 1822 A.D.], from the *Bayāẓ* of Miyān Jān.

«9»

Dā'eratul Ma'ārif Library, Tehran, No. 1834/2

Nasta'līq, fol.451, Faqīr Moḥammad Ghauth Qāderī, Thursday, Sha'bān, 1277 A.H./[February, 1861 A.D.].

Presented by Dr. Ṣādiq Kiyā.

Beginning:

باب‌الالف

آنکس که منزه است ز آب و گلِ مـا   بی‌او عدم است خلوت و محفلِ ما

Ending:

... ای حیرت فهم (کو موجود کیا) معدومی خویش از کجا می‌فهمی،

تمّت‌الرّباعیّاتِ بیدل (رح) به‌یدّالفقیر محمّد غوث قادری.

«10»

Upsala, No. 464 *Robā'īyāt.*

Nasta'līq, fol.152, Moḥarram, 1281 A.H./[June, 1864 A.D.].

«11»

Monīr-e 'Ālam Collection, No. Box 5, No. 27 Fārsiya

Nasta'līq, fol.189, scribed at the instance of Munshī Gholām Ghauth by Syed Mīrzā, [18th Rajab, 1292 A.H.]/20th August, 1875 A.D.

Beginning:

حمد دو جهان سزاست سلطانی را   کاو پست نخواست عجز بنیانی را

Ending:

عمری است بخواب بی‌نیازی مستیم   در سایهٔ آستان بی‌دیواری

Manuscripts of Robā'īyāt-e Bīdel (Undated)

«1»

N. Archives, Afghanistan, No. 15/186

Nasta'līq, fol.580, Laṭīf, incomplete in the end.

«2»

Hand list of Persian Mss. British Museum, No. Or.6594

Fol.424.

«3»

Hardayāl Library, No. R155.

Only 1840 *Robā'īs* out of 3619 in *Kolliyāt*.

Shikesta, fol.184, Hīrā Singh.

Beginning:

ای دانه ازین مزرع اندیشه بـرا   یعنی ز طلسم الفت ریشه بـرا

«4»

Ḥabībganj, No. 296 (H.G.50/65)

Nasta'līq, fol.116.

Beginning:

بی‌رنگی ما رنگِ نگار است اینجا   آزادیِ بندگی شعار است اینجـا

Ending:

بر خلق ببخشا که منِ ناکس هم   آیم بشـمار گـردِ دامـانِ کسـی

«5»

Malik Library, Tehran, No. 5169.

Fair *Nasta'līq*, fol.73, golden front-pieces.

Beginning:

آنکس که منزه است از آب و گِلِ مـا   بی‌او عدم است خلوت و محفـلِ مـا

Ending:

زان بارگهم چیزی اگر باید خواسـت   آن خواهم کز کسی نخـواهم چیـزی

«6»

Tonk, Rajasthan, No. 3151
Nasta'līq, p.138.

«7»

Aḥsan, AMU, Aligarh, No. Fārsiya 891.5513/2:1
Terjī'-Band and Robā'īyāt
Nasta'līq, fol.16.
Beginning:

ما حریفانِ بزم اسراریم   مست جام شهود و دیداریم

«8»

Aḥsan, AMU, Aligarh, No. Fārsiya 891.5513/2:1
Terjī'-Band: Mā Ḥarīfān (ما حریفان) **and *Robā'īyāt***
Nasta'līq, fol.3, bound with some other works.
Beginning:

ما حریفانِ بزم اسراریم   مست جام شهود و دیداریم

Ending:

که جهان نیست جز تجلّی دوست   این من و ما همه اضافت اوست

«9»

Idāreh-e Adabiyāt-e Urdū, Hyderabad, Volume V, No. 1005
This manuscript entitled *Mostazād* also contains some *Robā'īyāt* of Bīdel after the *Mostazād*.
Nasta'līq, fol.3.

Chapter VII

Manuscript of Motafarriqāt-e Bīdel

«1»

Motafarriqāt-e Bīdel (متفرّقاتِ بیدل)

Late Prof. Nurul Ḥasan Ansari, Department of Persian, University of Delhi, has referred to Bīdel's monumental work "Fārsī Adab Be-'Ahd-e Aurangzib," in Urdū (PhD).

It includes dilectic *Qaṣīdas*, *Mukhammas*, poetry in praise of prominent persons, elegies, *Moqaṭṭa'āt* and *Hajviyāt*.

Prof. Ansari has not given any information about its Ms. or printed edition.[1]

1. See *Fārsī Adab Be-'Ahd-e Aurangzīb*; Dr. Nūrul Ḥasan Anṣārī, Indo-Persian Society, Delhi, 1969, p.191.

Chapter VIII

Manuscripts of Bayāī -e Bẓdel*

Following the tradition of men of letters in the Persian world, Bīdel selected verses of his choice from a good number of Persian poets obviously for personal use. He has also written a *Dībācha* (preface) to it. Ṣā'ib Tabrīzī and Wāleh Dāghistānī are two prominent poets whose such selections have survived as manuscripts.

*

---

* Late Dr. Noorus Sa'id Akhtar, Department of Persian, Mahārāshtra College, Mumbai, imformed me of the presence of *Bayāẓ-e Bīdel* in Sindhia Oriental Library, Ujjain in India.

«1»

Rieu, No. Add.16,802 and 16,803.

Fair *Shikesta*, fol.429 and 453 (Two uniform Volumes), Ẕīqa'da, 1152 A.H./[January, 1740 A.D.] and Moḥarram, 1153 A.H./ [March, 1740 A.D.], Lahore.

It contains selected pieces by a large number of poets from the age of Khāqānī to the author's time, organized according to the various styles of poetical compositions and arranged alphabetically according to the rhymes in each class. Poems written by different authors in the same measure and with the same rhyme are grouped together. The names of the poets are given in versified headings like the following: معراج سخن کلام قدسی and بادشاه سریر معنی اسیر.

This *Jung* (*Bayāẓ*) also includes some letters of Bīdel's contemporaries to him and a story of a stupid Brahman. It also contains some jokes about 'Abdul Aḥad Waḥdat (d.1125 A.H.), a selection from a *Mathnavī* by *Bazmī* and *Me'rāj-ul Khayāl* by Mollā 'Alī Raẓā Tajallī Ardistānī (d.1088 A.H.), a dialogue between opium and tobacco, some *Ḥikāyat* of mystics, a selection from a *Tarjī'-Band* by 'Urfī Shīrāzī (d.999 A.H.) entitled *Golshan-e Rāz*. (Rieu, Vol. II, p.727).

«2»

Majlis-e Shorā-e Millẓ Library, Tehran, No. 14415/4

Dībācha-e Bayāẓ

Nasta'līq, fol.2.

Beginning:

مسجود اندیشی جبین قلم بهنگارش حمد واحدی که...

(This *Dībācha* is also included in *Majma'-ul Afkār*, p.434, published by National Mission for Manuscripts, New Delhi).

«3»

Sharaf-ul Mulk Library, Chenā'ẓ, No. 328.

Goldastah-e Bīdel

It may be a selection of Bīdel's poetry or the *Bayāẓ* of this poet.

Chapter IX

Manuscripts of Moḥīṭ-e A‘żam (The Great Ocean) (Dated)

Bīdel has composed four *Mathnavīs* (long poems), mainly characterized by mystical insight balanced by artful rhetoric. A deep study and thorough investigation of Bīdel's thought process, reveals a link between his four *Mathnavīs*. The first *Mathnavī Moḥīṭ-e A'żam* was completed in 1668 A.D., the second *Mathnavī Ṭelesm-e Ḥairat* in 1669 A.D., the third *Ṭūr-e Ma'refat* in 1687 A.D. and the fourth and the last one *'Irfān* with *Lāhūt* (divinity) as its backdrop in 1712 A.D. This concept places the last one at the beginning of the spirit's journey, which ends with *Moḥīṭ-e A'żam* going through *Ṭūr-e Ma'refat* and *Ṭelesm-e Ḥairat* on its way. Consequently, there is a plan in the four *Mathnavīs* in tune with the Ṣūfī travelogue of the spirit.[1]

Moḥīṭ-e A'żam was composed in 1078 A.H.[2]/1668 A.D. The number of the couplets in this *Mathnavī* differs in various manuscripts of it ranging from 2,000 to 6,000.[3] The same is the case with other works of Bīdel. It has a brief preface in the style of Mollā Żohūrī Tarshīzī's[4] *Sāqī Nāmeh*, which is why it is also

---

1. Mīrzā Bīdel's 'Irfān and Yogavasishtha: Wagesh Shukla, p.12 (footnote).
2. The title «محیطِ اعظم» (*Moḥīṭ-e A'żam*) is the chronogram for the year of its completion as composed by Bīdel himself:

   این نسخه که از خامهٔ الهام رقم   گردید مسمّی به‌محیطِ اعظم

   دریافت دبیر خرد از روی حساب   سال تاریخ هم به‌نامش مدغم

   Moḥīṭ-e A'żam (included in *Kolliyāt* published from Kabul), pp.3-4.
3. Nearly 6,000 couplets in Kābul edition.
4. Nūroddīn Moḥammad pen-named Żohūrī came to India from Tarshīz in Khorāsān and settled down in Bījāpūr where he enjoyed the favour of Ibrāhīm 'Ādil Shāh II (1580-1628 A.D.). He died in 1025 A.H./1616 A.D.

termed as *Sāqī Nāmeh* and *Maikhāneh* in some manuscripts. Bīdel also states in a letter: «محیطِ اعظم که ساقی‌نامه‌ایست». Bīdel states in this regard:

این میخانهٔ ظهور حقایق است نه ساقی‌نامهٔ اشعار ظهوری، آیینه‌پرداز کیفیت دقایق است، نه زنگار فروشِ خمار بی‌شعوری.

This *Mathnavī* is divided into eight chapters called دور (*Daur*), as in Ibn-e 'Arabī's *Fuṣuṣ-ul Ḥikam*. Each *Daur* is illustrated with several anecdotes. Among the many stories and anecdotes, some Indian stories are also related in it. An Indian tale of a Rāja and a wooden horse has been narrated. It is important to note that the great Indian spiritual and poetic classic Yogavasishtha and Mahābhārata had always interested Bīdel. Direct evidence of Yogavasishtha is available in this *Mathnavī*. The story, which starts with this verse in praise of India:

شنیدم در اقلیم هندوستان   که خاکش بود آبروی جهان

[*I have come to know that in India, the dust of which is the face glow of the world.*]

has been taken verbatim from Yogavasishtha.[1] Bīdel, not well acquainted with Sanskrit, certainly studied Persian translation of Yogavasishtha. One of the translations of this book was done during Akbar's reign, and the other at the instance of Dārā Shukoh.[2]

Among his other works, his *Sāqī Nāmeh* is particularly a celebrated poem. Almost all the contemporary and latter *Tazkirah* writers (biographers) have written about his life and literary achievements in their respective works. For his detailed life account and description of works see Żohūrī by Prof. Nazir Ahmed.

1. For details see: the article "Mīrzā Bīdel's 'Irfān and Yogavasishtha" by Wagesh Shukla included in Mīrzā 'Abdul Qādir Bīdel (a collection of articles edited by Prof. Qamar Ghaffar, New Delhi, 2017, pp.115-24).
2. For details see: A Descriptive Catalogue of Persian translations of Indian Works compiled by Sharif Husain Qasemi, National Mission for Manuscripts, New Delhi.

Apart from it, Bīdel scholars have traced widespread influence of Indian philosophy, intellect and wisdom on Bīdel's thought. While dealing with such a subject, Bīdel has demonstrated his grasp on Indian culture and intellectual traditions.

In brief, Bīdel following Ibn al-'Arabī's doctrine *Waḥdat-ul Wujūd* (وحدت‌الوجود) in illustrating how the universe not distinct from the pre-eternal divine essence, comes into fermentation like wine and finally develops into man.

The style of the poem is in conformity with Bīdel's general poetry obscure – delicate and philosophical. Its understanding, Bīdel claims, requires a good background of Ṣūfism:

لاجرم هر بی‌مغزی را کیفیّت مطالعه‌اش نشئه تردماغی نرساند و هر تنک ظرف را پیمانهٔ ورق گردانش جرعهٔ ادراک نچشاند.

*

«1»

Rampur, No. 4011M

Nasta'līq, fol.145, Shaikh Moḥammad, 1108 A.H./[1696 A.D.].

«2»

Peshawar University, Peshawar, No. 127, Monzavī 8, 1040

Nasta'līq, p.418, 1135 A.H. [1723 A.D.].

Beginning:

دیباچه: حمد بی‌حد نشئه آفرینی که میخانهٔ حقیقتِ انسانی را از نشئه...

آغاز مثنوی:

خوش آندم که در بزمگاه قدم   میی بود بی‌نشئه کیـف و کـم

«3»

Khodā Bakhsh, No. 382

***Moḥīṭ-e A'ẓam included in the Kolliyāt* (No. 382)**

Nasta'līq, fol.126a to 188a, Moḥammad Wārith b. Moḥammad Bāqer, Shawwāl, 1136 A.H./[June. 1724 A.D.].

Beginning:

حمد بی‌حد نشاه آفرینی که میخانهٔ حقیقت انسانی را از نشاء کرمنا بنی‌آدم علوّ مفاخرت ظهور بخشید...

Mathnavī begins:

خوش آندم که در بزمگاه قدم   میی بود بی‌نشاء کیـف و کـم

«4»

Tonk, No. 3331/3

Nasta'līq, p.78, 1140 A.H./[1727 A.D.].

«5»

Monīr-e'Ālam Collection, No. Box, 5, No. 20 ن

Nasta'līq, fol.241, Loṭfollāh, at the instance of Mīr Wilāyatollāh Khān, 1146 A.H./[1734 A.D.], 16th regnal year of Moḥammad Shāh.

Beginning: preface:

حمد بی‌حد نشئه آفرینی که میخانهٔ حقیقت انسانی را از نشئه...

خوش آندم که در بزمگاه قدم   میی بود بی‌نشاهٔ کیـف و کـم

Ending of the poem:

کنم صاف اســرار وحــدت بجــام   همه نشئه چون می‌شــود والسّــلام

مصرع دوّم بدین قرار است: «همه نشئه می شوم والسّلام».

«6»

ASB, No. 841

Nasta'līq, Qodratollāh Mīrzāpūrī, 1179 A.H./[1765 A.D.], two columns in the centre and one on the margins.

Beginning of preface:

حمد بی‌حد نشاء آفرینی که میخانهٔ حقیقت...

Beginning of the poem:

خوش آندم که در بزمگاه قدم   میی بود بی‌نشاء کیـف و کـم

«7»

Ethe, No. 1683

Shikesta-Nasta'līq, fol.32-74, Moḥammad Ja'far Ref'at, 26th Ṣafar, 1191 A.H./[5th April, 1777 A.D.].

Beginning:

حمد بی‌حد نشاء آفرینی که میخانهٔ حقیقتِ انسانی را...

«8»

Tajikistan, No. 1560/1

Shikesta-Nasta'līq, fol.61, 1193 A.H./1779 A.D.

In some catalogues it is also named as *Maikhāneh* (میخانه) and also *Sāqi Nāmeh* (ساقی‌نامه).

«9»

National Museum, Karachi, No. N.M.1972-110/A.B., Monzavī 8, 1040

Nasta'līq, 1201 A.H./[1787 A.D.], worm eaten.

«10»

Moḥd Shafī' Collection, Lahore, No. 185/214, Monzavī 8, 1040

Shikesta-Nasta'līq, fol.79, 'Alī Shīr Qāne' Shīrāzī Shokrollāhī Ḥusainī, 1202 A.H./[1788 A.D.].

Beginning:

دیباچه: حمد بی‌حد نشئه آفرینی که میخانهٔ حقیقتِ انسانی را از نشئه...

«11»

Tajikistan, No. 136

Shikesta-Nasta'līq, fol.84, 1204 A.H./1790 A.D.

«12»

Punjab University, Lahore, Shīrānī Collection No. 3131 Spi/ VI-103B, Monzavī 8, 1040

Nasta'līq, fol.102, Wāresta Mal, 1215 A.H./[1800 A.D.].

Beginning:

حمد بی‌حد نشئه آفرینی که میخانهٔ حقیقتِ انسانی را از نشئه...

«13»

Tajikistan, No. 402

Shikesta-Nasta'līq, fol.103, Moḥammad Qāsim b. Mollā Shafī'ollāh, 1223 A.H./1808 A.D.

«14»

Āṣafīya, No. 293

Nasta'līq, 1229 A.H./[1814 A.D.].

«15»

Tajikistan, No. 2964/2

Shikesta, fol.218, Mollā 'Abdur Reḥmān b. Mollā Yādgār, Ẕīqa'da, 1232 A.H./September, 1817 A.D.

«16»

Tajikistan, No. 18/1

Shikesta-Nasta'līq, fol.87, Sharīf Khāksār, 1235 A.H./1820 A.D.

«17»

Tajikistan, No. 836/3

Shikesta, fol.77, 1246 A.H./1830, Bukhara.

«18»

Tajikistan, No. 1239/1

Nasta'līq, fol.98, 1276 A.H./1859 A.D., Tashkent in the Mosque of Ḥāfiż Kuhokī.

«19»

Maulānā Qodratollāh Bahlwal, Sargodha, Monzavī 8, 1040

Nasta'līq, p.200, Mollā 'Abdur Raḥīm, 11th Ẕilḥijja, 1279 A.H./ [30th May, 1863 A.D.]. It lacks «دیباچه» in prose.
Beginning:

خوش آندم که در بزمگاه قدم میی بود بی‌نشئه کیـف و کـم

«20»

Ganj Bakhsh, Islamabad, No. 1939, Monzavī 8, 1040

Nasta'līq, p.16-316, 1288 A.H./[1871 A.D.], incomplete in the end.

«21»

Ganj Bakhsh, Islamabad, No. 1532, Monzavī 8, 1040

Nasta'līq, p.74-78, Fārigh, 1314 A.H./[1896 A.D.].

Manuscripts of Moḥīṭ-e A‘żam (The Great Ocean) (Undated)

«1»

Sālār, No. A./Nm.890

Good *Nasta‘līq*, fol.104, a late 11th century A.H. copy, heading in red, gold and coloured ruled borders.

Beginning:

حمد بی‌حد نشاهٔ آفرینی که میخانه حقیقتِ انسانی را از نشاهٔ...

Ending:

کنم صاف اسرار وحدت به‌جام   همه نشاء چون می شـوم والسّـلام

«2»

Peshawar University, Peshawar, No. 126, Monzavī 8, 1040

Beautiful *Nasta‘līq*, p.412, 12th century A.H, gold work.

Beginning:

حمد بی‌حد نشئه آفرینی که میخانهٔ حقیقتِ انسانی را از نشئه...

«3»

British Museum, London, No. Or.10923
Handlist of Persian Mss.

Fol.67, 18th century A.D.

«4»

Ganj Bakhsh, Islamabad, No. 10522, Monzavī 8, 1040

Nasta‘līq, p.138, 13th century A.H., incomplete in the end.

حمد بی‌حد نشئه آفرینی که میخانهٔ حقیقتِ انسانی را از نشئه...

«5»

National Museum, Karachi, No. N.M.1958-202/20-4, Monzavī 8, 1040

Contains *Dībācha* (preface) only.

Nasta‘līq, p.269-269, 13th century A.H.

Beginning:

حمد بی‌حد نشئه آفرینی که میخانهٔ حقیقتِ انسانی را از نشئه...

«6»

Ethe, No. 1882

Nasta'līq, fol.204.

Beginning:

خوش آندم که در بزمگاه قدم　　میی بود بی‌نشئهٔ کیف و کم

«7»

Punjab University, Lahore, No. 1526 PPi/VI46B, Monzavī 8, 1040

Also includes *Ṭūr-e Ma'refat*.

Nasta'līq, fol.44-247.

Beginning:

حمد بی‌حد نشئه آفرینی که میخانهٔ حقیقتِ انسانی را از نشئه...

«8»

Punjab University, Lahore, No. 1524 PPi/VI46, Monzavī 8, 1040

Nasta'līq, fol.184.

«9»

Ḥabībganj, No. 295 (H.G.50/308)

Beautiful *Nasta'līq*, fol.141, illustrated head-piece, transcribed within blue and gold ruled borders.

Beginning:

خوش آندم که در بزمگاه قدم　　میی بود بی‌نشاهٔ کیف و کم

Ending:

کنم صاف اسرار وحدت بجام　　همه نشئه چون می شوم والسّلام

مصرع دوّم در نسخه بدین‌قرار است: «همه نشئه می شوم والسّلام».

«10»

Tajikistan, No. 2670

Shikesta-Nasta'līq, fol.82.

«11»

Rampur, No. 6661

Nasta'līq, fol.79.

«12»

Rampur, No. 8482

Nasta'līq, fol.76, Nūr Moḥammad son of Moḥammad Fāẕil of Ambāla.

«13»

Tajikistan, No. 1/1434

Shikesta-Nasta'līq, fol.53.

«14»

Tajikistan, No. 502/5

Shikesta-Nasta'līq, fol.52.

«15»

Sprenger, No. 178

P.71.

It has a short preface in prose and then begins:

خوش آندم که در بزمگاه قدم   میی بود بی‌نشاء کیف و کم

منزّه ز اندیشهٔ حادثات   مبرا ز درد غبار صفات

«16»

Monīr-e'Ālam, Collection, No. Box, 5, No. 22/1

It is bound with some other works by different authors.

Nasta'līq, fol.28.

Beginning: preface:

حمد بی‌حد نشاه آفرینی که میخانهٔ حقیقت انسانی را از نشئه...

Ending:

بطوفان مژگان دریا خروش   به... ز خود رفتن رنگ هوش

«17»

Tonk, No. 4509/1

Dıḅācha-e Moı ḻt-e A'ẕam

Nasta'līq, p.8.

«18»

Brown, No. V.63 (10), P.253

1) *Maikhāneh* (the wine-tavern) in eight sections called *Daur* (Round or Circuit) of the wine-cup by a prose preface beginning:

بی‌حد نشئه آفرینی را که میخانهٔ حقیقت انسانی را...

Then:

اما بعد بدان که این خمخانهٔ ظهور حقایق است نه ساقی‌نامهٔ اشعار ظهوری...

Actual poem:

ازین میخانه نتوان بود غافل   که درها می‌کشاید بر رخ دل

«19»

Punjab University, Lahore, Shīrānī Collection No. 3421 Spi/ VI103D, Monzavī 8, 1040

Nasta'līq, transcribed in the life time of the author. Exact date not given.

Beginning:

خوش آندم که در بزمگاه قدم   میی بود بی‌نشئهٔ کیف و کم

«20»

Sharaful Mulk Lirary, Chenā'ī , No. 143

Chapter X

Manuscripts of Ṭelesm-e Ḥairat (The Talisman of Bewilderment) (Dated)

Composed in 1080 A.H.[1]/1669 A.D. only two years after his *Mathnavī Moḥīṭ A'żam*. It is allegorical and metaphysical in nature, dealing with the kingdom of human body. It contains about 4,000 couplets. (Khushgū). The essence and attributes of God, the scheme of creation as well as man's physical and spiritual existence are discussed in it. In its form, it resembles Farīdoddīn 'Aṭṭār's celebrated *Mathnavī-e Manṭequṭ Ṭair* and focuses on the ambivalent relationship of the soul to the body, elaborating the different faculties that serve the soul, the causes of its troubles and the ways these troubles can be alleviated. Bīdel substantiates the supremacy of the heart in the human body and advocates the sublimity of love over fear, enmity and other vicious sentiments.

Bīdel has conveyed its year of completion in these couplets:

به‌ملک مخترع چون یافت اتمام   چو عالم شد طلسم حیرتش نام
گهی تـاریخ عقـل زمـان یـاب   پی تاریخ نظمـش بـود بیتـاب
سر اندیشه‌ای تا دید در حبیـب   برون آورد گنج از عـالم غیـب

(۱۱۵۳-۷۳ = ۱۰۸۰ ه)

The numerical value of «گنج» (= 73) has to be deduced from the numerical value of «عالم غیب» (= 1153) which comes to 1080.

This *Mathnavī* was sent to Shokrollāh Khān, a friend and mentor of Bīdel who wrote the headings on different parts of the *Mathnavī*.[2]

*

1. Sprenger, p.379 and the Cataloguer of Sālārjung Museum have wrongly given 1125/ 1713-14 as the year of its completion. *Āwāzhāy-e Bīdel*, p.30.
2. *Ṭelesm-e Ḥairat*, included in the *Kolliyāt*, Kābul edition, p.1 and *Roqqa'āt*.

«1»

Monīr-e 'Ālam Collection, Box 5, No. 17

Khulāṣa Musamma be Mer'at-e Ṭelesm-e Ḥairat)

(خلاصه مسمّی به‌مرأت طلسم حیرت)

Nasta'līq, fol.103, 1093 A.H./[1682 A.D.].

Beginning:

بر محرمان اسرار حقیقت محتجب مباد که چون لطیفۀ روح...

آنچه درین دایرۀ صوت و صداست   پـــردۀ آرایـــش حمـــدِ خداســـت

به‌نام آن کـــه دل کاشـــانۀ اوســـت   نفـــس گـــرد متـــاعِ خانـــۀ اوســـت

Ending:

زبان را با خموشـــی روبـــرو کـــن   دگر چندان که خواهی گفتگو کن

«2»

University, No. (2) 101 Fārsiya

Nasta'līq, fol.180, Saturday, 19th Ẕīqa'da, 1147 A.H./[2nd April, 1735 A.D.], Hyderabad.

Beginning:

بنـــام آن کـــه دل کاشـــانۀ اوســـت   نفـــس گـــرد متـــاعِ خانـــۀ اوســـت

Ending:

زبان را با خموشـــی روبـــرو کـــن   دگر چندان که خواهی گفتگو کن

On the last pages, stray couplets from Maulānā Jalāloddīn Rūmī, Mīr Murād 'Alī Khān and Bīdel are transcribed.

«3»

Sālār, No. A./Nm.629

Good *Shikesta*, fol.119, Khushḥāl Chand, 26th Ṣafar, 1172 A.H./ 29th October, 1758 A.D., heading in red.

Beginning:

آنچه درین دایرۀ صوت و صداست   پـــرده آرایـــش حمـــدِ خداســـت

Ending:

زبان را با خموشـــی آشـــنا کـــن   دگر چندانکه خواهی گفتگو کن

«4»

Ganj Bakhsh, Islamabad, No. 766, Monzavī 8, 1036

Shikesta-Nasta'līq, p.238, 1201 A.H./[1787 A.D.].

Beginning:

آنچه در این دایرهٔ صوت و صداست — پـــردهٔ آرایـــش حمـــدِ خداســـت

بەنـــام آن کـــه دل کاشـــانهٔ اوســـت — نفـــس گـــردِ متـــاعِ خانـــهٔ اوســـت

«5»

National Museum, Karachi, No. N.M.1972-110/AB, Monzavī 8, 1036

Nasta'līq, 1201 A.H./[1787 A.D.], worm eaten.

Beginning:

بەنام آن که دل کاشانهٔ اوست — نفس گـــردِ متـــاعِ خانـــهٔ اوســـت

«6»

Patiala (Public Library), Patiala, No. 1575

Nasta'līq, fol.131, Sohamal Nanda, [1215 A.H.]/1800 A.D.

Beginning:

بنام آن که دل کاشانهٔ اوســـت — نفس گـــردِ متـــاعِ خانـــهٔ اوســـت

Ending:

زبان را با خموشی روبـــرو کـــن — دگر چندان که خواهی گفتگو کن

«7»

Tajikistan, No. 1849/5

Shikesta-Nasta'līq, fol.105, Bāi Moḥammad, 1235 A.H./1820 A.D., scribed in two columns.

«8»

Tajikistan, No. 836/4

Shikesta-Nasta'līq, fol.128, 'Abdur Reḥmān Khatlānī, 1246 A.H./ 1830 A.D., Sultanabad, Bukhara, with gold work, corrections made on margins by the scribe.

«9»

Tajikistan, No. 292/3

Beautiful-*Nasta'līq*, fol.105, Yūnos, 1246 A.H./1830 A.D., scribed in two columns.

«10»

Maulānā Qodratollāh, Bahlwal, Sargodha, Monzavī 8, 1036
Nasta'līq, p.172, 1255 A.H./[1839 A.D.].
Beginning:

آنچه در این دایرهٔ صوت و صداست   پـــردهٔ آرایـــش حمـــدِ خداســـت

«11»

Tajikistan, No. 1763
Shikesta-Nasta'līq, fol.133, 1263 A.H./1847 A.D., scribed in two columns, gold work.

«12»

Tajikistan, No. 2673
Shikesta-Nasta'līq, fol.136, 1264 A.H./1848 A.D.

«13»

Monīr-e 'Ālam Collection, Box 3, No. 16
Nasta'līq, fol.64, [14th Shawwāl, 1268 A.H.]/1st August, 1852 A.D.
Beginning:

آنچه درین دایرهٔ صوت و صداست   پـــردهٔ آرایـــش حمـــدِ خداســـت

به‌نام آن کـــه دل کاشـــانهٔ اوســـت   نفـــس گـــرد متـــاع خانـــهٔ اوســـت

Ending:

زبان را با خموشـــی روبـــرو کـــن   دگر چندان که خواهی گفتگو کن

«14»

Ganj Bakhsh, Islamabad, No. 12551, Monzavī 8, 1036
Ordinary script, p.270, 1280 A.H./[1863 A.D.].

کزو دریاست ساحل بی‌نشانست...

Eight verses are missing from the beginning.

«15»

Rampur, No. 760M
Nasta'līq, fol.210, Ilāhī Bakhsh Merjān Qalam, 1282 A.H./[1865 A.D.].

Manuscripts of Ṭelesm-e Ḥairat
(The Talisman of Bewilderment)
(Undated)

«1»

Sprenger, No. 176

P.300.

Beginning:

بنام آن که دل کاشانهٔ اوست　　نفس گردِ متاعِ خانهٔ اوست

«2»

Ethe, No. 1684

Nasta'līq, fol.105, seals of Qāsim 'Alī Mīr Khān, dated 1191 A.H./ [1777 A.D.].

Beginning:

بنام آن که دل کاشانهٔ اوست　　نفس گرد متاعِ خانهٔ اوست

«3»

N. Archives, Afghanistan, No. 31/24

Nasta'līq, fol.104, incomplete in the end.

«4»

Moḥammad Baig Library, Sargodha, Monzavī 8, 1036

Nasta'līq, p.180, 13th century A.H.

Beginning:

آنچه در این دایرهٔ صوت و صداست　　پردهٔ آرایش حمدِ خداست

«5»

Kitābkhāna-e Majlis-e Shorā-e Millī, Tehran, No. 733

Nasta'līq, fol.99.

Beginning:

آنچه در این دایرهٔ صوت و صداست　　پردهٔ آرایش حمدِ خداست

بەنــام آن کــه دل کاشــانۀ اوســت　　نفــس گــردِ متــاعِ خانــۀ اوســت

Ending:

الصلوای حق رضاجوی امرالقبل تین　　الســلام قبلــۀ عــالم بروئــی بــا صــفا

الصلوای در تو بســتم ذاتِ حــق بینــا　　السلام در تفکّر بــرد بــاری بــا هــر...

«6»

Tajikistan, No. 2559/1

Shikesta-Nasta'līq, fol.92, (1b to 92), with gold work, some additions and corrections are made on margins.

«7»

Madras, No. D75 (c)

Nasta'līq, fol.63, good condition.

Though recorded in the catalogue but could not be traced in the collection.

«8»

Ethe, No. 1685

Nasta'līq, fol.52.

Beginning:

بەنام آن که دل کاشانۀ اوست　　نفس گــردِ متــاعِ خانــۀ اوســت

«9»

Khodā Bakhsh, No. 382

Ṭelesm-e Ḥairat Included in the Kolliyāt

Nasta'līq, fol.189a to 225b.

Beginning:

بەنام آن که دل کاشانۀ اوست　　نفس گرد متــاعِ خانــۀ اوســت

«10»

Lucknow, No. 891.5513, B39T

Chapter XI

Manuscripts of Ṭūr-e Ma'refat (The Senai of Gnosis: Golgasht-e Ḥaqīqat) (Dated)

This third *Mathnavī* is mystical in its nature as well. Its concluding part is entitled *Golgasht-e Ḥaqīqat*[1], which was sent to 'Āqil Khān Rāzī.[2] It contains 3,000 couplets (2,000 couplets: Khushgū). In this poem, Bīdel primarily describes the mountain and the country side of Bairat, now in Rajasthan state. He visited this place with his friend-patron Shokrollāh Khān, the *Faujdār* (military commander) of the place.[3] While describing various fascinating manifestations of nature, Bīdel emphasises the spiritual aspects of natural phenomenon. It is interesting that Bīdel visited a goldmine in this region where mining was being carried out on regular basis.

Bīdel has referred to its title:

به‌یمنش آخر این مکتوب منظوم   به‌طور معرفت گردید موسـوم

There is no indication of its year of versification in this work. But as Shokrollāh Khān was engaged in confronting Bijay Rām in Mewat in 1097-98 A.H./1685-87 A.D., this may have been composed during the same period. Bīdel was proud of this *Mathnavī* and praised it as a work bearing hundred thousand thought-provoking pearls:

«صدهزار گوهر معانی به‌دامان»

*

1. It is not an independent poem as wrongly stated in the Edinburgh Catalogue, No. 313.
2, *Roqqa'āt*, p.96.
3. *Ibid.*, p.81.

«1»

Peshawar University, Peshawar, No. 134, Monzavī 8, 1037

Having 1100 couplets.

Nasta'līq, p.79, 1135 A.H./[1723 A.D.].

Beginning:

طپش فرسوده شوق ناله تمثال   ز تحریک نفس وا می‌کند بـال

«2»

Khodā Bakhsh, No. 382

Ṭūr-e Ma'refat Included in the Kolliyāt

Nasta'līq, fol.112b to 125, Moḥammad Wārith b. Moḥammad Bāqer, Ẕilḥijja, 1136 A.H./[August, 1724 A.D.]. (See No. 381)

Beginning:

طپش فرسوده شوق ناله تمثال   ز تحریک نفس وا می‌کند بـال

«3»

Idāreh-e Adabiyāt-e Urdū, Hyderabad, No. 36 (*Taẕkirah-e Makhṭūṭāt*, Vol. II)

Fine *Shikesta*, fol.83, Mīr Niżāmoddīn Ḥusain, Thursday, Sha'bān, 1189 A.H./[October, 1775 A.D.], Aurangabad, headings red.

«4»

Ethe, No. 1686

Shikesta-Nasta'līq, fol.75-85, Moḥammad Ja'far Ref'at, 2nd Rabī'I, 1191 A.H./[10th April, 1777 A.D.].

Beginning:

بینـوایی ز محفـل هسـتی   داشت پیمانهٔ تهـی دسـتی

«5»

National Museum, Karachi, No. N.M.1972-110/A-B, Monzavī 8, 1037

Nasta'līq, 1201 A.H./[1787 A.D.], worm eaten.

«6»

Tajik, No. 2559/2

Shikesta-Nasta'līq, fol.131, 1203 A.H./[1789 A.D.], scribed in two columns, gold work.

«7»

Tajikistan, No. 292/2

Beautiful *Shikesta-Nasta'līq*, fol.36, 1248 A.H./[1832 A.D.], gold work.

«8»

Ganj Bakhsh, Islamabad, No. 5983, Monzavī 8, 1037

Nasta'līq, p.89-220, Jumāda'I, 1268 A.H./[March, 1852 A.D.].

Beginning:

آغاز بیان سیر بیرات   تحقیق سواد قدرت آیات

«9»

Kitābkhāna-e Mālik, Tehran, No. 6433

Nasta'līq, fol.82, Moḥammad Ibrāhīm Gauharī, Friday, 8th Shawwāl, 1290 A.H./[29th November, 1873 A.D.].

Beginning:

آغاز بیان سیر بیرات   تحقیق سواد قدرت آیات

طپش فرسوده شوق ناله تمثال   ز تحریک نفس وا می‌کند بال

Ending:

بهار لفظ وقف مدحتش باد   گل معنی نثار فطرتش باد

End of Mostazād:

و آن فرقه که بی‌وجود اسباب غرور   سازند به عجز

یعنی چه روند به‌خاک یکسان باشند   معذورانند

Manuscripts of Ṭūr-e Ma‘refat (The Senai of Gnosis: Golgasht-e Ḥaqīqat) (Undated)

«1»

Sālār, No. A./Nm.620

Good *Naskh*, fol.43, late 12th century A.H. copy, gold and coloured borders, heading in red, defective in the end.

Beginning: as usual.

Ending:

دمی زین گفتگوی رشحه پردرد   بساط صفحه ابری می‌توان کرد

«2»

Punjab University, Lahore, No. 1526 PPi/VI 46 B

Also contains *Moḥīṭ-e A‘żam*.

Nasta‘līq, fol.1-43.

Beginning:

طبش فرسوده شوق ناله تمثال   ...

«3»

Rampur, No. 6625M

Nasta‘līq, fol.43.

«4»

Sālār, No. A./Nm.631

Good *Shikesta*, fol.34, Abul Ma‘nā transcribed from a copy of Dakhnī Rām Jīu, an early 13th century A.H. copy.

Beginning:

تپش فرسوده شوق نالـه تمثـال   ز تحریک نفس وا می‌کنـد بـال

Ending:

زر و سیم تویی و دنیـا دیـن اسـت   همین است و همین است و همین است

«5»

Sprenger, No. 177

Contains chiefly descriptions, as a description of a mountain, of a cloud, of the rainbow, of the dawn of morning and also religious and philosophical reflections.

P.26, this all is about Bairat now in Rajasthan.

Beginning:

طپش فرسوده شوق ناله تمثال   ز تحریک نفس وا می‌کند بـال

Ending:

بهار لفظ وقف مدحتش باد   گل معنی نثار فطرتش بـاد

Chapter XII

Manuscripts of Mathnavī-e 'Irfān (Gnosis) (Dated)

This longest, the most celebrated and the final *Mathnavī* comprising eleven thousand couplets, was completed in 1124 A.H./1712 A.D., after thirty years of hard labour. Bīdel in these verses records the number of the verses and the year of its composition:

شکر ایزد کـه نسـخهٔ عرفـان   یافـت اقبـال از اختتـام بیـان
وضع ابیات این خیـال نمـود   جز خطی چند در خیال نبـود
لیـک هرگـاه در شـمار آمـد   بـر زبـان یـازده هـزار آمـد
کـرده تـاریخ او نیـاز ارقـام   «هدیـهٔ ذوالجـلال والاکـرام»[1]
(١١٢٤ هـ)

'Irfān, as its title suggests, is a mystical poem. Bīdel regarded it as his best creation and was very proud of it.[2] Apart from it, *'Irfān* is rightly regarded among the most intellectual mystical poems in Persian literature. This highly mystical and philosophical work, illustrated with moral anecdotes, is classified into different sections, each of which has a *Mathnavī Bait* (couplet) for its *Rubric*. It especially elaborates the intermingling of the pre-existing soul with the lower material world, and its upward ascent culminating in the birth of human beings.

'Irfān's Style is vague and obscure, as is typical with other works of Bīdel.

---

1. 'Irfān, *Kolliyāt-e Bīdel*, Kābul, p.25; Khushgū, p.123-4.
2. Khushgū, p.123-4; Bīdel repeatedly used to say: «آنچه ما داریم نسخهٔ عرفان است» (Whatever we posses is 'Irfān).

As compared to other works, Bīdel has drawn his material from Indian sources in this *Mathnavī* more. Bīdel versifies a good number of anecdotes in this *Mathnavī* to support and illustrate his view points. Among them are some Indian stories, particularly taken from Yogavasishtha. The story of ten children of a Brahman, ten worlds and the Sun beginning with this couplet:

ذکر آن برهمن طالب دید   که تناسخ زد و کناس دمید

[*I narrate the story of a Brahman who wanted to see God and was re-born as untouchable.*]

falls under the same category. Similarly, the eighth-century Sanskrit play Malatimadhava by Bhavabhūtī has been very popular in vernacular literature. Moreover, the folk version of the Madhavanal and Kama Kundla story has been written a dozen times in medieval Hindī. It has also been rendered into Persian by a poet pen-named Ḥaqīrī.[1] But when Bīdel integrates it into *'Irfān* as the story of Kamādī and Madan, it becomes transformed into a philosophical opus, which cannot be matched by anybody except perhaps the original writer.[2]

*

1. Ḥaqīrī composed it in 1091 A.H./1680 A.D. under the title of E'jāz. It was edited by Dr. Yogdhayan Ahuja, Delhi, 1965. (*Mathnavī Madhonal Kam Kundla*). Dr. Ahuja in his preface to this edition refers to its two translations into Rājasthānī language, one by a poet Ganpatī in 1527 and another after thirty years by some other poet. Its actual popularity is the result of its narration in Hindī poetry by Shaikh 'Ālam in 991 A.H./ 1583 A.D. The Persian translation is based on its same Hindī version. For further details see: *Fārsī Adab Be-'Ahd-e Aurangzīb*, p.243.
2. For detaile see: Mīrzā Bīdel's 'Irfān and Yogavasistha, Wagesh Shukla, op.cit, p.123. This story has been studied in detail by Soviet scholars and repeatedly emulated by Tājīk poets.

«1»

Rieu, No. Add.7093

Nasta'līq, fol.332, Allāh Bakhsh, Rajab, the 4th year of the reign of Farrukhsiyar, 1128 A.H./June, 1716 A.D.

Beginning:

عشق از مشت خاک آدم ریخت آن‌قدر خون که رنگِ عالم ریخت

There is a note on the first page stating that the Ms was bought in 1159 A.H. by Mīrzā Moḥammad son of Mu'tamad Khān. A seal of Archibed Swinton is also affixed.

«2»

Khodā Bakhsh, No. 382

'Irfān Included in the Kolliyāt

This copy is the continuation of the copy of the Ms (No. 381).

Nasta'līq, fol.226a onward till the end, Moḥammad Wārith b. Moḥammad Bāqer al-Ṣiddīqī, Jumāda'II, 1136 A.H. [February, 1724 A.D.] (See No. 381).

Beginning:

عشق از مشت خاکِ آدم ریخت آنقدر خون که رنگ عالم ریخت

«3»

Madras, No. D141

***Mathnavī-e Mer'at* (a part of 'Irfān)**

Nasta'līq, fol.15, 15th Rajab, 1153 A.H./[25th September, 1740 A.D.], dilapidated condition.

Beginning:

ذکرِ بی‌پردگی ظلمت و نور اعتباراتِ کمالاتِ ظهور

ای حدوثت شعور اسم و صفات مذمت حیرت تقدّسِ ذات

Ending:

کرد اینجا فسان‌ها کوتاه معنی لا اله الّا الله

It is a part of *Mathnavī-e 'Irfān.*

«4»

Tājīkistān, No. 1560/2

Mathnavī-e Mer'atollāh (مثنوی مرأةالله)

It is an extract from the *Mathnavī-e 'Irfān*.

Shikesta-Nasta'līq, fol.54, 1193 A.H./1779 A.D.

«5»

National Museum, Karachi, No. N.M.1972-110/A.B., Monzavī 8, 1034

Ḥairat Afsūn

A *Mathnavī* included in the end of *Mathnavī-e 'Irfān* in Kabul edition.

Nasta'līq, 1201 A.H. [1787 A.D.].

Beginning:

ختم افسانۀ حیرت افسون سجدۀ شکر جناب بی‌چون

Ending:

از من و تو باو دعا چه رسد او هم او نیست تا بما چه رسد

«6»

Tājīkistān, No. 3131

Shikesta-Nasta'līq, fol.101, Mollā 'Abduż Żohūr b. Moḥammad Raḥīm, 11th Jumāda'I, 1205 A.H./16th January, 1791 A.D.

Some corrections and notes on the margins.

«7»

University, No. 891/5514/39

Nasta'līq, fol.208, 10th Rajab, 1228 A.H./[9th July, 1813 A.D.], the text also on margins.

Beginning:

عقل و حسن، سمع و بصر، جان و جسد

همه عشق است، هو الله احد

عشق از مشت خاک آدم ریخت

آنقدر خون که رنگ عالم ریخت

Ending:

کـــرد تـــاریخ او نیـــازِ اکـــرام   هدیـــهٔ ذوالجـــلال والاکـــرام

«8»

N. Archives, Afghanistan, No. 14/115

Mathnavī-e Mer'atollāh (مثنوی مرأةالله)

Nasta'līq, fol.251-301, copied during 1234-36 A.H./[1819-21 A.D.]. It is included in the Ms. of *Dīwān*.

This *Mathnavī* is a part of Bīdel's famous *Mathnavī "'Irfān"*.

«9»

Tājīkistān, No. 1849/3

Mathnavī-e Mer'atollāh (مثنوی مرأةالله)

Shikesta-Nasta'līq, fol.47, Warrāq Bāi Moḥammad, 1235 A.H./ 1820 A.D.

«10»

Tehran University, Tehran, No. 10042

Nasta'līq, fol.385, 1237 A.H./[1822 A.D.], illuminated with gold work.

Beginning:

عشق از مشت خاک آدم ریخـــت   آن‌قدر خون که رنگِ عالم ریخت

Ending:

کـــرده تـــاریخ او نیـــاز ارقـــام   هدیـــهٔ ذوالجـــلال والاکـــرام

«11»

N. Archives, Afghanistan, No. 19/80

Nasta'līq, fol.230, 1237 A.H./[1822 A.D.].

«12»

Tājīkistān, No. 381/1

Shikesta-Nasta'līq, fol.112, 1240 A.H./1825 A.D., it was bound by Moḥammad 'Āshūr Aḥmadī.

«13»

Jāmia, No. 18

Mer'at-ul Khayāl (Mathnavī-e Mirat)

A Ṣūfī *Mathnavī*.

Nasta'līq, fol.57, Moḥammad 'Ābid b. Shaikh Moḥammad Afẓal 'Abdur Reḥmān Ṣiddīqī, Jumāda'II, 1248 A.H./1832 A.D., worm eaten. Beginning:

ذکرِ بی‌پردگی ظلمت و نور   اعتباراتِ کمالاتِ ظهور

«14»

Tājīkistān, No. 292/4

Shikesta-Nasta'līq, fol.35, Yūnos, 1248 A.H./1832 A.D., scribed in two columns.

«15»

Hamdard, Nazimabad, Karachi, No. 5203A, Monzavī 8, 1031

Nasta'līq, p.260, 1269 A.H./[1853 A.D.], Fatehpur, incomplete in the beginning.

«16»

Foremen Christian College, Lahore, No. 891-55, 52A, Monzavī 8, 1031

Nasta'līq, fol.304, 1278 A.H. [1861 A.D.].

«17»

Mas'ūd Jahāngīr Library, Mailisī, Pakistan, No. 111/D,I

'Irfān-ul 'Āshaqīn (Mathnavī-e 'Irfān)

Shikesta-Nasta'līq, p.500, Moḥammad 'Ādil b. Mollā 'Abdur Razzāq Sayyadī, 1339 A.H./[1921 A.D.].

Manuscripts of Mathnavā-e 'Irfī n (Gnosis) (Undated)

«1»

Ganj Bakhsh, Islamabad, No. 8640, Monzavā8, 1031

Nasta'līq, fol.63, Allāh Bakhsh, 11th century A.H.

Beginning:

ذکرِ بی‌پردگی ظلمت و نور...

«2»

Khodī Bakhsh, No. 388

Fair *Nasta'līq*, fol.331, 18th century A.D.

Beginning:

عشق از مشت خاکِ آدم ریخت...

«3»

Khodī Bakhsh, No. 387

This copy is the continuation of the copy of the Ms (No. 381) Written in different hands, fol.330, 18th century A.D.

Beginning:

عشق از مشت خاکِ آدم ریخت...

«4»

ASB, No. 842

Nasta'līq, fol.201, 12th century A.H.

Beginning:

عشق از مشت خـاکِ آدم ریخـت   آنقدر خون که رنگ عـالم ریخـت

«5»

Ganj Bakhsh, Islamabad, No. 1102, Monzavā8, 1031

Nasta'līq, p.1-95, 12th century A.H., incomplete in the beginning.

«6»

Ganj Bakhsh, Islamabad, No. 492, Monzavā8, 1031

Shikesta-Nasta'līq, p.554, 13th century A.H.

One page in the beginning is missing.

«7»

Patiala, (Public Library), No. 1576

'Irfān-e Bīdel

Nasta'līq, fol.274, Moḥammad Wārith b. Moḥammad Bāqer.

Beginning:

عقل و حسن، سمع و بصر، جان و جسد

همــــه عشـــق اســـت، هـــو الله احـــد

Ending:

تا سرانجامش از غبـار قصـور　　ننمایـد بدیـدههـا مسـتور

کـرد تـاریخ او نیـازِ کـرام　　هدیـهٔ ذوالجـلال والاکـرام

«8»

University, No. 2/14

Nasta'līq, fol.168, Moḥammad Shākir, Bareilly, versified heading in red, text also scribed on margins.

Beginning:

عقل و حسن، سمع و بصر، جان و جسد

همــــه عشـــق اســـت، هـــو الله احـــد

عشـــق از مشـــت خـــاک آدم ریخـــت

آنقـدر خـون کـه رنـگ عـالم ریخـت

«9»

Madras, No. D1103

Mathnavī-e Mirat

Nasta'līq, fol.33.

«10»

Rieu, No. Add.6950

Nasta'līq, fol.579-591.

«11»

N. Archives, Afghanistan, No. 35/195

Nasta'līq, fol.376, incomplete in the end.

Chapter XIII

Manuscripts of Chahār 'Onṣor (Four Elements) (Dated)

This is an important work of Bīdel in 10,000 lines («بیتِ نثر», Khushgū) dealing to an extent with his life account. As its title suggests, it is divided into four chapters and was completed in a span of fifteen years from 1091 A.H./1680 A.D. to 1106 A.H./ 1694 A.D. It is in rhymed prose interspersed with couplets from *Ghazals*, *Robā'īyāt*, *Mathnavīs* and *Qiṭ'āt*. These poetic compositions are amazingly thought provoking and original. All of them have not been derived from Bīdel's other poetic works. Preceded by a short preface, its four chapters correspond to the four elements – air, water, fire and earth. Each *'Onṣor* has also a *Khātemeh* (conclusion). It has, however, been ranked as the most difficult book in the whole corpus of Indo-Persian literature.

It was completed in 1116 A.H./1704 A.D. as contained in the two complicated chronograms in this *Qiṭ'a*:

قطعهٔ تاریخِ ختمِ کتاب

به‌حمد لله ز ختم چار عنصر　　فرح پیش‌آمد و غم بر قفا رفت

به‌سیر آهنگی قانون اسرار　　ز ساز جهل سامانِ نوا رفت

بهاری دست بند رنگ و بو شد　　که اندوهِ خزان از باغِ ما رفت

دمی کاندیشهٔ تحقیق پرداز　　به‌فکر سال این تحریرها رفت

دو تاریخ از حساب آورد بیرون　　که دخل شبهه خون گشت و خطا رفت

نخست افسونی از اعجاز پرداخت　　که از افراد هر عنصر فنا رفت

دوم در اجتماع چار عنصر　　نحوست بود چون زنگ از صفا رفت[1]

(۱۱۱۶ هـ)

---

1. *Āwāzhāy-e Bīdel*, p.672. Unfotunately I could not make out 1116 A.H. from both the chronograms contained in the last two couplets of this *Qiṭ'a*.

In Chahār 'Onṣor, he states that:

از آن هنگام تا حال که نفس شماری عمر مقارن سال چهل و یکم است (۱۰۹۵ ه).

[*He was engaged in writing the work at the age of 41.*]

Though heavily intermixed with the narrations of Bīdel's supernatural and metaphysical experiences and observations, the importance of *Chahār 'Onṣor* lies in the fact that it helps to a great extent in solving the confusing statements about his life. It also gives an intimate picture of Bīdel's family, his early career, his wide tours and contacts with Ṣūfīs who shaped his life and thought. Strangely enough he does not mention his birthplace. The first and second sections give an account of the author's birth, parentage, early education and travels. A major part is devoted to interesting experiences which Bīdel had with Ṣūfīs of his time. The third and fourth parts are more reflective and deal with silence, speech, attributes of absolute spirit and other metaphysical subjects. Casual references are also found regarding some strange and curious happenings during the author's travels. According to some of Bīdel's statements, he is trying to describe himself as an extraordinary person gifted with unusual spiritual power since his boyhood. In the concluding part of the Fourth *'Onṣor*, Bīdel elaborates on some historical events such as Shāh Shujā's armed struggle to seize the central power and the ensuing social unrest, as well lawlessness in the wake of Aurangzīb's military campaign in the Deccan.

*

«1»

Anjuman-e Taraqqī-e Urdū, Aligarh, No. 198

It also contains *Roqqa'āt-e Bīdel* (143 letters).
Shikesta, fol.300, Nāth Mal, 11th Jumāda'II, 1136 and 1139 A.H./ [21th February, 1724 and 1727 A.D.].
Beginning:

عجز مراتب حمد و ثنا تسلیم بارگاه صمدی...

This Ms. also contains *Chahār 'Onṣor.*
The *Tarqīma* (Colophon) is:

ترقیمه: به‌عونِ عنایتِ الٰهی این کتاب فیضِ انتساب یازدهم شهر جمادی‌الآخر ۱۱۳۹ از هجرتِ رسول الله صلعم [۲۳ فوریه ۱۷۲۷ م] سمت اتمام و صورتِ اختتام پذیرفت از قلم نیاز رقم نته مل عفی الله ذنوبه.

It means the Ms. was transcribed only three years after the death of Bīdel in 1133 A.H./[1720 A.D.]. It is, thus, an important manuscript.

«2»

Banaras, No. 0164,61.32,1
First 'Onṣor

Different hands (scribes), fol.250, [1145 A.H]/1732 A.D.
Second, third and fourth *'Onṣors* are bound separately.

«3»

Sālār, No. A.N./88
Chahār 'Onṣor

Nasta'līq, fol.261, Golāl Chand, 1st Rabī'I, 1155 A.H./(25th Moḥammad Shāhī)/25th April, 1742 A.D., double gold ruled borders, lacking the last *Fourth 'Onṣor*.
This copy begins with:

غبار نشانی بساط (صور) عجائب و زنگ زدایی...

Beginning of *First 'Onṣor*:

ابجد اشغال شعله مقال و گرمی‌های صحبت ارباب فضل و کمال...

Beginning of *Second 'Onṣor*:

روایح شگفتگی بهار عالم منظوم و نسایم فیض غنایم فواید معلوم (عنوان)...

Beginning of *Third 'Onṣor*:

طراوت سنبلستان مراتب منشور و آبیاری نخلستان کیفیات شعور (عنوان)...

Ending:

... و هرکجا خموشی است، انفعال گفت و گو مبیناد.

«4»

ASB, No. 389

Second 'Onṣor* and *Third 'Onṣor

Nasta'līq, 1160 A.H./[1747 A.D.].

Contains only the *second* and the *Third 'Onṣor*.

The *Second 'Onṣor* begins with:

روایح شگفتگی بهار عالم منظوم و نسیم فیض غنایم...

The *Third 'Onṣor* begins:

طراوت شبنمستان مراتب منشور...

«5»

ASB, No. 388

Chahār 'Onṣor

Nasta'līq, 1164 A.H./[1751 A.D.], Azimabad (Patna).

Containing only the *First* and the *Fourth 'Onṣor*.

The first *'Onṣor* and the usual preface begin as usual.

The *Fourth 'Onṣor* begins:

غبار نشانی بساط صور عجائب...

«6»

Idāreh-e Adabiyāt-e Urdū, Hyderabad, No. 382 (*Tażkireh-e Makhṭūṭāt*, Vol. II)

First 'Onṣor

Shikesta-Nasta'līq, 7th Rabī'II/[1168 A.H./21st January, 1755 A.D.], first regnal year of 'Ālamgīr II, probably the scribe of this copy is the same who transcribed *'Onṣor-e Doyum* preserved in the collection (No. 381). Headings are in red ink.

«7»

Idāreh-e Adabiyāt-e Urdū, Hyderabad, No. 381 (*Taẕkireh-e Makhṭūṭāt,* Vol. II)

Second 'Onṣor

Shikesta-Nasta'līq, Thursday, 7th Ẕīqa'da, 1171 A.H./[13th July, 1758 A.D.], Elor Fort, *'Unwān* red.

Colophon (ترقیمه):

تمام شد عنصر دوّم مرزا عبدالقادر بیدل علیه‌الرحمة به‌تاریخ هفتم ذیقعده ۱۱۷۱ هجری مطابق (چهارم) سنهٔ عالمگیر (ثانی) روز پنجشنبه به‌وقتِ دوپهر در قلعهٔ ایلور.

«8»

Solaimān, No. 301/34

Only *First 'Onṣor* out of four

Shikesta, fol.54, Rām Kishan b. Kirpā Rām Qannaujī, Saturday, 22nd Ramaẓān, 1173 A.H./[8th May, 1760 A.D.].

Beginning:

خداوندا زبان معذور بی‌صرفه‌سرایی است...

Ending:

بی‌دلی‌هایم دلیل امتحان بیغشی است   نیستم قلب آشنا از بس گدازم کرده‌انــد

«9»

Idāreh-e Adabiyāt-e Urdū, Hyderabad, No. 381 (*Taẕkireh-e Makhṭūṭāt,* Vol. II)

Second 'Onṣor

Shikesta-Nasta'līq, 7th Ẕīqa'da, 1179 A.H./[17th April, 1766 A.D.] (on Thursday, at noon at Vellore Fort).

This copy also contains other Works of Bīdel.

«10»

Kitābkhāna-e Millī, Tehran, No. 7331

Second 'Onṣor

Fair *Nasta'līq*, fol.50, Ḥāfiż Moḥammad Ḥabībollāh b. Ḥāfiż Moḥammad Derwīsh, 1182 A.H./[1768 A.D.], Hyderabad, India, with two miniatures.

Beginning:

روایح شگفتگی بهار عالم منظوم...

«11»

Kitābkhāna-e Millī, Tehran, No. 7332

Third 'Onṣor

An incomplete copy.

Nasta'līq, Ḥāfiż Moḥammad Ḥabībollāh b. Ḥāfiż Moḥammad Derwīsh, 1182 A.H./[1768 A.D.], Hyderabad, India.

Beginning:

(هرچـــه دارد جهـــان بـــی‌بنیـــاد   مشت خاکی است) در قلمرو بـــاد

... بـــی‌ثبـــاتی بامتحـــان وقـــار   محملی مـــی کشـــد بـــدوش غبـــار

بسکه رنـــگ ثبـــات پـــرواز اســـت   کوه با ناله هـــم عنـــان نـــاز اســـت

Ending:

نفس پرده غفلت بس است باده‌فروش   کنون بساز ادب محو این نو است سخن

*

ز رمـــز نخـــل انـــا الله گـــوی ناآگـــاه   حدیث جلوه‌گه و موسی و عصا گویند

(غزلیّات: ۲۲۱)

کنون به‌ســـازِ ادب محـــو ایـــن نواســـت ســـخن

که مدّعای بیانِ وصف خامشی است، خمـــوش

غرض هرجا سخنی است، بی‌معنی افاده مباد و هرجا خاموشی است، انفعال گفت و گو مبیناد.

Colophon:

تمّت عنصر سیم و قصد کتابت عنصر چهارم... در اندک فرصت به‌اتمام خواهد رسید.

«12»

Kitābkhāna-e Millī, Tehran, No. 7329

Fourth 'Onṣor

Fair *Nasta'līq*, fol.80, Ḥāfiż Moḥammad Ḥabībollāh b. Ḥāfiż Moḥammad Derwīsh, 1183 A.H./[1769 A.D.], Kānjī Kota district Hyderabad.

There are some *Nekāt* of Bīdel in the end.

Beginning:

عنصر چهارم، غبار نشانی بساط صور عجائب، رنگ‌زدای آیهٔ نقوش غرایب حیرت انجامی قلم بدایع رقم تامل انشای حقیقی است که نقطهٔ شهودش انتخاب رموز یقین می‌داند...

Ending:

دوّم در اجتمـــاع چـــار عنصـــر نحوست بود چون زنگ از صفا رفت

«13»

Āṣafīya, No. 134
Chahār 'Onṣor
Nasta'līq, 1183 A.H./[1769 A.D.].

«14»

Idāreh-e Adabiyāt-e Urdū, Hyderabad, No. 26 (*Taẕkireh-e Makhṭūṭāt,* Vol. II)
Sormeh-e Aghnīyā
Shikesta, fol.5, Sha'bān, 1183 A.H./[December, 1769 A.D.], scribed at the instance of Durgā Prashād for Lāla Lachhmī Prashād, *'Unwān* red. It may be *Sormeh-e E'tebār*.

«15»

Jawāhar Museum, No. جف 497
Only three *'Onṣors* and so named in the catalogue as *Seh Nathr* (سه نثر)
Shikesta, fol.190, 20th Jumāda'II, 1184 A.H./[11th October, 1770 A.D.], (14th regnal year of Shāh 'Ālam), 1178 *Faṣlī*.
Beginning:

خداوندا زبان معذور بی‌صرفه سرائیست...

Ending:

نظر التفات از سرنگ‌های...

«16»

Tājīkistān, No. 2559/3
Chahār 'Onṣor
Shikesta, fol.57, 1203 A.H./1789 A.D.

«17»

Āṣafīya, No. 179

Chahār 'Onṣor

Nasta'līq, 1206 A.H./[1791 A.D.].

«18»

University, Supplement No. 144 Fārsī

Second 'Onṣor* and *Third 'Onṣor

Nasta'līq, fol.175, Friday, 17th Jumāda'II, 1211 A.H./[16th December, 1796 A.D.].

Beginning:

خداوندا زبان معذور بی‌صرفه‌سرایی است...

Ending:

بیدل چه قدر شور کلامت مزه دارد   کز یاد تو باید لب اندیشه مکیـدن

«19»

Tājīkistān, No. 1812

Chahār 'Onṣor

Shikesta-Nasta'līq, fol.268, 1215 A.H./1800 A.D.

«20»

Mozzammil, No. 180

Chahār 'Onṣor

Nasta'līq, fol.187, Bahādur Singh Saksena, 1217 A.H./[1802 A.D.].

Beginning:

خداوندا زبان معذور بی‌صرفه سرایی است عذر هرزه درایان بپذیر و بیان مجبور آشفته نوایی است...

Ending:

دویـــم در اجتمـــاع چـــار عنصـــر   نحوست بود چون زنگ از صـفا رفـت

والسّلام علی من اتبع الهدی (١١١٦ هـ).

(The following statement of Bīdel in *Chahār 'Onṣor*:

"از آن هنگام تا حال که نفس شماری عمر مقارن سال چهل و یکم است".

indicates that it was completed around 1094 A.H./1683 A.D. when Bīdel was forty-one years old.

«21»

Tājīkistān, No. 1837

Chahār 'Onṣor

Shikesta-Nasta'līq, fol.369, Moḥammad Ibrāhīm better known as Pūryāī, 21st Jumāda'II, 1218 A.H./8th October, 1804 A.D.

«22»

Āṣafīya, No. 171

Chahār 'Onṣor

Nasta'līq, 1225 A.H./[1810 A.D.].

«23»

Sālār, No. A.N./91

Chahār 'Onṣor

Shikesta-Nasta'līq, fol.26, Gholām Ḥusain, 11th Sha'bān, 1230 A.H./ 19th July, 1815 A.D., red ruled borders, defective in the beginning by a folio. It contains the last *'Onṣor* and a few letters of Bīdel in the margins of folios 1-7 by a different hand.

Beginning:

... فطرت از خاکستر نشان شعله این نیرنگ...

Ending:

دو تاریخ از حساب آورد بیرون — که دخل شبه خون گشت و خطا رفت
نخست افسونی از اعجاز پرداخت — که از افراد هر عنصر فنا رفت
دوّم در اجتماع چار عنصر — نحوست بود چون رنگ از حنا رفت

«24»

Sālār, No. A.N./89

Chahār 'Onṣor

Nasta'līq, fol.230, Syed Moḥīoddīn for Rashīduddaula, 27th Rabī'II, 1231 A.H./27th March 1816 A.D., heading in red, contains all four *'Onṣors* but defective at a few places.

Beginning:

یا همه را حسن نگار عشق مژگان بفسون‌ها...

Ending:

دوّم در اجتماع چار عنصر   نحوست بود چون رنگ از حنا رفت

(چون زنگ از صفا رفت).

«25»

N. Archives, Afghanistan, No. 30/82

Chahār 'Onṣor

Nasta'līq, fol.264, Khairollāh, 1233 A.H./[1818 A.D.].

«26»

Tājīkistān, No. 1849/6

Chahār 'Onṣor

Shikesta-Nasta'līq, fol.213, Bāi Moḥammad, 1237 A.H./1822 A.D.

«27»

Curzon, No. 152

Chahār 'Onṣor

Nasta'līq, fol.134, Saramal Guruharilāl Kāyath, 1st Ṣafar, 1246 A.H./ 22rd July 1830 A.D.

Stray notes on the fly-leaves.

«28»

Sobḥānallāh, Supplement, No. 891/552/34

Nasta'līq, fol.95, 'Azīzoddīn, Wednesday, 3rd Jumāda'II, 1247 A.H./ [9th November, 1831 A.D.].

Beginning:

خداوندا زبان معذور بی‌صرفه‌سرایی است...

Ending:

بیدل چه قدر شور کلامت مزه دارد   از یاد تو باید لب اندیشه مکیدن

«29»

Sobḥānallāh, Supplement, No. 891/552/34 (a)

Nasta'līq, fol.79, 'Azīzoddīn, Monday, 20th Sha'bān, 1248 A.H./ [12th January, 1833 A.D.].

Beginning:

طراوت شبنمستان مراتب منشور و آبیاری نخلستان کیفیت شعور...

Ending with a *Qiṭ'a* with chronogram:

... نحوست بود چون زنگ از صفا رفت.

«30»

Tājīkistān, No. 1854

Chahār 'Onṣor

Nasta'līq, fol.271, 'Abdul Khāliq Bukhārī b. Moḥammad Salīm Kolābī b. Niyāz Moḥammad Balkhī, 1248 A.H./1833 A.D.

«31»

Nadva, No. 99

Chahār 'Onṣor

Nasta'līq, p.482, 1256 A.H./[1840 A.D.], worm eaten, signature of the calligrapher on the last page.

Beginning:

خداوندا زبان معذور بی‌صرفه‌سرایی است عذر هرزه درایان بپذیر...

Ending:

نخست افسونی از اعجاز پرداخت   که از افراد هر عنصر فنا رفت
(دوّم در اجتماع چار عنصر   نحوست بود، چون زنگ از صفا رفت)
(۱۱۱۶ ه ق)

«32»

Tonk, Rajasthan, No. 2741/1

Chahār 'Onṣor

Nasta'līq, p.187, 1269 A.H./[1853 A.D.].

«33»

Bū'Alī Tomb Library, Hamedan, No. 2

Roqqa'āt in the end of the manuscript, year 1299 A.H./[1882 A.D.].

Beginning:

عجز مراتب حمد و ثنا تسلیم بارگاه صمدی که خامه را در معرکهٔ...

Ending:

... بسعی اندیشه تهیّهٔ این اقبال...

Manuscripts of Chahār ‘Onṣor (Four Elements) (Undated)

«1»

Tājīkistān, No. 1561
Chahār ‘Onṣor
Shikesta-Nasta‘līq, fol.352.

«2»

Tonk, Rajasthan, No. 4327
Chahār ‘Onṣor
Nasta‘līq, p.666.

«3»

Kitābkhāna-e Adabiyāt, Tehran University, Tehran, No. 106ب
All the Four *‘Onṣors*
Nasta‘līq, fol.278.

«4»

Handlist of Persian Mss. British Museum, No. Or.6443
Chahār ‘Onṣor
Fol.251.
Chahār ‘Onṣor is followed by some poems of Bīdel in this Ms.

«5»

Tonk, Rajasthan, No. 3676
Chahār ‘Onṣor
Shikesta-Nasta‘līq, p.494.

«6»

Rieu, No. Or.1622
Intekhāb-e Nathr-e Bīdel
It is Ṣifāt-e Kā’enāt (Description of things) in which some prose pieces of Bīdel are included. This is a collection of selected examples of ornate prose-compostions and arranged according to the objects described.

Nasta'līq, fol.206b.
May be, it is a work by Siyālkotī Mal. (See Rieu, Or.1762, fol.453-458).

«7»

Sobḥānallāh, No. 891/552/18
It also contains *Nekāt* (71 in total) in the beginning.
Shikesta-Nasta'līq, fol.202, Moḥammad Jān b. Moḥammad Sulṭān, 15th Jumāda'II, 3rd regnal year of … (?).
Beginning:

خداوندا زبان معذور بی‌صرفه‌سرایی است...

Ending:

و هرکجا خموشی است، انفعال گفت و گو میبناد

«8»

Sobḥānallāh, No. 891/552/8
Nasta'līq, fol.171. It also contains *Nekāt* in the beginning.
Beginning:

خداوندا زبان معذور بی‌صرفه‌سرایی است...

Ending:

به‌سیر آهنگی قانون اسرار ز راز جهل سامان نوا رفت

«9»

Jawāhar Museum, No. 461 ج ف
Nasta'līq, fol.156.
Beginning:

صریر الفت صفیر خامهٔ بیدل در تحریر این عنصر عنان رنگهای رفته...

Ending:

دوم در اجتماع چار عنصر نحوست بود چون زنگ از صفا رفت

«10»

Tājīkistān, No. 1093
Chahār 'Onṣor
Shikesta-Nasta'līq, fol.128.

«11»

Jāmia, No. 653

Chahār 'Onṣor

Shikesta, fol.96, two seals of Moḥammad Żohūr Aḥmadī and Moḥammad Mashkūr.

Beginning:

خداوندا زبانِ معذور بی‌صرفه‌سرایی است عذر هرزه درایان بپذیر...

بهاری دسته بند رنگ و بو شد که اندوه خزان از باغِ ما رفت

«12»

Hardayāl, No. R171

First 'Onṣor

Shikesta, fol.71, worm eaten.

Beginning:

خداوندا زبانِ معذور بی‌صرفه‌سرایی است عذر هرزه درایان بپذیر...

«13»

Sālār, No. A.N./90

Chahār 'Onṣor

Nasta'līq, fol.60, an early 13th century A.H. copy, only the third *'Onṣor*.

Beginning:

طراوت شبنمستان مراتب منشور و آبیاری نخلستان...

«14»

Tājīkistān, No. 502/2

Chahār 'Onṣor

Shikesta-Nasta'līq, fol.54.

«15»

Tonk, Rajasthan, No. 4509/2

Fourth 'Onṣor

Incomplete in the end.

Nasta'līq, p.66.

«16»

Tājīkistān, No. 1551/2

Chahār 'Onṣor

Shikesta-Nasta'līq, fol.31.

«17»

Idāreh-e Adabiyāt-e Urdū, Hyderabad, No. 384 (*Tazkireh-e Makhṭūṭāt*, Vol. II)

Third 'Onṣor

Shikesta-Nasta'līq, fol.15, headings red, incomplete in the end.

«18»

Hamidiya Bhopal, No. 344

Chahār 'Onṣor

Nasta'līq, Moḥammad Wārith son of Moḥammad Bāqer Ṣiddīqī.
Beginning:

ابجد، اشغال شعلۀ مقال و گرمی‌های صحبت ارباب فضل و کمال...

It is the heading of the 1st *'Onṣor*.

«19»

ASB, No. 387

Chaḥār 'Onṣor

Nasta'līq, 12 century A.H., good condition.
This copy contains only the first and the second *'Onṣor* out of four in total.
The preface to the work begins:

خداوندا زبان معذور بی‌صرفه‌سرایی است...

The *first 'Onṣor* begins:

ابجد اشغال شعلۀ مقال و گرمی‌های صحبت...

The *Second 'Onṣor* begins:

روایح شگفتگی بهار عالم منظوم و نسیم فیض غنایم...

«20»

Sharaf-ul Mulk Library, Chenā'ī, No. 146

Chahār 'Onṣor

«21»

Banaras, No. 0164,61.32,1

First 'Onṣor

First part of the work.

Nasta'līq, fol.302.

Beginning:

خداوندا زبانِ معذور بی‌صرفه‌سرایی است عذر هرزه درایان بپذیر...

«22»

Banaras, No. 0164,61.32,1

Second 'Onṣor

Second part of the work.

Nasta'līq, fol.249, worm eaten.

Beginning:

عنصر دوّم: روایح شگفتگی بهار عالم منظوم و نسایم فیض غنایم فواید معلوم...

«23»

Banaras, No. 0164,61.32,1

Third 'Onṣor & Fourth 'Onṣor

Third and fourth parts of the work.

Nasta'līq, fol.360.

Beginning:

عنصرِ سوّم: طراوتِ شبستان مراتب منشور و آبیاری نخلستان کیفیاتِ شعور...

«24»

Majlis-e Shorā-e Millī Library, Tehran, No. 1355/2

Nasta'līq, Moḥammad 'Ālam b. Moḥammad Yousof Nawgānvī.

«25»

Majlis-e Shorā-e Millī Library, Tehran, No. 16715

«26»

Sharaf-ul Mulk Library, Chenā'ī, No. 3718

«27»

Sharaf-ul Mulk Library, Chenā'ī, No. 5200

«28»

Sharaf-ul Mulk Library, Chenā'ī, No. 5602

«29»

Sharaf-ul Mulk Library, Chenā'ī, No. 5966

«30»

Hamidiya, Bhopal, No. 351
Chahār 'Onṣor
Incomplete in the end.

«31»

Tehran University Library, Tehran, No. 9642
Chahār 'Onṣor
Incomplete from both the ends.
Nasta'līq, fol.232, 12th century copy.

«32»

Majlis-e Shorā-e Millī, Library, Tehran, No. 14209/207
Sormeh-e I'tebār (سرمهٔ اعتبار)
An article in prose and verse composed extempore at the instance of Kāmgār Khān, son of Jumdatul Mulk Ja'far Khān, praising «گرد و غبار».
Nasta'līq, p.5 (530-534), transcribed by the poet himself. It is on page 573 in *Āwāzhāy-e Bīdel*.
Beginning:

نه غبار است کزین دشت پرافشان برخاست
نگهی بال تماشا زد و مژگان برخاست
حسن گر موج زند این‌قدرش طوفان کو
شوق اگر ناله شود این همه نتوان برخاست
سبحان الله دلنشین غباری که تا مصوّر خیال به‌نقشِ تصویر پرداخته...

Chapter XIV

Manuscripts of Roqqa'āt-e Bīdel (Letters of Bīdel) (Dated)

Bīdel was a prolific letter-writer. His acquaintances wrote letters to him and Bīdel responded regularly to them and, thus, a great number of 285 letters[1] have been accumulated in the collection of his letters. However, it should be noted that the number of letters differ in different manuscripts. A long list of his addressees attests to his relationship with people from different social classes. His letters have been addressed to nobles, men of letters and ordinary people. His letters provide a glimpse into his personal life, his ambitions and his failings, *Faqr* and Ṣūfism. Some of them even throw light on social conditions of the day. Interestingly, the personality of Bīdel that emerges from these letters is not in total conformity with that generally evolved by his biographers. We find him endeavouring seriously to get an access to Prince A'żam, only to be met with disappointment and then resignation. His staunch advocacy of the cause of Prince Mo'ażżam for the throne, and his indecent attack on Moḥammad A'żam and his supporters is also observed. A letter written in a highly obscene language reveals that he was espousing the company of the nobles, not in the capacity of a friend, but for the sake of material gain.

Shokrollāh Khān Khāksār, his three sons – Loṭfollāh Khān, 'Ināyatollāh Khān and 'Karamollāh Khān – Rūḥollāh Khān, Mīrzā Fażā'il Khān, Mīrzā Mon'em Beg, 'Āqil Khān Rāzī,[2] the Syed

---

1. In *Āwāzhāy-e Bīdel.*
2. Father in law of Shokrollāh Khān.

brothers are among the prominent nobles with whom Bīdel corresponded. A larger number of letters are written to Shokrollāh Khān and his sons. He has also written some recommendation letters to men of authority seeking their favour for poets and the needy. Though a good number of poets were in contact with him, yet he was in correspondence with only a few of them like his teacher Shaikh 'Abdul 'Azīz 'Izzat, Īzad-Bakhsh Rasā and Rafī' Khān Bāẕil.

Bīdel has written his letters in a highly ornate and difficult style and profusely intermixed with verses. Most of such verses are not included in his *Dīwān* or other works in verse-form. It means Bīdel composed these couplets especially for these letters. The most impressive and touching are those written in condolence. These are written in fluent style and charged with emotions, displaying the sentimental attachment of the writer with the deceased.

It should be stated that Jan Rypka has rightly said in his "History of Iranian Literature" about his style in prose, "The language of his prose is very difficult, even in the poets letters so that the argument that Bīdel used complex form only for the purpose of obscuring his ideas is untenable."

*

«1»

Sālār, No. A.N./352

Included in a *Majmū'a* (مجموعه)

Nasta'līq, fol.5-111, Mākhan Singh, 1095 A.H./1684 A.D. or 1195 A.H./ 1781 A.D., Hyderabad, coloured paper, seal of Syed Moḥammad 'Alī Khān Bahādur, 1221 and 1237 A.H./[1806 and 1822 A.D.].

سیّد محمّد علی خان بهادر ۱۲۲۱ ه [۱۸۰۶ م] بود جانشین محمّد علی ۱۲۳۷ ه [۱۸۲۲ م].

«2»

Sālār, No. A./Nm.522

Nasta'līq, fol.329, Moḥammad Wārith b. Moḥammad Bāqer, 22nd Ṣafar, 1138 A.H./19th October, 1725 A.D., good condition, seal of Ḥasbīallāh.

Beginning:

آنکس که منزّه است از آب و گلِ ما   بی‌او عدم است خلوت و محفلِ ما

Ending:

بر خلق ببخشا که منِ ناکس هم   آیم بشمار گردِ دامانِ کسی

«3»

Shiblī Academy, A'zamgarh (Uttar Pradesh), No. 800/493/30

Nasta'līq, fol.124, Moḥammad Wārith b. Moḥammad Bāqer Ṣiddīqī, 1145 A.H./[1732 A.D.], in good condition and having 289 letters.

«4»

Sālār, No. A.N./148/1

Good *Shikesta*, fol.108, Sath Sohai, surnamed Hazārī Mall Khatrī, 21st Rabī'I, 1146 A.H./21st August, 1733 A.D., Aurangabad, coloured ruled borders, heading in red, fair condition, 284 letters chiefly addressed to Shokrollāh Khān and his son Shākir Khān and 'Āqil Khān, father-in-law of Shokrollāh Khān. All these three were patrons of Bīdel.

Beginning:

عجز مراتب حمد و ثنا تسلیم بارگاه صمدی...

Ending:

الحاصل احسان احسان است باقی همه حرف است، والسّلام.

«5»

Kāżimīnī Library, Yezd, No. 145

Nasta'līq, fol.107, Moḥammad Kāżim b. Moḥammad Zamān Khaṭīb, Salakh-e (last day of) Ramażān, 1160 A.H./[24th September, 1747 A.D.].

«6»

Jawāhar Museum, No. ج ن 486

Nasta'līq, fol.92, 10th Ṣafar, [1161 A.H./30th January, 1748 A.D.], 30th regnal year of Moḥammad Shāh.

Incomplete from the beginning.

Beginning:

... یا در ذات رحمت آیات ایشان باد و سایهٔ التفات شما...

Ending:

باقی همه حرف والسّلام.

«7»

Pīrmoḥammad Shāh Library, Aḥmedābād, No. 1620

***Jonūn-e Bahīriya* (جنونِ بهاریه)**

An extract from Bīdel's *Roqqa'āt*.

Shikesta-Nasta'līq, fol.6, Moḥib 'Alī Derwīsh Āzād, Thursday, 27th Ramażān, 1163 A.H./[19th August, 1750 A.D.], Surat.

Beginning:

زبیم نازکی‌های گل آنجا نفس دزدیده...

Ending:

نگه بر رنگِ گل چون مو بر آتش   ز بس اسباب عشرت شد مرتب

Its microfilm is available in Noor Microfilm Centre, Culture House, Islamic Republic of Iran, New Delhi.

«8»

Madras, No. D210

Inshī -e Būlel

Nasta'līq, fol.82, Moḥammad Ḥasan, Friday, 12th Rajab, 1164 A.H./[26th May, 1751 A.D.].

Beginning:

عجز مراتب حمد و ثنا تسلیم بارگاه صمدی که خامه را در معرکهٔ...

Ending:

دماغ اهلِ سودا نیست پرشـــور الهـــی خانـــهٔ زنجیـــر معمـــور

It was purchased at Milapur on 9th Ẕīqa'da, 1173 A.H./[23rd June, 1760 A.D.].

«9»

Āṣafīya, No. 132

Roqqa'ī t-e Būlel: Jonān-e Bahī riya

An extract from *Roqqa'āt*.

Nasta'līq, 1165 A.H./[1752 A.D.].

«10»

Deoband, No. 939/3

***Inshī -e Būlel* (Vol. II)**

Nasta'līq, fol.104, 1179 A.H./[1765 A.D.].

«11»

Tājīkistān, No. 2559/4

Nasta'līq, fol.85, 1203 A.H./1789 A.D.

«12»

Anjuman-e Taraqqī-e Urdū, Aligarh, No. 197

Shikesta, fol.96, Thursday, 24th Sha'bān, 1205 A.H./[28th April, 1791 A.D.], Karnaul (Hyderabad).

Beginning:

رقّعه در تحسین مکتوب مرزا خسرو بیگ: بارک الله، امروز کرم‌نامهٔ خسرو لفظ...
ترقیمه: روز پنجشنبه بست و چهارم شعبان‌المعظّم ۱۲۰۵ ه [۲۸ آوریل ۱۷۹۱ م]، درِ مَقام کرنول.

«13»

Anjuman-e Taraqqī-e Urdū, Delhi, No. 8916552/3

Nasta'līq, p.192, 24th Sha'bān, 1205 A.H./[28th April, 1791 A.D.].

Beginning:

مسطر چون رشتهٔ نگاه، بال وحشت می‌گشاید راه تشنگی‌های زلال وصال به‌سراب موج سطور بستن محال...

It is from the beginning of the preface to *Roqqa'āt*. Almost a paragraph is missing in the beginning.

Its microfilm is available in Noor Microfilm Centre, Culture House, Islamic Republic of Iran, New Delhi.

«14»

Tehran University Library, Tehran, No. 9798

Nasta'līq, fol.166, Kharak Rai, Wednesday, 15th Rabī'I, 1222 A.H./ [23rd May, 1807 A.D.].

Colophon:

کهرک رای پسرِ جسونت رای پسرِ گاسی رام کایسته شری باست کری از چکله کوره جهان‌آباد به‌فرمایشِ غوث صَاحب در اودگیر نیلور صوبهٔ کرناتکا در سه‌پهر روز چهارشنبه ۱۵ ربیع‌الاوّل ۱۲۲۲ ه [۲۳ مه ۱۸۰۷ م].

«15»

Tājīkistān, No. 124

Nasta'līq, fol.78, 1228 A.H./1813 A.D.

«16»

Nadva, Lucknow, No. 222

Nasta'līq, p.112, Shitāb Rai, 16th regnal year of Moḥammad Akbar Shāh Ghāzī II, [1237 A.H./1822 A.D.].

Beginning:

عجز مراتب حمد و ثنا تسلیم بارگاه صمدی که خامه را در معرکهٔ...

Ending:

... آن حاصل احسان احسان است و باقی همه حرف است.

«17»

Anjuman-e Taraqqī-e Urdū, Delhi, No. 167

Shikesta, fol.106, 14th Rabī'I, 1239 A.H./[18th November, 1823 A.D.].
Beginning:

عجز مراتب حمد و ثنا تسلیم بارگاه صمدی که خامه را در معرکهٔ...

Its microfilm is available in Noor Microfilm Centre, Culture House, Islamic Republic of Iran, New Delhi.

«18»

Patiala (Public Library), No. 2086

289 Letters

Nasta'līq, fol.67, Gol Shīr 'Alī, 1247 A.H./[1831 A.D.].
Beginning:

عجز مراتب حمد و ثنا تسلیم بارگاهِ صمدی که خامه را در معرکهٔ آغاز...

Ending:

... سربلند نیاز سرشتان عالم فرمود من از مروّت طبع دانستم.

«19»

Sālār, No. A.N./149/1

Ordinary script, fol.119, 21st Sha'bān, 1250 A.H./23rd December, 1834 A.D., seals of Moḥtaramuddaula, dated 1257 A.H./ [1841 A.D.], E'teṣām-ul Mulk, dated 1274 A.H./[1857 A.D.], containing 290 letters.
Beginning: as usual.
Ending:

... مسرور و مشکور باشد زیاده گلزار عرش‌نگار.

«20»

Moḥammadan Public Library, Madras, No. 266PM

Shikesta-Nasta'līq, fol.132, 9th Shawwāl, 1254 A.H./[26th December, 1838 A.D.], beautiful copy.
Beginning:

عجز مراتب حمد و ثنا تسلیم بارگاه صمدی که خامه را در معرکهٔ...

Ending:

... در کنف فضل ازل راحت اندوزد و آن درد و ملال.

«21»

N. Archives, Afghanistan, No. 25/22

Nasta'līq, fol.45, 1257 A.H./[1841 A.D.].

«22»

Jawāhar Museum, No. ج‌ن 487

Nasta'līq, fol.30, Najmoddīn b. Maulavī Ḥamīdollāh Chistī, 18th Moḥarram, 1264 A.H./[26th December, 1847 A.D.].

It was trancribed for Nūroddīn b. Qāẓī Aḥmad Ḥusain Reẓavī.

Beginning:

عجز مراتب حمد و ثنا تسلیم بارگاه صمدی...

Ending:

آفت کمین خموشی مباد و راز جمعیت این نوا خارج آهنگی انقلاب مبیناد.

«23»

Persian Academy, Tehran, No. 620,24

Majma'-ul Inshī

By Munshī Rai Dakhānī

Nasta'līq, fol.259, Ṣafar, 1265 A.H./[January, 1849 A.D.], Madras.

Only a few *Roqqa'āt* of Bīdel are included in this collection of letters.

«24»

Tājīkistān, No. 232/3

Nasta'līq, fol.90, 1265 A.H./1849 A.D.

«25»

University, No. 151 Fārsiya (3)

Nasta'līq, fol.56, 15th Rajab, 1274 A.H./[1st March, 1858 A.D.].

Beginning:

عجز مراتب حمد و ثنا تسلیم...

Ending:

از بسکه نگاه هرزه نازیبا داشت   مژگان یکسر جو جاده گردید سپید

«26»

Deoband, No. 949/13

Nasta'līq, fol.100, 1274 A.H./[1858 A.D.].

Manuscripts of Roqqaʻāt-e Bīdel
(Letters of Bīdel)
(Undated)

«1»

ASB, No. 843

At the end there are a few artificial *Ghazals* and quatrains written with letters not requiring diacritical dots. Another short series of quatrains in contradistinction to the preceding ones, are written only with letters requiring diacritical dots. A long *Mathnavī* describing the elephant and a series of *Terjīʻ-Bands*.

Shikesta, fol.392, 12th century A.H., folios misplaced.

«2»

Sālār, No. A./Nm/523

Good *Nastaʻlīq*, fol.299, an early 12th century A.H. copy, most folios damaged.

Beginning as usual.

Ending as usual.

«3»

Saulat Public Library, Rāmpūr, No. 222 (131)

Nastaʻlīq, fol.189, Muradabad (at Amroha), copied from the Mss. of Lāla Mangal Sen.

«4»

Banaras, No. 0164,4

Nastaʻlīq, fol.174.

Beginning:

عجز مراتب حمد و ثنا تسلیم بارگاهِ صمدی که خامه را در معرکهٔ آغاز...

«5»

Madras, No. 213

***Inshā-e Bīdel*, bound with Tārīkh-e ʻĀdil Shāh**

Nastaʻlīq, fol.142, good condition.

Beginning:

عجز مراتب حمد و ثنا تسلیم بارگاه صمدی که خامه را در معرکهٔ...

«6»

Hardayāl, No. R271
289 Letters
Nasta'līq, fol.136.
Beginning:

عجز مراتب حمد و ثنا تسلیم بارگاهِ صمدی که خامه را در معرکهٔ آغاز...

Heading in red, also explanatory notes on the margins on some pages in the beginning.

«7»

Patiala (Archives), No. 179
289 Letters mostly to Shokrollāh Khān and his son Shākir Khān and father-in-law 'Āqil Khān.
Nasta'līq, fol.131.
Beginning:

عجز مراتب حمد و ثنا تسلیم بارگاهِ صمدی که خامه را در معرکهٔ آغاز ثنایش...

Ending:

... الحاصل احسان احسانِ توست باقی همه حسرت (حرف است) والسّلام والاکرام.

«8»

Madras, No. 212
Nasta'līq, fol.113.

«9»

Anjuman-e Taraqqī-e Urdū, Aligarh, No. 199
Shikesta, fol.106.

«10»

Rieu, No. Add.7690
Nasta'līq, fol.139-241 (103).
Beginning:

عجز مراتب حمد و ثنا تسلیم بارگاه صمدی...

«11»

Madras, No. 211 P.Ms.
Inshā
Shikesta-Nasta'līq, fol.98.
Beginning:

عجز مراتب حمد و ثنا تسلیم بارگاه صمدی که خامه را در معرکهٔ...

Ending:

... دولت ابد مدّت تفرقه امور دیگر مبیناد.

«12»

Madras, No. D967
Inshā-e Bīdel
Nasta'līq, fol.96.
Beginning:

عجز مراتب حمد و ثنا تسلیم بارگاه صمدی که خامه را در معرکهٔ...

Ending:

... و جبین نیاز غیرسعادت سجود بهره دیگر مبیناد ظلکم مدود و عافیتکم محمود باد.

«13»

Āyātollāh-e Golpāyegānī Library, Qom, No. 14/51-2601
Nasta'līq, fol.93.
Beginning:

عجز مراتب حمد و ثنا تسلیم بارگاهِ صمدی که خامه را در معرکهٔ...

Ending:

... نصرت و فتح قرین احوال باد... خیراندیشان را امان بخشد از آشوب ملال این یکی در کنف فضل ازل راحت اندوزد و آن درد و ملال، تمّت.

«14»

Anjuman-e Taraqqī-e Urdū, Delhi, No. 464
Shikesta, fol.92.

عجز مراتب حمد و ثنا تسلیم بارگاه صمدی که خامه را در معرکهٔ آغاز...

«15»

Fort William, 121 (Acc.No. 410)
Naskh, p.178.
Beginning:

عجز مراتب حمد و ثنا تسلیم بارگاه صمدی...

«16»

Fort William College Collection (National Archives), No. 410
Naskh, p.178.
Beginning:

عجز مراتب حمد و ثنا تسلیم بارگاه صمدی که خامه را در معرکهٔ آغاز ثنایش از نقطهٔ سپر انداختن است...

«17»

Madras, No. D1081 (a)
Nasta'līq, fol.80.
It could not be traced in the collection but recorded in the catalogue.

«18»

Sālār, No. A./Nm.524
Ordinary *Nasta'līq*, fol.76, a late 12th century A.H. copy, worm eaten. Containing selections from *Robā'īs* and followed by *Mukhammasāt*, letters etc.
Beginning:

ای جوهر هوش محرم راز بـرآ   رندانه ز زهد مکـر پـرواز بـرآ

Ending:

سرمو مرنجـان دل هـیچ کـس   که مغز عبادت همین است و بـس

«19»

Solaimān, No. 323/56
Inshā-e Bīdel
Shikesta, fol.74.
Beginning:

عجز مراتب حمد و ثنا تسلیم...

Ending:

... بقربان حال بیدل اگر نه این برق بی‌نیازی بی‌گناه که می‌خرامد.

«20»

University, No. (3) 97

Shikesta, fol.66.

Beginning:

عجز مراتب حمد و ثنا...

Ending:

... احسان احسان است باقی همه حرف، والسّلام.

«21»

Sālār, No. A./Nm.676/2

Nasta'līq, fol.62, late 12th century A.H. copy, fair condition.

Beginning: as usual.

Ending:

دماغ اهلِ سودا نیست بی‌شور　　الهی خانهٔ زنجیر معمور

«22»

Tājīkistān, No. 1849/1

Nasta'līq, fol.51, Bāi Moḥammad.

«23»

Tājīkistān, No. 502

Nasta'līq, fol.50.

«24»

Idāreh-e Adabiyāt-e Urdū, Hyderabad, No. 40 (*Tazkireh-e Makhṭūṭāt*, Vol. I)

Beautiful *Nasta'līq*, fol.45.

«25»

Idāreh-e Adabiyāt-e Urdū, Hyderabad, No. 40 (*Tazkireh-e Makhṭūṭāt*, Vol. II)

Beautiful *Nasta'līq*, fol.45.

«26»

Madras, No. D954 (a)

Nasta'līq, fol.44 (from 13 to 61).

Beginning:

عجز مراتب حمد و ثنا تسلیم بارگاه صمدی که خامه را در معرکهٔ...

It contains *Waṣīlat-un Nijāt*, some *Roqqa'āt* of Bīdel and a selection of *Dīwān* of Amīr Khusrau.

«27»

Wazīrī Library, Yezd, No. 2405/4

Nasta'līq, fol.43, (102-144).

Beginning:

عجز مراتب حمد و ثنا تسلیمِ بارگاه صمدی که خامه را...

«28»

Khodā Bakhsh, No. 381

Roqqa'āt-e Bīdel Included in the Kolliyāt

Nasta'līq, fol.109a to 142 (34), Moḥammad Wārith b. Moḥammad Bāqer. (See Khudā Bakhsh, No. 381 *Kolliyāt*)

Beginning:

عجز مراتب حمد و ثنا تسلیم بارگاه صمدی...

«29»

Idāreh-e Adabiyāt-e Urdū, Hyderabad, No. 382 (*Tazkireh-e Makhṭūṭāt*, Vol. II)

Sormeh-e Aghnīyā

Beautiful minute script, fol.22. It is one of the most beautiful manuscripts of this collection.

Some verses in Urdū on the pages in the beginning and end of the manuscript.

«30»

Idāreh-e Adabiyāt-e Urdū, Hyderabad, No. 385 (*Tazkireh-e Makhṭūṭāt*, Vol. II)

Sormeh-e Aghnīyā

Shikesta-Nasta'līq, fol.22.

«31»

Shīfta, No. 180/144

Shikesta-Nasta'līq, fol.16.

Beginning:

دیدهٔ مشتاق را تا حصول سعادت دیدار به‌هرچه مژگان گشاید...

«32»

Kitābkhāna-e Majlis-e Shorā-e Millī, No. 14215/13

Only a few letters.

Nasta'līq, fol.11, (47-57).

Beginning:

... هستی نقد انفاسی است که بی‌توقّف از گنج خانه...

«33»

Majlis-e Shorā-e Millī Library, Tehran, No. 14209/209

Only one letter to 'Abduṣ Ṣamad pen-named Sokhan.

Nasta'līq, p.1, Moḥammad Ḥakīm Hindī.

«34»

Majlis-e Shorā-e Millī Library, Tehran, No. 14209/98

A letter in words without dots (بی‌نقط).

Nasta'līq, p.1 (303), Moḥammad Ḥakīm Hindī.

«35»

Majlis-e Shorā-e Millī Library, Tehran, No. 14215/23

A letter in words without dots.

Nasta'līq, fol.1.

«36»

Anjuman-e Taraqqī-e Urdū, Delhi, No. 135/2:3B:171

Majmū'a-e Roqqa'āt

This Ms. is entitled *Majmū'a-e Roqqa'āt*.

«37»

Shīfta, Aligarh, No. Fārsiya,144/180

Only few letters.

Shikesta-Nasta'līq, fol.16.

Beginning:

دیدهٔ مشتاق را تا حصول سعادت دیدار به‌هرچه مژگان گشاید...

Ending:

... درجهٔ کمال و اعتبار بهمرسانده تلافی شداید روزگار نماید.

This is the concluding part of a letter (4th in Tehran edition) to Nawwāb Shokrollāh Khān.

«38»

ASB (First Supplement), No. 811

A few letters in the end of the manuscript entitled *Risāla-e Ḥaq Numā* by Dārā Shukoh (d.1069 A.H./1659 A.D.).

Nasta'līq, only a few pages, slightly worm eaten.

«39»

Rieu, No. Or.1599

Some letters of Bīdel are included in *Majma'-ul Inshā* by Moḥammad Amīn Banī-Isrā'īl.

Shikesta.

«40»

Āṣafīya, No. 97

Nasta'līq.

«41»

Fort William College Collection (National Archives, New Delhi), No. 891.556, R879R

«42»

Research Library, Kashmīr University, Srinagar

«43»

Kotobkhāna-e Alqarshia Qiladar (Pakistan), Kotob-e Adab, No. 113

«44»

Sharaf-ul Mulk Library, Chenna'ī, No. 432

Inshā

«45»

Sharaf-ul Mulk Library, Chenna'ī, No. 702
Inshā

«46»

Sharaf-ul Mulk Library, Chenna'ī, No. 759

«47»

Sharaf-ul Mulk Library, Chenna'ī, No. 770
Inshā

«48»

Sharaf-ul Mulk Library, Chenna'ī, No. 1534
Inshā

«49»

Sharaf-ul Mulk Library, Chenna'ī, No. 1550K
Inshā

«50»

Sharaf-ul Mulk Library, Chenna'ī, No. 1609
Inshā

«51»

Sharaf-ul Mulk Library, Chenna'ī, No. 1619
Inshā

«52»

Sharaf-ul Mulk Library, Chenna'ī, No. 1651K
Inshā

«53»

Sharaf-ul Mulk Library, Chenna'ī, No. 2562

«54»

Sharaf-ul Mulk Library, Chenna'ī, No. 4788
Inshā

«55»

Sharaf-ul Mulk Library, Chenna'ī, No. 5201

«56»

Sharaf-ul Mulk Library, Chenna'ī, No. 5290
Inshā

«57»

Sharaf-ul Mulk Library, Chenna'ī, No. 6206
Inshā

(Inspite of best efforts, I could not see the collection in this library)

«58»

Sālār, No. A.N/342

Included in a *Majmū'a* (مجموعه).

Nasta'līq, fol.57-146 (90), early 13th century A.H., incomplete in the end.

Beginning: as usual.

Ending:

امید که ثمرهٔ اعتقاد اخلاص‌کیشان بباغ...

«59»

Jawāhar Museum, No. ج‌ف 514

Nasta'līq, fol.65, incomplete in the end.

Beginning:

عجز مراتب حمد و ثنا تسلیم بارگاه صمدی...

Ending:

... آفتاب عطوفت مشاهده نمودیم صبح عالم اقبال شام غبار.

«60»

Madras, No. 214
Inshā-e Bīdel

Nasta'līq, fol.60.

An incomplete Ms.

Chapter XV

Manuscripts of Nekāt-e Bīdel (Statements of Bīdel) (Dated)

It is a collection of philosophic and didactic aphorisms written by Bīdel in ornate (مسجّع) and obscure prose. Each *Nukta* is followed, for the sake of illustration, by a set of verses which generally includes a pair of *Ghazals* and a fragment in the form of *Mathnavī*. A quatrain is also sometimes added to it. This poetic part conforms to the theme of the related *Nukta*. Apart from it, the poetry part skirts social and satirical themes as well. Consequently, the prose portion is hardly one-fourth of the whole work. The *Nekāt* vary in their themes from higher philosophy, mysticism to mere depiction and come to an end with some verses under the title of *Ishārāt*.

There is no reference to its date of composition. As one of its manuscripts was transcribed in 1091 A.H./1680 A.D.,[1] it may be alluded that it was completed in 1091 A.H. or a little before it. As is the case with the number of letters of Bīdel in different manuscripts, the number of *Nekāt* in its different manuscripts also differ with each other. There are seventy-five *Nekāt* in the Tehran edition. Apart from it, there are also some *Nekāt* in *Chahār 'Onṣor* not included in the work named *Nekāt*.[2]

*

1. *Catalogue of the Āṣifīya Library*, Vol. I, p.136.
2. *Āwāzhāy-e Bīdel*: Akbar Bahdarwand.

«1»

Āṣafīya, No. 107

Fair *Nasta'līq*, 'Arab Shāh Bukhārī, 1091 A.H./[1680 A.D.], gold work.

«2»

Dargāh Library, Ūch, No. 379

It is a very fine Ms. containing four different treatises. One of them is probably *Nekāt* of Bīdel as its opening line indicates.
Fair *Nasta'līq*, fol.90, 1151 A.H./[1738 A.D.] (*Nekāt* from fol.7a-52a).
Beginning:

این هفتاد و یک نکته از جمله کتاب نکات و اشارات...

Headings in red ink and with an illustrated headpiece.
It is one of the rare Mss. of this collection.

«3»

Rieu, No. Add.16,866

Nasta'līq, fol.83, Rabī'I, 1154 A.H./[May, 1741 A.D.].
Beginning:

اگر منکر نبوّت نه‌ای با حضرات جز بتعظیم پیش میا...

«4»

Public Library, Khairpur, Monzavī 14, p.123

Shikesta-Nasta'līq, p.158, 'Abdul Qādir, 3rd Ẕīqa'da, 1163 A.H./[23rd September, 1750 A.D.].
Beginning:

اگر منکر نبوّت نه‌ای با حضرات جز بتعظیم پیش میا...

«5»

ASB, No. 384

Nasta'līq, 1169 A.H./[1756 A.D.], Mohammadpur, good condition.
Beginning:

اگر منکرِ نبوّت نه‌ای...

«6»

Solaimān, Khwāja Ḥasan, No. Taṣawwuf, 297-7

Shikesta, fol.46, Wednesday, 5th Ṣafar, 4th regnal year of 'Ālamgīr II, (1170 A.H.)/[30th October, 1756 A.D].

«7»

ASB, No. 385

Nasta'līq, fol.45, Gholām Aḥmad, 1182 A.H./[1768 A.D.], good.
It contains a preamble but fragmentary.
Beginning abruptly with:

ز دو جای نرسید...

«8»

National Museum, Karachi, No. N.M.1958.360/1, Monzavī 14, p.123

Shikesta, fol.82, 1st Moḥarram, 1190 A.H./[21st February, 1776 A.D.].
Beginning:

اگر منکر نبوّت نه‌ای با حضرات جز بتعظیم پیش میا...

«9»

Ghālib Institute, New Delhi, No. ف091.50123

Shikesta, fol.74, 11th Rabī'II, 1193 A.H./[28th April, 1779 A.D.], worm eaten.
In the end of the Ms. some *Isṭeleḥāt* (اصطلاحات) of Bīdel have been written.
Beginning:

اگر منکر نبوّت نه‌ای...

Ending:

کنون به‌ساز ادب محو این نواست سخن

که مدّعای بیانِ وصف خامشی است، خموش

غرضِ هرجا سخنی است، بی‌معنی افاده مباد و هرجا خاموشی است، انفعال گفتگو مبیناد تمّت‌الکتاب؛ بعون الله تعالی.

Two seals: one of Moḥammad 'Abdur Razzāq and the second of Moḥammad 'Abdul Wahhāb.

Microfilm of the Ms. is available in Noor Microfilm Centre, Culture House, Islamic Republic of Iran, New Delhi.

«10»

Nadva, Lucknow, No. 262

Nasta'līq, p.136, Syed Amjad 'Alī, [1202 A.H./1788 A.D. in the beginning of the Ms].

Beginning:

نکتهٔ اوّل از نکات سرِحلقهٔ ارباب صاحبِ دل مرزا عبدالقادر بیدل...

Ending:

گوش هوس بپرداز از خامشی بیانـان بوی گل است بیـدل تقریـر ناتوانـان

در ساز ما صدایی است پرغنچه می‌سراییم

(از نکتهٔ ۶۸ چاپِ تهران).

«11»

Dār-ul 'Ulūm Farīdiya Library, Sāhiwāl, Monzavī 14, p.124

Nasta'līq, p.71, Żahūroddīn Aḥmad Shīrāzī, 1212 A.H./[1797 A.D.].

Beginning:

اگر منکر نبوّت نه‌ای با حضرات جز بتعظیم پیش میا...

«12»

Hāshemī Library, Naushehra district Shaikhūpūra, Monzavī 14, p.124

Nasta'līq, p.146, Moḥammad Aḥmad, 16th Sha'bān, 1219 A.H./[20th November, 1804 A.D.].

Beginning:

حمد مبدعی که تردّد اعیان کیف و کم موقوف...

It is the beginning of the *Dībācha* of Bīdel on his *Kolliyāt*.

«13»

Tājīkistān, No. 1558/3

Nasta'līq, fol.72, 1222 A.H./1807 A.D.

«14»

Browne, No. V.63 (10), P.253 (2nd Part)

Along with *Moḥīṭ-e A'żam*.
Ta'līq, fol.210, 1223 A.H./1808 A.D.

«15»

Tājīkistān, No. 201

Nasta'līq, fol.72, Mollā Khodā'ī Nażar, 1225 A.H./1829 A.D.

«16»

Deoband, No. 996/6

Nasta'līq, fol.97, 1227 A.H./[1812 A.D.].

«17»

ASB, No. 386

Nasta'līq, 1228 A.H./[1813 A.D.].
Beginning:

اگر منکرِ نبوّت نه‌ای...

«18»

Tājīkistān, No. 1884/4

Nasta'līq, fol.104, 1230 A.H.[/1815 A.D.].

«19»

Sālār, No. A.N.326

Nasta'līq, fol.50, Lāla Bishan Lāl, 29th Rabī'I, 1231 A.H./28th February, 1816 A.D., coloured red borders.
Beginning:

اگر منکرِ نبوّت نه‌ای با خطرات جز بتعظیم پیش میا...

Ending:

... هرکجا خاموشی است، انفعال گفتگو مباد.

«20»

Tājīkistān, No. 836/2

Nasta'līq, fol.68, 1246 A.H./1830 A.D., Bukhara.

«21»

Mozzammil, No. 504

Nasta'līq, fol.96, 1248 A.H./[1832 A.D.].

Begins with the first *Nukta* in the published edition:

نکته: اگر منکرِ نبوّت نه‌ای با حضرات، جز بتعظیم پیش میا و اگر بر تجلّی حق ایمان داری بی‌ادب چشم مکشا...

Ending:

گـر بـه‌طبـع کـرم نباشـد بـار رنـج افعـال مـا ز مـا بـردار

This is the ending of *Nukta* No. 53 in the Tehran published edition.

«22»

Tājīkistān, No. 3024/2

Nasta'līq, fol.89, Rabī'II, 1256 A.H./June, 1840 A.D.

«23»

Record Office, Peshawar, No. 182, Monzavī 14, p.124

Shikesta-Nasta'līq, p.128, Gholām Qādir Khān Kātib Bāshī, Sunday 25th Ṣafar, 1257 A.H./[18th March, 1841 A.D.].

Beginning:

اگر منکر نبوّت نه‌ای با حضرات جز بتعظیم پیش میا...

«24»

Peoples District Library, Faiṣalābād, Monzavī 14, p.124

Defective in the beginning.

Nasta'līq, p.206, 26th Ṣafar, 1260 A.H./[17th March, 1844 A.D.].

Beginning:

(به‌هرجا کمال یقین نشـه‌ایسـت) برون زین دو کیفیتش جلوه‌ایست

It is a verse from second *Nukta* in printed edition.

«25»

Tājīkistān, No. 2395

Shikesta-Nasta'līq, fol.80, 1261 A.H./1845 A.D.

«26»

N. Archives, Afghanistan, No. ...

Nasta'līq, fol.174, 'Abdur Reḥmān, 1263 A.H./[1847 A.D.].

«27»

Sālār, No. A./Nm.999

Shikesta, fol.50, 1st Ẕilḥijja, 1268 A.H./16th September, 1852 A.D., European paper.

«28»

Tājīkistān, No. 289/1

Nasta'līq, fol.63, 1270 A.H./1854 A.D.

«29»

National Museum, Karachi, No. N.M.1971-295, Monzavī 14, p.124

Nasta'līq, fol.6+90, Mīrzā Faẓl Aḥmad Peshāwarī, 6th Ṣafar, 1271 A.H. [29th October, 1854 A.D.], Lahore.

Beginning:

اگر منکر نبوّت نه‌ای با حضرات جز بتعظیم پیش میا...

«30»

Ḥabībganj, No. 105/21 Fārsiya

Majlis-e Āb-o-Gil

Nasta'līq, fol.76, Faẓl-Jī Bihārī, 2nd Ẕilḥijja, 1272 A.H./[27th July, 1759 A.D.], Lucknow.

Beginning:

اگر منکر نبوّت نه‌ای با خطرات جز بتعظیم پیش میا...

Ending:

... غرضِ هرجا سخنی است، بی‌معنی افاده مباد و هرجا خاموشی است، انفعال گفتگو مبیناد.

«31»

Tājīkistān, No. 217/1

Nasta'līq, fol.81, 1275 A.H./1859 A.D.

«32»

Tājīkistān, No. 1178/4

Nasta'līq, fol.73, 1298 A.H./1881 A.D.

«33»

Tājīkistān, No. 2939

Nasta'līq, Mollā Mīr Qāsim, Bukhara, 1299 A.H./1882 A.D.

«34»

Maḥmūd Beg Library. Naunānwālā, Bahlwal, Monzavī 14, p.124

Nasta'līq, p.158, [5th Rajab, 1347 A.H.]/18th December, 1928 A.D.
Beginning from the *Dībācha* on Bīdel's *Kolliyāt*:

حمد مبدعی که تردّد اعیان کیف و کم موقوف...

Manuscripts of Nekāt-e Bīdel (Statements of Bīdel) (Undated)

«1»

Sālār, No. Tas.223

Shikesta-Nasta'līq, fol.114, a late 12th century A.H. copy, seals of Syed 'Abdur Reḥmān, 1167 A.H., Mīr Moḥammad Ṣāleḥ, Syed Ḥusain, 1167 A.H.

Beginning:

اگر منکر نبوّت نه‌ای با حضرات به‌جز تعظیم پیش میا...

«2»

Sa'diya Library, Mīyānwālī, Monzavī 14, p.124

Shikesta-Nasta'līq, p.196, 12th century A.H.

Beginning:

اگر منکر نبوّت نه‌ای با حضرات به‌جز تعظیم پیش میا...

«3»

Syed Shamsoddīn Gīlānī, Ūch, 379, Monzavī 14, p.123

A selection of 71 *Nekāt* out of 75 in the published edition.

Nasta'līq, p.118, 12th century A.H.

Beginning:

این هفتاد و یک نکته ازجمله کتاب نکات و اشارات و چهار عنصر انتخاب نمود تا نسخهٔ مختصری دست... اگر منکر نبوّت نه‌ای...

«4»

Shahābuddīn Library, Sargodha, Monzavī 14, p.124

Nasta'līq, p.112, 12th century A.H.

Beginning from *Dībācha* to Bīdel's *Kolliyāt*:

حمد مبدعی که تردّد اعیان کیف و کم موقوف...

«5»

Qāẓī 'Abdul Karīm Library, Ḥasan Abdāl, Kembalpūr, Monzavī 14, p.124

Shikesta-Nasta'līq, p.109, 13th century A.H.

Beginning:

اگر منکر نبوّت نه‌ای با حضرات به‌جز تعظیم پیش میا...

«6»

Tājīkistān, No. 502/1

Nasta'līq, fol.85.

«7»

Tājīkistān, No. 2267

Nasta'līq, fol.85, 'Ubaid Faiẓ.

«8»

Madras, No. 820

Nasta'līq, fol.64.

Beginning:

اگر منکر نبوّت نه‌ای با حضرات جز به‌تعظیم پیش میا...

Ending:

... و هرکجا خموشی است انفعال.

Three couplets one each from Bīdel, Hāshim Kashmīrī and Amīr Khusrau have been copied on the last page.

«9»

Panjab Public Library, Lahore, No. 95, Monzavī 14, p.125

Containing 71 *Nekāt*.

Nasta'līq, fol.52, 'Abdollāh Khalīfa Ḥayātollāh Qādirī Sahāranpūrī.

«10»

Solaimān, No. 149/49

It is bound with the Ms. No. 806/81 in this collection.

«11»

Dānishkada-e Ilāhīyāt, Mashhad, No. 19326/2

Nasta'līq.

Beginning:

اگر منکر نبوّت نه‌ای با حضرات به‌جز تعظیم پیش میا...

«12»

N. Archives, Afghanistan, No. 2/69

Nasta'līq.

«13»

N. Archives, Afghanistan, No. 18/136

Nasta'līq.

«14»

Sharaf-ul Mulk Library, Chenna'ī, No. 4861

«15»

Sharaf-ul Mulk Library, Chenna'ī, No. 4856

Sharḥ-e Dah Fiqrah-e Awwal-e Nekāt-e Mīrzā 'Abdul Qādir-e Bīdel

It is a commentary on ten first *Nekāt* and probably the only work of its kind in Persian.

«16»

Moḥammad Akram Library, Malikābād, Jhang, Monzavī 14, p.124

Incomplete copy from the end.

Nasta'līq, p.185, 'Abdul Mo'īn b. Gholām Rasūl b. Pīran Bakhsh, 13th century A.H.

Beginning from *Dībācha* to *Kolliyāt*:

حمد مبدعی که تردّد اعیان کیف و کم موقوف...

«17»

Majlis-e Shūrā-e Millī, Tehran, No. 17029/2

Incomplete copy from the end.

Naskh-Nasta'līq, p.257 (193-449).

Beginning:

اگر منکر نبوّت نه‌ای با حضرات به‌جز تعظیم پیش میا...

Ending:

... طینتِ آدمی بحکم النّاس نیام مخمر اثبات غفلت است و اطلاق بیداری بر حقیقت غنودن انجامش...

«18»

Āyātollāh-e Mar'ashī, Library, Qom, No. 11659/2

Incomplete copy from end.

Nasta'līq, fol.60.

Beginning:

اگر منکر نبوّت نه‌ای با حضرات به‌جز تعظیم پیش میا...

Ending:

هزار گل ز لب هرزه گوست رنگین‌تـر   تبسّم لب زخمی اگر کشـد آغـوش

(«تبسّمِ لب زخمی که واکند آغوش» در چاپی).

Chapter XVI

Published Works of Bīdel

Kolliyāt (کلیّات)

«1»

***Kolliyāt-e Bīdel* (کلیّاتِ بیدل)**

Only after 145 years of the death of Bīdel, his *Kolliyāt* was published from Maṭba'-e Aḥmadī, Delhi (i.e., in 1278 A.H.)/ [1861 A.D.] in two volumes. Its first volume is preserved in Khodā Bakhsh Oriental Public Library, Patna. The 2nd volume was in possession of Prof. 'Aṭā-ur Reḥmān 'Aṭā Kākvī, Patna.

«2»

***Kolliyāt-e Bīdel* (کلیّاتِ بیدل)**

Nawal Kishore Press, Kanpur, published the *Kolliyāt* for the first time in [1292 .A.H.]/1875 A.D. It contains *Nekāt*, *Roqqa'āt* and *Chahār 'Onṣor* in one volume. The famous Urdū fiction writer Pandit Ratan Nāth Sarshār, serving at the press at that time, played an important role in its publication. During the same period *Dīwān of Bīdel* along with *Nekāt-e Bīdel* was also published from the same press. During the same period *Dīwān-e Bīdel* along with *Nekāt* was also published from Nawal Kishore Press.

«3»

***Kolliyāt-e Bīdel* (کلیّاتِ بیدل)**

Published by Maṭba'-e Ṣafdarī, Bombay in [1299 A.H.]/1882 A.D. It is a voluminous edition on large size and includes *Ghazals*, *Chahār 'Onṣor*, *Nekāt* and *Roqqa'āt-e Bīdel*.

«4»

***Kolliyāt-e Bīdel* (کلیّاتِ بیدل)**

Kolliyāt in four volumes, Kabul, 1342 Khorshīdī/[1963 A.D.].

«5»

Kolliyāt-e Bīdel **(کلیّاتِ بیدل)**

Al-Kitāb Publication, Lahore, [1398 A.H.]/1978 A.D.

«6»

Kolliyāt-e Bīdel **(کلیّاتِ بیدل)**

Kolliyāt compiled by Akbar Behdārwand and Perviz 'Abbāsī Dākānī, published by Ilhām, Tehran, 1st edition in 1376 H.S./ [1997 A.D.].

«7»

Kolliyāt-e Bīdel **(کلیّاتِ بیدل)**

Kolliyāt-e Dīwān-e Maulānā Bīdel Dehlavī, the greatest composer of India, compiled by Khāl Moḥammad Khasteh, Ḥusain Āhī, Ostād Khalīlollāh-e Khalīlī, Forūghī Publication, Tehran, published in 1381 H.S./[2002 A.D.].

«8»

Kolliyāt-e Bīdel **(کلیّاتِ بیدل)**

In three volumes, edited by Akbar Behdārwand and Perviz 'Abbāsī Dākānī, published by Āgāh, Tehran, 1385 H.S./[2006 A.D.].

Dīwān (دیوان)

«1»

Dīwān-e Bīdel **(دیوانِ بیدل)**

Compiled by Khairīya-e Jadīda in Samarqand City, published by Maṭba'-e Taimūro, scribe: 'Abdul Ghafūr, 1301 A.H./[1884 A.D.]. Containing *Ghazaliyāt* and *Robā'īyāt*.

«2»

Dīwān-e Bīdel with Nekāt **(دیوانِ بیدل مع نکات)**

Dīwān-e Bīdel with *Nekāt*, *Ishārāt* and *Moḥīṭ-e A'żam*, compiled and supervised by Ibrāhīm-ush Shān with the cooperation of Moḥammad Murād entitled "Dīwān Begī", Maṭba'-e Khorshīd-e Maṭla', Dārul Khilāfa-e Khuyūq, 1301 A.H./[1884 A.D.].

«3»

Dīwān-e Ghazaliyāt (دیوانِ غزلیّات)

Edited by Ostād Khalīlollāh-e Khalīlī, Nashr-e Bainul Milalī, (Tehran), 1st edition, 1263 H.S./[1884 A.D.].

«4»

Dīwān with Nekāt (دیوانِ مع نکات)

Nawal Kishore Press, Kanpur, [1303 A.H.]/1886 A.D.
Containing 258 pages.

«5»

Dīwān-e Bīdel with Nekāt (دیوانِ بیدل مع نکات)

Compiled by Raḥīm Khwāja Īshān Ibn-e ‘Alī Khwāja Īshān, published by Maṭba‘-e Lākhtīn, Tashkent, in 1309 A.H./1892 A.D.
This *Dīwān* comprises of *Ghazaliyāt* from p.2 to p.210, *Robā‘īyāt* from p.210 to p.216 and *Nekāt* from p.212/216 to p.216/260.

«6»

Dīwān-e Bīdel (دیوانِ بیدل)

Compiled by Mollā Fāẓil Ākhund Khūqandī Ibn-e Mollā ‘Abdollāh Ākhund with the permission of Ma‘ārif-e Nażārat-e Jalīla-e Patīrbūrkh, published by Maṭba‘-e Lākhtīn, Tashkent, 1310 A.H./1893 A.D. or 1315 A.H./1898 A.D.
Colophon on p.162:

"تمام شد غزلیّاتِ میرزا عبدالقادر بیدل با همراهی رباعیات در حاشیه در بیست و دوّم شهر شوّال در سنهٔ ۱۳۱۵ هجری مطابق بیست و ششم افریل (آوریل) در سنهٔ ۱۸۹۳ عیسوی [۲۲ شوّال ۱۳۱۰ برابر با ۹ مه ۱۸۹۳ م است] یا [۲۲ شوّال ۱۳۱۵/۱۶ مارس ۱۸۹۸ م] در روز دوشنبه".

«7»

Dīwān-e Bīdel with Nekāt (دیوانِ بیدل همراه با نکات)

Published from Nawal Kishore Press, Kanpur, [1310 A.H.]/1893 A.D.

«8»

Dīwān-e Bīdel (ديوانِ بيدل)

Published by Maṭba'-e Lākhtīn, scribe: Moḥammad Shāh Murād, 20th Moḥarram 1311 A.H./[4th August, 1893 A.D.]

Having *Ghazaliyāt* from p.2 to p.217, and *Robā'īyāt* from p.217 to p.227.

«9»

Dīwān-e Bīdel (ديوانِ بيدل)

Compiled by Mollā Gholām Rasūl Khwāja bin Moḥammad Rasūl Khwāja, published by Maṭba'-e Barīdīnbākh, Tashkent, [1311 A.H.]/ 1893 A.D.

Having *Ghazaliyāt* and *Robā'īyāt*.

«10»

Dīwān-e Bīdel (ديوانِ بيدل)

Compiled by Khairulḥājj Mollā 'Abdul Malik Ḥājī son of 'Abdun Nabī, Maṭba'-e Futūkhof, Tashkent, 1313 A.H./[1895 A.D.].

«11»

Dīwān-e Bīdel (ديوانِ بيدل)

Compiled by Aṣghar Khwāja Ibn-e Sa'ādat Khwāja Īshān, published by Maṭba'-e Barīdīnbākh, Tashkent, 1314 A.H./ [1896 A.D.].

«12»

Dīwān-e Bīdel (ديوانِ بيدل)

Published from Shirkat-e Jadīda, Tashkent, 1314 A.H./[1896 A.D.].

«13»

Dīwān-e Bīdel (ديوانِ بيدل)

Compiled by Mollā Gholām Rasūl Khwāja bin Moḥammad Rasūl Khwāja, published by Maṭba'-e Barīdīnbākh, Tashkent, [1314 A.H.]/ 1896 A.D.

Having *Ghazaliyāt* and *Robā'īyāt*.

«14»

***Dīwān-e Bīdel* (دیوانِ بیدل)**

Compiled by Rāqim, published by Maṭba'-e Barīdīnbākh, Tashkent, 1316 A.H./[1898 A.D.].

Having *Ghazaliyāt* from p.2 to p.181 and *Robā'īyāt* from p.182 to p.192.

«15»

***Dīwān-e Bīdel* (دیوانِ بیدل)**

Under the supervision of Ya'qūb Khwāja Ṣaḥḥāf Ibn-e Pādshāh Khwāja Ṣaḥḥāf, printed by Ellīyīn Press, Tashkent, 1318 A.H./[1900 A.D.].

«16»

***Dīwān-e Bīdel* (دیوانِ بیدل)**

Published from Ellīyīn Press, Tashkent, scribe: Shāh Islām, 1318 A.H./1900 A.D.

Containing *Ghazals* from p.2 to p.132 and *Robā'īyāt* from p.132 to p.144.

«17»

***Dīwān-e Bīdel* (دیوانِ بیدل)**

Published from Shirkat-e Jadīda, Tashkent, 1319 A.H./[1901 A.D.].

«18»

***Dīwān-e Bīdel* (دیوانِ بیدل)**

Ellīyīn Press, Tashkent, scribe: Moḥammad Shāh Murād, 1319 A.H./[1901 A.D.].

Ghazals from p.2 to p.137 and *Robā'īyāt* from p.137 to p.144.

«19»

***Dīwān-e Bīdel* (دیوانِ بیدل)**

Printed by Pūr-e Ṣūf Press, Tashkent, 1319 A.H./[1901 A.D.].

Containing *Ghazals* from p.2 to p.157 and *Robā'īyāt* from p.158 to p.168.

«20»

***Dīwān-e Bīdel* (دیوانِ بیدل)**

Printed by Pūr-e Ṣūf Press, Tashkent, scribe: Moḥammad Shāh Murād, 1321 A.H./[1903 A.D.].

Containing *Ghazals* from p.2 to p.130 and *Robā'īyāt* from p.130 to p.144.

«21»

Dīwān-e Bīdel **(دیوانِ بیدل)**

With grants from Shirkat-e Khairīya-e Jadīda, printed by Chāpkhāneh-e Pādshāhī, scribe: Najmoddīn Khwāja Al-Khūqandī, 1321 A.H./[1903 A.D.].

«22»

Dīwān-e Bīdel **(دیوانِ بیدل)**

Under the supervision of Moḥammad Ṣāleḥ Khwāja Bukhārī with cooperation of Mīrzā 'Abdul Wāḥid Bukhārī, Maṭba'-e Taimūro, 1322 A.H./[1904 A.D.].

It contains *Ghazals* and *Robā'īs*.

«23»

Dīwān-e Bīdel **(دیوانِ بیدل)**

Edited by Syed Akbar Khwāja bin Syed 'Umar Qārī, Chāpkhāneh-e Ellīyīn, Tashkent, scribe: Shāh Islām, 1323 A.H./[1905 A.D.].

«24»

Dīwān-e Bīdel **(دیوانِ بیدل)**

Compiled by Ya'qūb Khwāja Īshān, Maṭba'-e Pūr-e Ṣūf, Tashkent, scribe: Mollā Shāh Islām Shāhī, 1324 A.H./[1906 A.D.].

«25»

Dīwān-e Bīdel **(دیوانِ بیدل)**

Under the supervision of Gholām Rasūl Khwāja bin Moḥammad Rasūl Khwāja, Chāpkhāneh-e Pūr-e Ṣūf, Tashkent, 1325 A.H./[1907 A.D.].

P.128 has the following line:

"تمّت‌الکتاب بعون‌الملک الوهاب سنهٔ ۱۳۲۵ ق، محمّد شاه مراد العبدالمذنب".

Moḥammad Shāh Murād named in this line may be its scribe.

«26»

Dīwān-e Bīdel **(دیوانِ بیدل)**

Kitāb-e Ghazaliyāt, Maṭba'-e Taimūro, 1325 A.H./1907 A.D.

«27»

Dīwān-e Bīdel (دیوانِ بیدل)

Compiled by Ḥājī 'Abdur Ra'ūf, Maṭba'-e Gholāmīya, Tashkent, scribe: Shāh Islām Al-Shāshī, 1326 A.H./[1908 A.D.].

«28»

Dīwān-e Bīdel (دیوانِ بیدل)

Compiled by Mollā Moḥammadī Makhdūm, printed from Maṭba'-e Kāgān, Bukhara Sharīf, 1326 A.H./[1908 A.D.].
Containing *Ghazals* and *Robā'īyāt*.

«29»

Dīwān-e Bīdel (دیوانِ بیدل)

Chāpkhāneh-e Kāgān, scribe: Mīrzā Dāūd Khwāja, 1327 A.H./ [1909 A.D.].

«30»

Dīwān-e Bīdel (دیوانِ بیدل)

At the instance of Mollā Gholām Ḥasan Makhdūm printed by Maṭba'-e Gholāmī, Tashkent, scribe: Munshī Shāh Islām, 1327 A.H./ [1909 A.D.].
Having *Ghazals* and *Robā'īyāt*.

«31»

Dīwān-e Bīdel (دیوانِ بیدل)

Printed by Gholāmīya Press, Tashkent, scribe: Mollā Autib Shāshī, 1328 A.H./[1910 A.D.].
Containing *Ghazals* from p.2 to p.104 and *Robā'īyāt* from p.104 to p.110.

«32»

Dīwān-e Bīdel (دیوانِ بیدل)

Maṭba'-e Kāgān, Bukhara, scribe: 'Abdul Mū'min Shāh Darwāzī, 1328 A.H./[1910 A.D.].

«33»

Dīwān-e Bīdel (دیوانِ بیدل)

At the instance of Mollā 'Abdul Ḥakīm and Mollā 'Abdur Raḥmān, printed by Maṭba'-e Solemānof and Ghazarof, Samarqand, scribed by a teacher of Kabul Mīrzā Syed 'Abdus Salām Makhdūm bin Mollā Syed 'Abdul Ḥamīd Muftī son of Mollā Syed 'Abdollāh, 5th Shawwāl, 1329 A.H./[29th September, 1911 A.D.].

«34»

Dīwān-e Bīdel (دیوانِ بیدل)

Compiled by Ḥājī 'Abdur Ra'ūf, Maṭba'-e Pūr-e Ṣūf, Tashkent, 1330 A.H./[1912 A.D.].

«35»

Dīwān-e Bīdel (دیوانِ بیدل)

Gholāmī Press, Tashkent, scribe: Mollā 'Abdul Ghafūr entitled Mollā Autib Rasūl Moḥammad Oghlī of Tashkent, 1330 A.H./[1912 A.D.].

«36»

Dīwān-e Bīdel with Qaṣā'īd-e Foyūẓ (دیوانِ بیدل مع قصایدِ فیوض)

Maṭba'-e Lowīn, Bukhara, 1330 A.H./[1912 A.D.].

Qaṣā'īd-e Foyūẓ printed on the margins.

«37»

Ghazaliyāt-e Bīdel with Qaṣā'īd-e Foyūẓ on Margins (غزلیّاتِ بیدل مع قصایدِ فیوض در حاشیه)

With monetary grant of the chief businessman Mollā 'Abdul Qādir Bāi and Mollā 'Abdul 'Aẓīm Bāi son of Qārī 'Abdur Raḥīm Bāi of Tashkent. Printed at Maṭba'-e Pūr-e Ṣūf, Tashkent, 1330 A.H./[1912 A.D.].

Qaṣā'īd-e Foyūẓ Bīdel have been printed on the margins of this edition.

«38»

Dīwān-e Bīdel (دیوانِ بیدل)

Under the supervision of and financial aid by the chief of traders Mollā Mīrzā Aḥmad bin Mīrzā Karīm Ḥājib Marḥūm Tāshkendī, Maṭba'-e Āryā, Tashkent, scribe: Mollā 'Abdul Ghafūr entitled Autib bin Rasūl Moḥammad Shāshī, 1331 A.H./[1913 A.D.].

«39»

Dīwān-e Bīdel (دیوانِ بیدل)

Edited by Rāqim and with financial assistance from Mollā 'Abdul Qādir Bāi and Mollā 'Abdul 'Ażīm Bāi, sons of 'Abdur Raḥīm Bāi of Tashkent, Chāpkhāneh-e Pūr-e Ṣūf, Tashkent, 1332 A.H./ [1914 A.D.].

It has a note on p.192:

"العبدالمذنب محمّد شاه مراد".

Indicating the name of the scribe Moḥammad Shāh Murād.

«40»

Dīwān-e Bīdel (دیوانِ بیدل)

Having *Ghazaliyāt* and *Robā'īyāt*, printed from Maṭba'-e Nāmī Girāmī, 1333 A.H./[1915 A.D.] at the instance of 'Umdat-ut Tujjār-e Kuṭub Mollā Mīrzā Aḥmad bin Mīrzā Karīm Marḥūm.

«41»

Dīwān-e Bīdel with Qaṣā'īd-e Foyūẓ (دیوانِ بیدل مع قصایدِ فیوض)

Dīwān-e Ghazaliyāt with Qaṣā'īd-e Foyūẓ, edited by Mīrzā Aḥmad bin Mīrzā Karīm, Tashkent, 1333 A.H./1915 A.D. Printer's name not given.

Ghazaliyāt with *Qaṣā'īd-e Foyūẓ* printed on the margins.

«42»

Dīwān-e Bīdel with Qaṣā'īd-e Foyūẓ (دیوانِ بیدل مع قصایدِ فیوض)

Dīwān-e Ghazaliyāt with Qaṣā'īd-e Foyūẓ, under the guidance and with financial aid from chief trader Mollā Taimūr Khwāja bin Ḥājī Moḥammad Khojandī, Maṭba'-e Gholāmī, Tashkent, 1333 A.H./ 1915 A.D.

Qaṣā'īd-e Foyūẓ printed on the margins.

«43»

Dīwān-e Bīdel (دیوانِ بیدل)

Edited by Mollā Moḥammad Nāṣeḥ Makhdūm bin Mollā 'Alī Rāmulla, Chāpkhāneh-e Gholāmī, Tashkent, scribe: Yousof Nauqalamī Jollābī of Tashkent, 1333 A.H./[1915 A.D.].

«44»

Dīwān-e Bīdel (دیوانِ بیدل)

Under the supervision of Mollā Żahūroddīn Makhdūm b. Mollā Mūsā Qārī, Gholāmī Press, Tashkent, 1333 A.H./[1915 A.D.]. *Ghazaliyāt* from p.2 to p.97 and *Robā'īyāt* from p.97 to p.120.

«45»

Dīwān-e Bīdel (دیوانِ بیدل)

Under the supervision of Ḥājī 'Abdur Ra'ūf b. 'Abdun Nabī, Gholāmī Press, Tashkent, 1335 A.H./[1917 A.D.].
Ghazals from p.2 to p.76 and *Robā'īyāt* from p.76 to p.92.

«46»

Dīwān-e Bīdel (دیوانِ بیدل)

Under the supervision of Mollā Moḥammad Żafar Beg Moḥammad Oghlī, Maṭba'-e Pūr-e Ṣūf, Tashkent, 1366 A.H./[1947 A.D.].

«47»

Dīwān-e Bīdel (دیوانِ بیدل)

Compiled by Ḥusain Āhī, Forūghī Publication, Tehran, 2nd edition in 1368 H.S./[1989 A.D.].

«48»

Kitāb-e Ārzū (گزیدهٔ غزلیّات و تک بیت‌های بیدل)

Kitāb-e Ārzū: Guzīda-e Ghazaliyāt-o-Tak-Baithāy-e Maulānā 'Abdul Qādir Bīdel, Amīr Kabīr Publication, Tehran, 1st edition 1378 H.S./[1999 A.D.].

«49»

Guzīdah-e Ghazaliyāt-e Bīdel-e Dehlavī (گزیدهٔ غزلیّاتِ بیدل دهلوی)

Guzīda-e Ghazaliyāt-e Bīdel Dehlavī, Sa'īd Yūsufniyā, Qadyānī, Tīr, 1384 H.S./[July, 2005 A.D.].

«50»

Barguzīdeh-e Ghazaliyāt-e Ṣā'ib-o-Bīdel-e Dehlavī
(برگزیدهٔ غزلیّاتِ صائب و بیدل دهلوی)

By Aḥmad Golī, Nāṣir 'Alīzādeh, Hāshimī Sūdmand Publication, 1383 H.S./[2005 A.D.].

«51»

Dīwān-e Bīdel (دیوانِ بیدل)

Dīwān-e Bīdel (غزلیّاتِ حرف الف تا آخر خ), Preface by Moḥammad Sarwar Maulā'ī, 'Ilmī Publication, Tehran, Mordād, 1386 H.S./ [August, 2007 A.D.].

«52»

Dīwān-e Bīdel (دیوانِ بیدل)

Dīwān-e Bīdel (غزلیّاتِ حرف د تا آخر ل), Preface by Moḥammad Sarwar Maulā'ī, 'Ilmī Publication, (Tehran), Mordād, 1386 H.S./ [August, 2007 A.D.].

«53»

Dīwān-e Bīdel (دیوانِ بیدل)

Dīwān-e Bīdel (غزلیّاتِ حرف م تا آخر ی), Preface by Moḥammad Sarwar Maulā'ī, 'Ilmī Publication, (Tehran), Mordād, 1386 H.S./ [August, 2007 A.D.].

«54»

Guzīdah-e Ghazaliyāt-e Bīdel-e Dehlavī (گزیدۂ غزلیّاتِ بیدل دهلوی)

Guzīda-e Ghazaliyāt-e Bīdel-e Dehlavī, Moḥammad Kāẓim Kāẓmī, Shari'atī, Moḥammad Ibrahim, Ābān, 1386 H.S./[November, 2007 A.D.].

«55»

Dīwān-e Bīdel (دیوانِ بیدل)

(In two volumes)

Only *Ghazaliyāt*, edited by Moḥammad Sarwar Maulā'ī, Nashr-e 'Ilmī, Tehran, 1386 H.S./[2007 A.D.].

This is the same as recorded above.

«56»

Guzīda-e Ghazaliyāt-e Bīdel (گزیدۂ غزلیّاتِ بیدل)

By Moḥammad Kāẓim Kāẓmī, 'Irfān Publication, Tehran, 1386 H.S./[2007 A.D.].

«57»

Dīwān-e Maulānā Bīdel-e Dehlavī (دیوانِ مولانا بیدل دهلوی)

Dīwān-e Maulānā Bīdel-e Dehlavī (Two Volumes), edited by Moḥsin Āthārjūi based on the edited text of Khāl Moḥammad Khasteh and Ostād Khalīlollāh-e Khalīlī, Sanā'ī Publication, Tehran, Behman, 1386 H.S./[February, 2008 A.D.].

«58»

Bīdel beh-Intekhāb-e Bīdel (بیدل به‌انتخاب بیدل)

A selection of Bīdel's *Ghazals* and *Robā'īyāt*

Introduction and editing by Sharif Husain Qasemi and Ali Reza Ghazveh, Persian Research Centre, I.R. Iran Culture House, New Delhi, 1388 H.S./2009 A.D. and afterwards published by Sūr-e Mehr, Tehran, 1393 H.S./2014 A.D. Then it was reprinted in 1394 H.S./2015 A.D. from the same publisher.

It was first published by Persian Research Centre, I.R Iran Culture House, New Delhi in 1388 H.S./2009 A.D. It's only Ms. is preserved in Sālārjung Museum, Hyderabad (No. 2056). It has 782 *Ghazals* and 235 *Robā'īs*. Bīdel has added some of his *Ghazals* in his own hand in *Shafī'ā* script on the margins of some of the pages of it. Probably it was transcribed before 1131 A.H/1719 A.D., i.e. two years before his death (1133 A.H./1721 A.D.).

«59»

Dīwān-e Abul Ma'ānī Mīrzā 'Abdul Qādir-e Bīdel-e Dehlavī (دیوانِ ابوالمعانی میرزا عبدالقادر بیدل دهلوی)

The manuscript of the *Dīwān* in Rampur Razā Library, Rampur (No. 3656), fol.848 has been published in facsimile in two volumes from *Inteshārāt-e Shirkat-e Ta'āwonī-e Kār Āfrīnān-e Farhang-o-Honar*, Tehran, Iran, in *Tābistān*, 1388 H.S./2009 A.D. Dr. Ali Reza Ghazveh a reputed poet of Iran, has written an informative preface to it dealing with different important manuscripts of *Dīwān-e Bīdel*.

The manuscript was transcribed in *Naskh* by Moḥammad Wārith Ṣiddīqī in 1131 A.H/1719 A.D. Some *Ghazals* have been added in it by Bīdel in his own hand. Hence it was in possession of Bīdel. This note on the first page is relevant to realize its importance:

تمّت بالخیر، پانزدهم شهر صفر ختم الله بالخیر والظفر سنهٔ ۱۱۳۱ یکهزار و یکصد و سی و یک هجری مبارک بخطِّ اعجزالعباد محمّد وارث ابنِ باقرالصدّیقی باتمام رسید الحمدلله علی ذٰلک.

«60»

Guzīda'ī Az Tak-Baithāy-e Ghazaliyāt-e Bīdel
(گزیده‌ای از تک بیت‌های غزلیّاتِ بیدل)

By Alḥāj Gholām Moḥammad Fā'īz, Kabul, Winter, Year 1390 H.S./ [2011 A.D.].

«61»

Montakhab-e Ījād-e Bīdelī, Guzīda'ī Az She'r Az Khūd-e Bīdel
(منتخب ایجادِ بیدل، گزیده‌ای از شعر از خودِ بیدل)

Introduction and editing by Sharif Husain Qasemi, National Mission for Manuscripts, New Delhi, 1st edition, 1438 A.H./ 2017 A.D.

Manuscript copy of selected verses from 340 *Ghazals* and a *Mukhammas* is preserved in the Khānqāh-e Reḥmānia, Monger, Bihar (India).

It was copied from the author's own handwritten copy as indicated in this colophon:

"نقل از نسخهٔ منقولهٔ دستخطِّ میرزا عبدالقادر بیدل قدس‌سرّه نوشته شد و بی‌استعدادی کاتب معذور باد".

From the following note in the beginning of the Ms., it appears that it was presented to Nawwāb Ḥusain 'Alī Khān Shahīd (one of the famous Syed brothers who was assassinated in 1132 A.H./ [1720 A.D.]) a friend of Bīdel.

نامِ این انتخاب «ایجادِ بیدلی» که طرزی که میرزا جدا از همه شعرا خود مخصوصِ خود دارد، به‌همان‌طور خاصِّ این همهٔ اشعار انتخاب کرده به‌نوّاب حسین علی شهید داده بود.

«62»

Ghazaliyāt-e Bīdel, Taṣḥīḥ-e Inteqādī-e Ghazaliyāt-e Abul Ma'ānī Mīrzā 'Abdul Qādir-e Bīdel
(غزلیّاتِ بیدل، تصحیح انتقادی غزلیّاتِ ابوالمعانی میرزا عبدالقادر بیدل)
Critically edited by Syed Mehdi Tabataba'i and Ali Reza Ghazveh, *Moassaseh-e Farhangī-e Honarī Shehristān-e Adab*, Iran, 1400 H.S/ [2021 A.D.]

«63»

Dīwān-e Bīdel (دیوانِ بیدل)
Under the supervision of Mollā Akmal Khān Ibn-e Mollā Islām Khān Marḥūm, Maṭba'-e Ellīyīn, Tashkent.

«64»

Dīwān-e Bīdel (دیوانِ بیدل)
At the instance of Mollā Aḥmad Khwāja Solemān Khwāja Oghlī, published by Chāpkhāneh-e Gholāmī, Tashkent, scribe: Mollā Ārtūq.

«65»

Dīwān-e Bīdel (دیوانِ بیدل)
At the instance of Mollā Taimūr Khwāja bin Ḥājī Moḥammad Khojandī, Chāpkhāneh-e Gholāmī, Tashkent.
It has both *Ghazaliyāt* and *Robā'īyāt*.

«66»

Dīwān-e Bīdel (دیوانِ بیدل)
At the instance of Mollā Zāfrīn Shokūr Moḥammad of Tashkent, Gholāmī Press, Tashkent, scribe: Mīr 'Alī.
Containing *Ghazals* from p.2 to p.73 and *Robā'īyāt* from p.73 to p.96.

«67»

Dīwān with Qaṣā'īd-e Foyūẓ (دیوان مع قصایدِ فیوض)
Gholāmī Press, Tashkent.
Containing *Ghazals* from p.2 to p.114 and *Robā'īyāt* from p.115 to p.120 and *Qaṣā'īd-e Foyūẓ* printed on margins from p.120 to p.122.

«68»

Dīwān-e Bīdel (دیوانِ بیدل)

Compiled by Ḥusain Āhī, Tehran.

«69»

Dīwān-e Bīdel (دیوانِ بیدل)

Scribe: 'Abdul Mannān Ḥājī bin 'Abdul Wahhāb Marḥūm, Maṭba'-e Bukhara.

«70»

Dīwān-e Bīdel (دیوانِ بیدل)

Compiled by Ḥājī 'Abdur Ra'ūf bin 'Abdun Nabī, Maṭba'-e Pūr-e Ṣūf, Tashkent.

«71»

Dīwān-e Bīdel (دیوانِ بیدل)

Compiled by Ḥājī 'Abdur Ra'ūf bin 'Abdun Nabī, Pūr-e Ṣūf Press, Nainak Bāṣma Khāneh-e Syeda, Tashkent.

Bīdel's stray couplets are also written on the margins.

«72»

Dīwān-e Bīdel Ma'-e Robā'īyāt-e 'Umar Khayyam fī Al-Ḥāshia (دیوانِ بیدل مع رباعیاتِ عمر خیام فی الحاشیه)

Compiled by Qāẓī Wilāyat-e Tashkent, Mollā Gholām Rasūl Khwāja bin Moḥammad Rasūl Khwāja, printed in Tashkent.

Contains *Ghazaliyāt-e Bīdel* from p.2 to p.137 and *Robā'īyāt* from p.137 to p.147; the biography of 'Umar Khayyām on the margins pp.2-8 and *Robā'īyāt*-e 'Umar Khayyām on pp.137-9 have been printed.

«73»

Dīwān-e Bīdel (دیوانِ بیدل)

Compiled by Ḥājī 'Abdur Ra'ūf bin 'Abdul Ghanī, Maṭba'-e Gholāmī, Tashkent.

«74»

Dīwān-e Bīdel (دیوانِ بیدل)

Published by Shirkat-e Khairīya-e Jadīda, Tashkent.

Roqqa'āt (رقّعات)

«1»

Roqqa'āt **(رقّعات)**
Nawal Kishore Press, Lucknow, 1261 A.H./[1845 A.D.].
It has 139 pages.

«2»

Roqqa'āt **(رقّعات)**
Maṭba'-e Aḥmadī, Shahdara, District Meerut, at the instance of Ḥāfiż Moḥammad Ḥusain under the supervision of Amujān, scribe: 'Abdur Razzāq, 1271 A.H./[1855 A.D.].

«3»

Roqqa'āt-e Bīdel **(رقّعاتِ بیدل)**
Nawal Kishore, Lucknow, 2nd edition Shawwāl, 1297 A.H./ September, 1880 A.D.

«4»

Roqqa'āt **(رقّعات)**
Maṭba'-e Ṣafdarī, Bombay, scribe: Nithār 'Alī b. Ḥāfiż Neyāz Aḥmad of Bareilly, 1299 A.H./[1882 A.D.].

«5»

Roqqa'āt-e Bīdel **(رقّعاتِ بیدل)**
Nawal Kishore, Lucknow, Jumāda'II, 1302 A.H/April, 1885 A.D.

«6»

Āwāzhāy-e Bīdel **(آوازهای بیدل)**
(*Nathr-e Adabī*: *Roqqa'āt*, *Nekāt*, *Ishārāt*, *Chahār 'Onṣor*), edited by Akbar Behdārwand, Nigāh Publication, Tehran, Iran, 1386 H.S./ [2007 A.D.].

«7»

Two Letters of Bīdel in Words without Dots **(دو رقّعهٔ بیدل)**
Majma'-ul Afkār, pp.618-9.
A letter condoling the death of Mīrollāh, p.1323. Both these letters are selected from Bīdel's *Roqqa'āt*, *Majma'-ul Afkār*, edited by Prof. Chander Shekhar, National Mission for Manuscripts, New Delhi, [1438 A.H.]/2016 A.D.

Robā'īyāt (رباعیّات)

«1»

Guzīda-e Robā'īyāt-e Bīdel (گزیدۀ رباعیّاتِ بیدل)

By Dr. 'Abdul Ghafūr Ārzū, Tarāna Publication, Mashhad, 1375 H.S./ [1996 A.D.].

«2»

Gol-e Chār Barg (Guzīda-e Robā'īyāt-e Bīdel) (گل چار برگ: گزیدۀ رباعیّاتِ بیدل)

A Selection of Bīdel's *Robā'īyāt*, compiled by Mehdī Almāsī, Madrasa, 1381 H.S./[2002 A.D.].

«3»

Robā'īyāt (رباعیّات)

By Akbar Behdārwand, Nigāh Publication, Tehran, Urdībahisht, 1385 H.S./[May, 2007 A.D.].

«4»

Robā'īyāt-e Bīdel-e Dehlavī (رباعیّاتِ بیدل دهلوی)

Edited by Mehdī Nizhād, Sarūsh-e Milal, Tehran, Tīr, 1386 H.S./ [August, 2007 A.D.].

«5»

Robā'īyāt-e Bīdel-e Dehlavī (رباعیّاتِ بیدل دهلوی)

Edited by Perviz 'Abbāsī Dākānī, Ilhām Publication, Tehran, Ābān, 1386 H.S./[November, 2007 A.D.].

Nekāt (نکات)

«1»

Nekāt (نکات)

Maṭba'-e Aḥmadī, Shahdara, District Meerut, at the instance of Ḥāfiż Moḥammad Ḥusain Dehlavī, under the supervision of Amujān, correction by Mīrzā Āghājān, scribe: Raḥmat 'Alī, 1271 A.H./[1855 A.D.].

«2»

Nekāt **(نکات)**

Its English translation by Johnson Pasha was published from Dublin in [1326 A.H.]/1908 A.D. along with the English translation of *Golshan-e Rāz* and *Robā'īyāt-e Khayyām*.

«3»

Nekāt **(نکات)**

Maṭba'-e Nawal Kishore, Kanpur, [Shawwāl, 1332 A.H.]/ September, 1914 A.D., on the margins of *Bīdel's Dīwān*, 6th edition.

«4»

Nekāt-e Bīdel **(نکاتِ بیدل)**

Translated into Urdū by Prof. 'Aṭā-ur Reḥmān Aṭā Kākvī, Khodā Bakhsh Oriental Public Library, Patna, [1419 A.H.]/1998 A.D.

Chahār 'Onṣor (چهار عنصر)

«1»

Chahār 'Onṣor **(چهار عنصر)**

Maṭba'-e Aḥmadī, Shahdara, District Meerut, at the instance of Ḥāfiż Moḥammad Ḥusain Dehlavī, scribe: Moḥammad Maqṣūd, 10th Ẕilḥijja, 1277 A.H./[19th June, 1861 A.D.].

«2»

Chahār 'Onṣor **(چهار عنصر)**

Printed by Nawal Kishore Press, Lucknow (India).

Mathnavī Moḥīṭ-e A'żam (مثنوی محیطِ اعظم)

«1»

Moḥīṭ-e A'żam **(محیطِ اعظم)**

Maṭba'-e Ṣafdarī, Bombay, scribe: Ḥabībollāh Shīrāzī, 1299 A.H./ [1882 A.D.].

«2»

Moḥīṭ-e A'ẓam **(محیطِ اعظم)**

Mīrzā 'Abdul Qādir Bīdel-e Dehlavī, edited by Teḥsīn Yūsuf 'Alī Mīr Shakkāk, Barg Publication, Tehran, 1370 H.S./[1991 A.D.].

'Irfān (عرفان)

«1»

'Irfān **(عرفان)**

Maṭba'-e Ṣafdarī, Bombay, 1299 A.H./[1882 A.D.].

Sharḥ-e Ṭūr-e Ma'refat (شرحِ طورِ معرفت)

«1»

Sharḥ-e Ṭūr-e Ma'refat **(شرح طور معرفت)**

It was accomplished by A.M. Athīr and published from Kabul, in 1356 Khorshīdī/[1977 A.D.].

Chapter XVII

Published Works on Bīdel

«1»

Ḥall-e Nekāt-e Bīdel

Aḥmad Ḥusain Shaukat, Shehneh-e Meerut, [1323 A.H.]/1905 A.D. It is an Urdu translation of Bīdel's *Nekāt*.

«2»

Bīdel Cheh Mī-Guft

Faiẓ Moḥammad Zakarīya, Kabul, 1322 Khorshīdī/[1943 A.D.].
It was reprinted from Tehran in 1334 H.S./[1955 A.D.]. It is believed that the same small book of 47 pages heralded the studies on Bīdel in Iran.

«3»

Bīdel

'Ibādollāh Akhtar, *Idāreh-e Thaqāfat-e Islāmīa*, Lahore, [1371 A.H.]/ 1952 A.D.
It was reprinted from Lahore in [1401 A.H.]/1981 A.D.

«4»

Mīrzā 'Abdul Qādir-e Bīdel

Ṣadroddīn 'Ainī (1878-1954 A.D), Istalinabad, [1373 A.H.]/1954 A.D.

«5»

Namūneh-e Adabiyāt-e Tājīk

Ṣadroddīn 'Ainī (1878-1954 A.D), the Tājīk poet and scholar, has dedicated a lengthy chapter on Bīdel in this book. In [1374 A.H.]/ 1955 A.D., he published a selection of Bīdel's poetry with a detailed preface of more than hundred pages. He also wrote a series of articles to introduce Bīdel and his contribution to Persian literature and published them in the journal *Sharq-e Surkh* in [1365 A.H.]/1946 A.D.

«6»

Faiẓ-e Quds

Ostād Khalīlollāh-e Khalīlī, Kabul, [1374 A.H.]/1955 A.D. Afterwards it was reprinted from Ostād Khalīlollāh-e Khalīlī, *Anjuman-e Tārīkh-e Afghanistan*, 1342 Khorshīdī/[1963 A.D.] and International Al-Hodā Publication, Tehran, 1383 H.S./[2004 A.D.].

It was reprinted twice in Iran in 1383 H.S./[2005 A.D.] by Al-Hodā Publication and then again by Inteshārāt-e 'Irfān, Tehran, in 1386 H.S./[2007 A.D.] by 'Iffat Mustashār Nīyā.

This 102-page book deals with the life of Bīdel as described by him in his *Chahār 'Onṣor*. Khalīlī has also discussed the prose style of Bīdel in this work.

«7»

Ḥairat Zār

'Aṭā Kākvī, Patna, 1st edition [1375 A.H.]/1956 A.D. and 2nd edition [1401 A.H.]/1981 A.D.

About more than fifty years ago Niyāz Fateḥpūrī wrote some valuable articles on Bīdel's poetry which along with some similar articles by Syed Solaimān Nadvī, were published together in this book by Prof. 'Aṭā Kākvī of Patna.

«8»

Yād-e Bīdel

Moḥammad Ḥaider Zobal, Ministry of Education, Kabul, 1335 Khorshīdī/[1956 A.D.].

«9»

Bīdel and His Poem 'Irfān

H. 'Ainī, Istalinabad, [1376 A.H.]/1956 A.D.

«10»

The Philosophical Views of Mīrzā Bīdel

I.M. Mūminov, Tashkent, [1377 A.H.]/1957 A.D. (in Russian).

«11»

Life and Works of 'Abdul Qādir-e Bīdel

'Abdul Ghanī, Lahore, [1380 A.H.]/1960 A.D. It is an important work of its kind.

«12»

Sharḥ-e Aḥwāl-o-Afkār-e Bīdel-e 'Aẓīmābādī

Dr. Kāshī Nāth Pandita (an Indian scholar).

It is a PhD thesis submitted in Tehran University, Tehran, in [1382 A.H.]/1962 A.D. It has not been published so far.

«13»

Montakhab-uz Zamān

Khāl Moḥammad Khasteh, in 200 Pages.

A part of it was published in Journal Zhondūn in 1342 H.S./ [1963 A.D.].

«14»

Bīdel

Ṣalāḥoddīn Saljūqī, Kabul, 1343 Khorshīdī/[1964 A.D.].

«15»

Naqd-e Bīdel

Ṣalāḥoddīn Saljūqī, 'Irfān Publication, Kabul, 1343 H.S./[1964 A.D.] and reprinted in 1380 H.S./[2001 A.D.].

It is an important work. The author has attempted to critically evaluate Bīdel's works particularly poetry. It is a pioneer work.

«16»

Bīdel as a Narrator

A. Bausānī, Yādnāmeh-e Jan Rypka, Prague, [1387 A.H.]/1967 A.D.

«17»

Rūḥ-e Bīdel

Dr. 'Abdul Ghanī, Majlis-e Taraqqī-e Adab, Lahore, [1388 A.H.]/ 1968 A. D.

«18»

Bīdel Shanāsī

Gholām Ḥasan Mujaddedī, Pohantun-e Kabul (University of Kabul), Kabul, 1350 Khorshīdī/[1971 A.D.].

It is in two volumes. It contains mostly extracts from the published works on Bīdel like *Faiẓ-e Quds*, *Naqd-e Bīdel* and *Aḥwāl-o-Āthār-e Bīdel* by Dr. 'Abdul Ghanī.

«19»

Aḥwāl-o-Āthār-e Mīrzā 'Abdul Qādir-e Bīdel

'Abdul Ghanī

It was translated into Persian by Mīr Moḥammad Āṣif Anṣārī, Faculty of Literature and Human Sciences, Kabul, 1351 Khorshīdī/[1972 A.D.].

«20»

Bīdel: Shā'ir-e Zamānehā

Dr. Asadollāh Ḥabībī, Kabul, 1393 A.H./[1973 A.D.].

It consists of six articles by the author on various aspects of Bīdel's thought.

«21»

Bīdel and His Work Chahār 'Onṣor

Dr. Asadollāh Ḥabībī, Moscow, [1393 A.H.]/1973 A.D. (in Russian).

«22»

Sharḥ-e Ṭūr-e Ma'refat

'Abdul Ḥamīd Asīr, Kabul, 1356 Khorshīdī/1977 A.D.

«23»

Mīrzā Bīdel (Swāneḥ, Inteqād, Intekhāb)

Dr. Nabī Hādī, Department of Persian, Aligarh Muslim University, Aligarh, 1st edition in [1401 A.H.]/1981 A.D. (Urdu).

«24»

Mīrzā Bīdel

Same as above. Dr. Nabī Hādī, Allahabad, [1401 A.H.]/1981 A.D. (Urdū).

«25»

Faiẓ-e Bīdel

'Abdul Ghanī, Lahore, [1402 A.H.]/1982 A.D.

«26»

Mīrzā 'Abdul Qādir-e Bīdel

Articles on Mīrzā 'Abdul Qādir Bīdel presented in a seminar on Bīdel in Patna, edited by Syed Aṭhar Shīr and published by the Institute of Post-Graduate Studies and Research in Arabic and Persian, Patna, 1402 A.H./1982 A.D. (Urdū). The articles are as follows:

۱) میرزا عبدالقادر بیدل کا مولد و نسب: پروفیسر سیّد حسن، پٹنا یونیورسٹی، پٹنا.

۲) رقّعاتِ بیدل کا ادبی و لسانی مطالعه: دکتر نذیر احمد، علیگره مسلم یونیورسٹی، علیگره.

۳) بیدل اور سبکِ هندی: دکتر سیّد امیر حسن عابدی، دهلی یونیورسٹی، دهلی.

۴) چهار عنصر: دکتر نورالحسن انصاری، دهلی یونیورسٹی، دهلی.

۵) مثنوی طورِ معرفت، ایک جائزه: دکتر کلیم سهسرامی، راجشاهی یونیورسٹی، بنگلادش.

۶) میرزا عبدالقادر بیدل کی کهانی تونک کے مخطوطات کی زبانی: شوکت علی خان، تونک، راجستهان.

۷) بیدل اور تصوّف: دکتر محمد صدّیق، پٹنا یونیورسٹی، پٹنا.

۸) بیدل کی سهل‌نگاری: دکتر آصفه زمانی، لکهنو یونیورسٹی، لکهنو.

۹) اقبال اور بیدل: دکتر محمّد سمیع‌الحق.

۱۰) بیدل کی آثارِ منثور اور اُن کا ادبی جائزه: دکتر محمّد رضوان‌الحق.

۱۱) بیدل عظیم‌آبادی اور راجستهان: سیّد منظورالحسن برکاتی، تونک، راجستهان.

۱۲) بیدل: ایک مطالعه: دکتر سیّد علی حیدر نیّر، پٹنا.

۱۳) وحدتِ وجود و شهود در کلامِ بیدل: دکتر طلحه رضوی برق، پٹنا.

۱۴) سخنورانِ همزمانِ میرزا عبدالقادر بیدل: دکتر غلام مجتبی انصاری، پٹنا.

15) Bīdel's Achievement and Influence: Dr. 'Abdul Mughnī.
16) What Bīdel gave to Persian Literature: Prof. Aṭā Karīm Burke.

«27»

Beḥthī Dar Aḥwāl-o-Āthār-e Bīdel

Ḥasan Shāh, Faculty of Language and Literature, University of Kabul, Kabul, 1363 Khorshīdī/[1984 A.D.].

It is a Persian translation of a part on Bīdel from the thesis of Dr. Nūrul Ḥasan Anṣārī. Prof. Anṣārī's thesis for PhD is entitled "Indo-Persian Literature under Aurangzīb" submitted in the University of Delhi, Delhi. This thesis was translated into Urdū by Prof. Anṣārī himself and published in 1969 A.D. From the same published thesis, the portion on Bīdel has been translated into Persian.

«28»

Bīdel-o-'Ilm-e Kalām

Dr. 'Ināyatollāh Iblāgh, *Moassaseh of 'Ilmī-e Dār-ul Ma'refeh-e Iblāgh*, Peshawar, Pakistan, [1405 A.H.]/1985 A.D.

«29»

Sī Maqāleh Darbāreh-e Bīdel

Compiled by Moḥammad Sarwar Pākfar, Millīyah-e Brāder, Kabul, Mīzān, 1365 H.S./[1986 A.D.].

Thirty articles by different scholars on Bīdel.

«30»

Shā'ir-e Āyīnehā

Moḥammad Reẓā Shafī'ī Kadkanī, Āgāh Publication, Tehran, 1366 H.S./[1987 A.D.].

Because of its relevance and importance, it has repeatedly been published from Iran. Its sixth edition came out in 1384 H.S./[2005 A.D.] from Āgāh Publication, Tehran. It is actually a collection of essays by Prof. Kadkanī followed by a short anthology. The book ends with a glossary of keywords in Bīdel's poetry; each entry is followed by concise but comprehensive explanations. In addition to *Āyīneh* (آیینه) the entries in the glossary also include جوهر آیینه, آیینهٔ زانو, آیینه خانه, خانهٔ آیینه, آب آیینه.

«31»

Bīdel in the Light of Bergson

'Allāma Iqbāl

Edited and Annotated by Dr. Teḥsīn Firāqī, Universal Books, Lahore, Pakistan, [Rabī'I, 1409 A.H.]/November, 1988 A.D.

Text in handwriting of Iqbāl and its Dr. Firāqī's fair transcription and Urdū translation of Iqbāl's handwritten text. It was translated into Persian by 'Alī Bayāt along with its original in 'Allāma's handwriting and published from Print Expert, Lahore, [1421 A.H.]/ 2000 A.D.

«32»

Bīdel-o-Chahār 'Onṣor

Dr. Asadollāh Ḥabībī, Pashtun, University of Kabul, Kabul, 1367 Khorshīdī/[1988 A.D.].

«33»

Bīdel, Sipehrī wa Sabk-e Hindī

Ḥasan Ḥusainī, Sarūsh Publication, Tehran, 1367 H.S./[1988 A.D.].

«34»

Bīdel, Sipehrī wa Sabk-e Hindī

Ḥasan Ḥusainī, Sarūsh Publication, Tehran, 2nd edition 1368 H.S./ [1989 A.D.].

«35»

Bīdel, Sipehrī and Sabk-e Hindī

Ḥasan Ḥusainī, Firdausī Publication, Tehran, 3rd edition 1368 H.S./ [1989 A.D.].

«36»

Az Chīdmān-e Rang

Moḥammad Kāẓim Kāẓmī, Mashhad, 1371 H.S./[1992 A.D.].

«37»

Bīdel Shanāsī: Āthārī Dar Shanākht-e She'r-o-Andīsha-e 'Abdul Qādir-e Bīdel-e Dehlavī

Moḥammad 'Ārif Pazhmān, University of Hormozgan, Bandar-e Abbas, 1376 H.S./[1997 A.D.].

«38»

'Abdul Qādir Bīdel-e Dehlavī

A book originally in Urdū by Prof. Nabī Hādī entitled "Mīrzā Bīdel" was subsequently translated into Persian by Dr. Taufīq Hāshimpūr Sobḥānī, a professor of Iran. It was printed by Nashr Publication, Tehran, 1376 H.S./[1997 A.D.].

This book has *Zindagīnāma, Naqd-o-Barrasī-o-Guzīda-e Āthār-e Bīdel.*

«39»

Būtīqāy-e Bīdel

Ārzū, 'Abdul Ghafūr, Tarāna Publication, Mashhad, Iran, 1378 H.S./ [1999 A.D.]

«40»

Bīdel Shanāsī: (Collection of articles on Bīdel)

Pazhmān, Moḥammad 'Ārif, Hormozgan University, [1421 A.H.]/ 2000 A.D.

A collection of 11 articles on Bīdel by Afghān, Iranian, Indian, Tājīk and Uzbek scholars.

«41»

Bīdel in the Light of Bergson

'Allāma Iqbāl Lāhorī

'Allāma Iqbāl attempted to compare some of Bīdel's thoughts with those of Bergson, famous French philosopher, in this article. He has indicated that Bīdel is more successful in describing and solving some of the philosophical matters than Bergson. This article in English has been translated into Urdū by Dr. Teḥsīn Firāqī, published in Lahore, Pakistan (as above).

It was translated into Persian by 'Alī Bayāt under the title: «مطالعهٔ بیدل در پرتو اندیشه‌های برگسون» and published by Iqbāl Academy, Pakistan, Lahore, [1421 A.H.]/2000 A.D.

«42»

Āyīn-e Zāhid Dar Āyīneh-e Dīwān-e Bīdel

Dr. Syed Nūrul Ḥaque Kāvish, Germany, [1423 A.H.]/2002 A.D.

«43»

Khūshehā'ī Az Jahān-Bīnī-e Bīdel

Ārzū, 'Abdul Ghafūr, Tarāna Publication, Mashhad, Iran, 1381 H.S./ [2002 A.D.].

«44»

Tajallī-e Qur'ān-o-Ma'ārif-e Islāmī Dar Ash'ār-e Bīdel-e Dehlavī

Māshā'Allah Jashnī Ārānī, Hastī-Numā Publication, 1383 H.S./ [2004 A.D.].

«45»

Wāzhehnāmeh-e She'r-e Bīdel

Dr. Asadollāh Ḥabībī, Hamburg, [1426 A.H.]/2005 A.D.

«46»

Mīrzā 'Abdul Qādir-e Bīdel

Ṣadroddīn 'Ainī (d. 1333 H.S./1954 A.D.), translated from Russian into Persian by Shehbāz Īraj, Sūra-e Mehr Publication, Urdībahisht, 1384 H.S./[May, 2005 A.D.].

It is actually a reproduction of Ṣadroddīn 'Ainī's work in Serelic script in Persian script. 'Ainī is a known and reputed poet and scholar from Tajikistan.

«47»

Asīr-e Bīdel, Montakhab-e Āthār-e Moḥammad 'Abdul Ḥamīd "Qandī Āghā"

Moḥammad Kāẓim Kāẓmī, Sharī'atī, Moḥammad Ibrāhīm Publication, Mehr, 1385 H.S./[October, 2006 A.D.].

«48»

Bīdel-e Dehlavī

Ḥaider Karīmpūr, Tīrgān Publication, Āẕar, 1385 H.S./[December, 2006 A.D.].

«49»

Asīr-e Bīdel (Montakhab-e Āthār-e Moḥammad 'Abdul Ḥamīd Asīr ("Qandī Āghā")

Compiled by Moḥammad Kabīr Rāziqī, 'Abdul Wahhāb Fā'īz, edited by Moḥammad Kāżim Kāżmī, published by Ministry of Islamic Culture & Guidance Publication, Tehran, 1385 H.S./ [2006 A.D.].

It has three main chapters:

1) *Kelīd-e 'Irfān*: Commentary on some difficult couplets of Bīdel.
2) *Panj Banāy-e Taṣawwuf*: Commentary on some *Robā'īs* of Bīdel.
3) *Guzīdah-e She'rhā*: Divided into *Paiwand-e Dil*, *Shākh-e Nabāt*, *Manāqib* and other poems. Under *Paiwand-e Dil*. Qandī Āghā has included his *Mukhammasāt* (five) on some *Ghazals* of Bīdel. There are also Qandī Āghā's own poems composed in imitation of Bīdel.

«50»

Faiẓ-e Quds: Aḥwāl-o-Āthār-e Mīrzā 'Abdul Qādir-e Bīdel

Ostād Khalīlollāh-e Khalīlī, Introduction by 'Iffat Mustashār Nīyā, edited by Moḥammad Kāżim Kāżmī, Sharī'atī, Moḥammad Ibrāhīm Publication, Shehrīvar, 1386 H.S./[September, 2007 A.D.].

«51»

Faiẓ-e Dil Az Mashrab-e Bīdel (Sharḥ-e Nukhustīn Ghazal-e Dīwān-e Mīrzā 'Abdul Qādir-e Bīdel)

Commentator: Ostād Maulānā Gholām Moḥammad Khadīm Sarpolī, Kitābkhāna-e Amīr 'Alī Shīrnawā'ī, Bayānī Social and Cultural Foundation, Sarpol, Hamal, 1387 H.S./[2008 A.D.].

«52»

Kelīd-e Dar-e Bāz

Moḥammad Kāẓim Kāẓmī, Sūra-e Mehr Publication, 1387 H.S./ [2008 A.D.].

Some of the contents of this work published very earlier in *Faṣlnāmeh-e She'r*, from Nos. 37 to 52, Tābistān 1383 to Tābistān 1386 H.S./[Summer, 2007 A.D.].

«53»

Dar Khāneh-e Āftāb, Saīrī Dar Aḥwāl-o-Āthār-e Bīdel

Dr. 'Abdul Ghafūr Ārzū, Kabul, 1387 H.S./[2008 A.D.].

«54»

Tarkībāt-e Khāṣṣ-e Bīdel Dar Chahār 'Onṣor

Mahjabīn 'Umar, Persian Research Centre, I.R. Iran Culture House, New Delhi, Behman, 1387 H.S./[February, 2009 A.D.].

«55»

Mīrzā 'Abdul Qādir Bīdel: Ḥayāt aur Kārnāme

Dr. Syed Aḥsan-al Żafar, Rampur Razā Library, Rampur, [1430 A.H.]/ 2009 A.D. (In two Volumes).

«56»

Iṣṭelāḥāt-e Nuskheh-Pardāzī Dar Dīwān-e Bīdel-e Dehlavī

Ḥamīd Reẓā Ghalīchkhānī, Persian Research Centre, I.R. Iran Culture House, New Delhi, 1390 H.S./2011 A.D.

«57»

Bīdel-o-Ghālib

Dr. Syed Aḥsan-al Żafar, Ghālib Institute, New Delhi, [1433 A.H.]/ 2012 A.D.

«58»

Saīrī Dar Nekāt-e Bīdel

Editor and Commentator: Moḥammad 'Abdul 'Azīz Mahjūr, *Anjuman-e Dūstādārān-e Bīdel*, Kabul, Hamal, 1392 Khorshīdī/ [2013 A.D.].

«59»

Jahān-e Bīdel

Moḥammad Ḥusainī Fiṭrat, ʻIrfān Publication, Tehran, 1393 H.S./ [2014 A.D.].

«60»

Wāzheh-e Dil Dar Kalām-e Bīdel Az Leḥāẓ-e Maʻnā-o-Mafhūm

A thesis submitted [1436 A.H.]/2015 A.D. in five Chapters by Syed Naʻīm ʻĀlamī for obtaining PhD in Persian from Jāmia Millia Islāmīa, New Delhi.

«61»

Mīrzā ʻAbdul Qādir-e Bīdel

(Mīrzā ʻAbdul Qādir-e Bīdel: Delineator of 17th-18th century Indo-Central Asia, Afghanistan and Iran Cultural and Historical Relations).

Collection of Articles presented at an *International Seminar on Bīdel* held from 17th to 21st March, 2003, in Jāmia Millia Islāmīa, New Delhi. This collection was published in [1438 A.H.]/2017 A.D. It comprises the following articles in English, Persian and Urdū.

Articles in English:

1. Short Introduction of Mīrzā ʻAbdul Qādir Bīdel; Prof. Qamar Ghaffār, Jāmia Millia Islāmīa, New Delhi.
2. Mīrzā ʻAbdul Qādir-e Bīdel: An Introduction; Prof. Wārith Kirmānī, Aligarh Muslim University, Aligarh.
3. Mīrzā ʻAbdul Qādir and His Contemporaries; Prof. Nabī Hādī, Aligarh Muslim University, Aligarh.
4. Mīrzā Bīdel and His Popularity; Prof. Walīul Ḥaque Anṣārī, Lucknow University, Lucknow.
5. Bīdel and Socio-Cultural Environment of His Age; Prof. S.M. ʻAzīzoddīn Ḥusain, Jāmia Millia Islāmīa, New Delhi.
6. A Computer-Assisted Analysis of Bīdel's Ṭūr-e Maʻrefat; Dr. Riccardo Zipole, University of Venice, Italy.

7. A New Approach to Analyze the Use of the Word (Āyīneh) mirror in Bīdel's *Ghazals*; Dr. Daniela Meneghini, Associate Professor, Persian Language and Literature, University of Venice, Italy.
8. Bīdel in Central Asia; Dr. Ninel Gafurova, Institute of Oriental Studies of the Academy of Science of Russia.
9. Bīdel and Bihar; Prof. Moḥammad Sharaf-e 'Alam, Patna.
10. Mīrzā 'Abdul Qādir Bīdel, Life and Works; Dr. Mażhar 'Alam Ṣiddīqī.
11. Mīrzā Bīdel's 'Irfān and Yogavasishtha; Dr. Wagesh Shukla.
12. Historical and Cultural Relations between India and Central Asia during 17th and 18th centuries with special reference to Bīdel; Dr. Ṣadr 'Alam.

Articles in Persian:

۱) تجلّی دوست در آیینهٔ کلامِ بیدل، صاحبدلی چو بیدل در جستجوی دلدار؛ دکتر حکیمه دبیران، ایران.

۲) بیدل در ایران؛ اسماعیل متعصب دیانی، ایران.

۳) بررسی ایماژهای خیالی و نقش عنصر در شعرِ بیدل؛ دکتر حسین فقیهی، استاد اعزامی ایران در دانشگاه دهلی، دهلی.

۴) تصویر بیدل؛ عبدالغفور هروی، افغانستان.

۵) بیدلی و دل‌شناسی بیدل: محمّد حنیف حنیف بلخی، افغانستان.

۶) نشهٔ بی‌خمار آزادگی در شعرِ بیدل؛ دکتر عباس علی وفایی، دانشگاه علّامه طباطبایی، ایران.

۷) تولّدِ مجدّد؛ عبدالغفور آرزو، افغانستان.

۸) سخنِ عشق یا حکایت بیدلی بیدل در غزلیاتش؛ خانم دکتر مهوش واحددوست، دانشگاه ارومیه، ایران.

۹) غزلی تاریخی از بیدل؛ پروفسور شریف حسین قاسمی، دانشگاه دهلی، دهلی.

۱۰) سبکِ هندی یا قند پارسی در آیینه؛ پروفسور خالق رشید، دانشگاه جواهرلعل نهرو، دهلی‌نو.
۱۱) بیدل و عرفان (به‌اشارۀ مخصوص به‌وحدة‌الوجود)؛ دکتر احسن‌الظّفر، دانشگاه لکهنو، لکهنو.
۱۲) تحلیل زیبانگری بیدل دهلوی؛ دکتر مهین پناهی، دانشگاه الزهرا، ایران.
۱۳) نگاهی به‌چهار عنصر بیدل؛ پروفسور سیّد انوار احمد، پتنا.
۱۴) دل بیدل؛ دکتر شمیم‌الحق صدّیقی، دانشکدۀ ذاکر حسین، دهلی.
۱۵) صدای پای خیال در غزلیات بیدل؛ خانم نرگس جابری‌نسب، ایران.
۱۶) ذهن و زبان بیدل؛ دکتر ابوالقاسم رادفر، ایران.
۱۷) عرفان بیدل؛ خانم فاطمه مقدم‌پور، ایران.
۱۸) تاثیر عرفای مسیحی و مسلمان بر عرفان و ادبِ بیدل دهلوی؛ دکتر فاطمه سمواتی، تهران، ایران.
۱۹) بیدل و اقبال؛ اخلاق احمد آهن، دانشگاه جواهرلعل نهرو، دهلی‌نو.
۲۰) میرزا عبدالقادر بیدل؛ دکتر غلام حیدر.
۲۱) بیدل عظیم‌آبادی (دهلوی): احوال و آثار؛ فخر عالم، دانشگاه دهلی، دهلی.

Articles in Urdū:

۱) بیدل‌شناسی؛ پروفیسر امیر حسن عابدی، دهلی یونیورستی، دهلی.
۲) بیدل اور زهدِ ریایی؛ پروفیسر محمّد ولی‌الحق انصاری، لکهنو یونیورستی، لکهنو.
۳) کچھ کلام بیدل کے متعلّق؛ پروفیسر محمّد ولی‌الحق انصاری، لکهنو یونیورستی، لکهنو.
۴) میرزا غالب اور بیدل؛ پروفیسر نثار احمد فاروقی، دهلی یونیورستی، دهلی.
۵) بیدل‌شناسی اقبال؛ پروفیسر عبدالحق، دهلی یونیورستی، دهلی.
۶) فقیدالعصر سی‌پارۀ دل بیدل (مثنوی ساده و پرکار)، صاحبزاده شوکت علی خان، تونک، راجستهان.

۷) بیدل: حیات اور تخلیقی شعور؛ پروفیسر احسان کریم برق، کلکتہ یونیورستی، کلکتہ.

۸) ابوالمعانی میرزا عبدالقادر بیدل اور اُن کے صوفیانہ افکار؛ پروفیسر محمّد سمیع الحق، رانچی یونیورستی، جھارکند.

۹) بیدل کے پنجابی معاصرین؛ دکتر طارق کفایت‌الله، پنجابی یونیورستی، پتیالہ.

۱۰) میرزا بیدل کی وطنیت، اسناد کی روشنی میں؛ دکتر عبدالحلیم اخگر، جامعۂ ملّیہ اسلامیہ، نئی دھلی.

۱۱) بیدل اور مغل سلاطین؛ دکتر احمد حسن، جامعہ ملیہ اسلامیہ، نئی دھلی.

«62»

Āyīneh-Gran, Shāgirdān-e Abul Ma'ānī 'Abdul Qādir-e Bīdel

Syed Faiẓ-ul Raḥmān Qureshī, Bunyād-e Afghanistan-o-Hind, Sifārat-e Jamhūrī-e Islāmī-e Afghanistan, Dehli-Nau (Embassy of the Islamic Republic of Afghanistan, New Delhi), [Isfand, 1397 H.S.]/February 2019 A.D.

57 disciples of Bīdel and their contribution to Persian has been described in this work.

«63»

Bīdel Shanāsī

Prof. Gholām Ḥasan Mujaddedī (Two Volumes), University of Kabul, Kabul, Afghanistan.

It contains mostly extracts from the published works on Bīdel like Faiẓ-e Quds, Naqd-e Bīdel and *Aḥwāl-o-Āthār-e Bīdel* by Dr. 'Abdul Ghanī.

«64»

Sharḥ-e Aḥwāl-o-Afkār-o-Āthār-e Abul Ma'ānī Mīrzā 'Abdul Qādir-e Bīdel

This is a thesis for PhD submitted in the Faculty of Arts and Humanities, University of Kabul, Kabul. It has been accomplished by Qayāmoddīn and Gholām Ḥasan Mujaddedī, see *Fehrist-e Āthār-e 'Ilmī-e Ostādān and Monograph-e Moḥaṣṣilān-e Pohantun*, p.45.

«65»

Muqāysa-e Insān-e Kāmil Az Dīdgāh-e Bīdel-o-Ḥāfiẓ

Dr. 'Abdul Ghafūr Ārzū, Sūra-e Mehr Publication, Iran.

«66»

Life and Works of Bīdel

Dr. 'Abdollāh, Pakistan.

«67»

Bīdel and Sabk-e Hindī

Ḥasan Ḥabībī, Tehran.

Chapter XVIII

Published Articles on Bīdel

«1»

Mīrzā ʻAbdul Qādir-e Bīdel

ʻAbdollāh Qārī, *Majallāh-e Kābul*, Volume I, No. 4, 1310 A.H./ [1892 A.D.].

«2»

ʻAbdul Qādir-e Bīdel

Niyāz Fateḥpūrī, *Nigār*, Lucknow.

Articles of Niyāz Fateḥpūrī on Bīdel published in his journal *Nigār*, Lucknow, in 12 numbers from [1344 to 1380 A.H.]/1925 to 1960 A.D.

«3»

Tazkireh-e Bīdel

Yāsīn Khān Niyāzī, *Oriental College Magazine*, Lahore, [Rabīʻ II-Rajab-Shawwāl 1351 A.H.]/August-November 1932-February 1933 A.D.

«4»

Mīrzā ʻAbdul Qādir-e Bīdel and Ajūdīyat-e Ao

Sharq-e Surkh, [1365 A.H.]/1946 A.D.

«5»

Kiyā Bīdel ʻAẓīmābādī Na They

Syed Solaimān Nadvī, Maʻārif, [Shawwāl, 1366 A.H.]/August, 1947 A.D.

«6»

ʻOrs-e Bīdel

Moḥammad Ibrāhīm Khalīl, *Majallāh-e Āryānā*, No. 14, IX Period, 1330 H.S./[1951 A.D.].

«7»

Pardesī Ke Khuṭūṭ Bīdel Ke Silsile Mein

Majnūn Gorakhpūrī, *Sawerā*, [1336 H.S.]/1957 A.D.

It is a long article in 28 pages.

«8»

Article on Bīdel: Encyclopedia of Islām

New Edition, Leiden and London, [1339 H.S.]/1960 A.D.

«9»

Bīdel Shanāsī Dar Shoravī

Sī Maqāleh, Kabul, 1345 Shamsī/[1966 A.D.].

«10»

Mīrzā Ghālib WA Maktab-e Bīdel

Sī Maqāleh, Kabul, 1345 Shamsī/[1966 A.D.].

«11»

Mīrzā 'Abdul Qādir-e Bīdel-o-Afghanistan

Syed Dāwūd Ḥusainī, *Majallāh-e Adab*, Nos. 5 & 6, 1347 H.S./[1968 A.D.].

«12»

Bīdel Az Afghanistan Ast

Badakhshī, Moḥammad Ṭāhir, *Adab*, Nos. 5 & 6, 1347 H.S./[1968 A.D.].

«13»

Ghālib and Bīdel's Style

A. Sandre Bausānī, International Ghālib Seminar, edited by Yousof Ḥusain Khān, New Delhi, [1390 A.H.]/1970 A.D.

«14»

Bīdel Shanāsī Dar Itteḥād-e Jamāhīr-e Shoravī

Dr. Asadollāh Ḥabībī, *Majallāh-e Adab*, Kabul, Nos. 5 & 6, 1352 H.S./[1973 A.D.].

«15»

Bīdel Shā'ir-e Fiṭrat-o-Ḥairat

Moḥammad 'Ārif Pazhmān, *Nashrīa-e Gauhar*, No. 9, Year V, Serial 56, Āẓar Māh, 1356 H.S./[December, 1977 A.D.].

«16»

Mīrzā 'Abdul Qādir Kā Maulad-o-Maskan

Prof. Syed Ḥasan, *Majallāh-e Nayā Daur*, Lucknow, [Rabī'I, 1400 AH.]/January, 1980 A.D.

«17»

Barkhī Az Wīzhgīhāy Dastūrī-e She'r-e Bīdel

Ḥasan Yāmīn, *Majallāh-e Khurāsān*, Year V, Nos. 4 & 5, 1364 H.S./ [1985 A.D.].

«18»

Wāzhegān, Ta'bīrāt-o-Moṣteleḥāt-e 'Āmmah Dar She'r-e Bīdel

Pazhmān, Moḥammad 'Ārif, *Khurāsān*, Nos. 24 & 25, 1364 H.S./ [1985 A.D.].

«19»

Iqbāl-e Lāhorī WA Dīgar Sho'arā-e Pārsī-Gūy

Moḥammad Riyāẓ, *Majallāh-e Kābul*, 1365 H.S./[1986 A.D.].

«20»

Bīdel Shanāsī

Moḥammad Riyāẓ, *Dānish*, No. 12, 1366 H.S./1987 A.D.

«21»

Bīdel

Mo'aẓẓam Ṣiddīqī, Encyclopedia Īrānīca, Vol. IV, Fascicle 3, Rutledge and Kegan Paul, London and New York, [1368 H.S.]/ 1989 A.D.

«22»

Aḥwāl-o-Āthār-e Mīrzā 'Abdul Qādir-e Bīdel

Farḥat Nāz, *Majmū'a-e Sokhanrānīhāy-e Nukhustīn Semīnār-e Paiwastgīhāy-e Farhangī-e Iran-o-Shibeh Qārreh* (Collection of articles presented at the First Seminar on Cultural Relations between Iran and the Sub-continent), Volume II, Persian Research Centre of Iran & Pakistan, Islamabad, 1372 H.S./[1993 A.D.].

«23»

Sabk-e She'r-e Bīdel-o-Ghālib-e Dehlavī

A. Sandre Bausānī, translated into Persian by Ẕīā'oddīn Torābī, *Kaihān-e Farhangī*, 1372 H.S./[1993 A.D.].

«24»

Dīwān-e Bīdel Kā Aik Ahm Qalmī Nuskha

Prof. Syed Amīr Ḥasan 'Ābidī, *Ghālibnāma*, Ghālib Institute, New Delhi, [Ramaẓān, 1418 A.H.]/January, 1998 A.D.

«25»

Bīdel Apnī Nathr Ke Āyīneh Mein

Prof. Syed Amīr Ḥasan 'Ābidī, *Ghālibnāma*, Ghālib Institute, New Delhi, [Ramaẓān, 1418 A.H.]/January, 1998 A.D.

«26»

Article on Bīdel: Encyclopedia of Persian Literature in the Sub-Continent (India, Bangladesh & Pakistan)

Ḥassan Anūsheh, Inteshārāt-e Wizārat-e Farhang-o-Irshād-e Islāmī, Tehran, Iran, 1378 H.S./[1999 A.D.].

«27»

Bīdel: Shakhṣiyat aur Māḥaul

Prof. Kabīr Aḥmad Jā'isī, *Khodā Bakhsh Library Journal*, Patna, [Ṣafar-Rabī'II, 1422 A.H.]/April-June, 2001 A.D.

«28»

Saīr-e Dil Az Nażar-e Bīdel

Dr. Syed Aḥsan-al Żafar, *Dānish*, *Quarterly Journal of Persian Research Centre of Iran and Pakistan,* Islamabad, Nos. 64-65, 1380 H.S./[2001 A.D.]

«29»

Mīrzā Ghālib Aur Bīdel

Nithār Aḥmad Fārūqī, *Sabras*, Hyderabad, Deccan, [1424 A.H.]/ 2003 A.D.

«30»

Ghālib kī She'riyāt Aur Bīdel

Wārith Kirmānī, *Adab-Sāz*, New Delhi, [Rabī'I 1428 A.H.]/April, 2007 A.D.

«31»

Qand-e Pārsī: Special Issue on Mīrzā Abdul Qādir-e Bedil Dehlavī

The Quarterly Journal of Persian Culture, Language and Literature, Persian Research Centre, Office of the Cultural Counsellor, I.R. Iran, New Delhi, Nos. 39-40, Zamistān 1386-Bahār 1387 H.S./Winter 2007-Spring 2008.

It includes the following articles on Bīdel:

۱) بیدل آزاد می‌اندیشد؛ دکتر سیّد مهدی نبی‌زاده (ایران).
۲) سیری در رقّعات بیدل؛ پروفسور نذیر احمد (هند).
۳) دریچهٔ آشنایی با بیدل؛ دکتر محمّد رضا شفیعی کدکنی (ایران).
٤) بیدل و سبک هندی؛ پروفسور سیّد امیر حسن عابدی (هند).
٥) نگاهی به‌اوضاع تاریخی عصر بیدل؛ دکتر کریم نجفی (ایران).
٦) عبدالقادر بیدل در قلمرو تئوری ادبیّات و نقد ادبی؛ دکتر اسدالله حبیب (افغانستان).
۷) بیدل‌شناسی ـ مروری بر کتاب فیض قدس؛ دکتر محمّد ریاض (پاکستان).
۸) بیدل و بهزاد؛ دکتر خسرو احتشامی هونه‌گانی (ایران).
۹) نگاهی به‌میرزا عبدالقادر بیدل عظیم‌آبادی؛ پروفسور محمود عالم (هند).
۱۰) سپهری و سبک هندی؛ دکتر سیّد حسن حسینی (ایران).
۱۱) بیدل‌شناسان؛ دکتر سیّد احسن‌الظّفر (هند).
۱۲) بررسی اندیشه‌های فلسفی در شعر بیدل دهلوی؛ دکتر سیّد عبدالحمید ضیایی (ایران).
۱۳) میرزا عبدالقادر بیدل در تذکره‌های شعری؛ پروفسور شریف حسین قاسمی (هند).

۱٤) نشئهٔ بی‌خمار آزادگی در شعر بیدل؛ دکتر عبّاس علی وفایی (ایران).
۱۵) وحدتِ وجود و شهود در کلامِ بیدل؛ دکتر طلحه رضوی «برق» (هند).
۱٦) هزلیّات در غزلیّات بیدل؛ دکتر محمّد افسر رهبین (افغانستان).
۱۷) عوامل شاعرانگی در شعر بیدل دهلوی؛ دکتر پروین سلاجقه (ایران).
۱۸) سخنوران همزمان میرزا عبدالقادر بیدل؛ دکتر غلام مجتبٰی انصاری (هند).
۱۹) رباعیّات بیدل، محمل ایجاز؛ دکتر سعید یوسف‌نیا (ایران).
۲۰) محلّ اقامت بیدل در دهلی؛ دکتر ادریس احمد (هند).
۲۱) بیدل شاعر بزرگ ناشناخته؛ دکتر محمّد کاظم کاظمی (افغانستان).
۲۲) درنگی در معانی و الفاظ بیدل؛ دکتر محمّد عابد حسین (هند).
۲۳) موسیقی شعر بیدل دهلوی؛ دکتر احمد ذاکری (ایران).
۲٤) بیدل و بیدل‌شناسی؛ دکتر محمّد محسن (هند).
۲۵) وحدتِ وجود در شعر بیدل دهلوی؛ دکتر لیلا هاشمیان (ایران).
۲٦) معرّفی کتاب «بیدل» نوشتهٔ خواجهٔ عباداللہ اختر؛ علیم اشرف خان (هند).
۲۷) بیدل در سفینهٔ خوشگو؛ دکتر ضمیره غفّاراوا (تاجیکستان).
۲۸) به‌کلام بیدل اگر رسی؛ دکتر خان محمّد عامر (هند).
۲۹) عکّاسی از اشعارِ بیدل: گفتگو با ریکاردو زیپولی (ایتالیا).
۳۰) کتابی آسمانی خَواندم و این است تفسیرش؛ گفتگویی با دکتر محمّد عبدالعزیز مهجور (افغانستان).
۳۱) بیدل را هنوز به‌مدرسه نیاورده‌اند؛ گفتگوی دکتر علی رضا قزوه با مرتضٰی امیری اسفندقه (ایران).
۳۲) از چیدنِ رنگ؛ محمّد رضا شالبافان (ایران).
۳۳) یاران نرسیدند به‌دادِ سخنِ من؛ دکتر نزهت هروی (افغانستان).

«32»

Kitāb Shanāsī-e Bīdel

Qira Dāghī Farībā and ʻAlī Ḥusainī, *Nashr-e Sarfarāz*, Karaj, 1388 H.S./[2009 A.D.].

«33»

Tāthīr-e Bīdel Bar Ghazal-e Shā'irān-e Nasl-e Awwal-e Inqelāb-e Islāmī

Yagāneh, Sapīdeh; Nīk-Manesh, Mehdī, *Adabiyāt-e Inqelāb-e Islāmī*, 1st issue, No. II (Pā'īz, 1394 H.S.)/[Autumn, 2015 A.D.].

«34»

A List of Printed Editions of the Works of Bīdel Dehlavī in Transoxiana-Uzbekistan (in litho)

Dr. Ibrāhīm Khodāyār, Teachers Training University and Gholām Karīmove, Bīrūnī Institute, Tashkent, published in *Bīdel Dar Āyīneh-e 'Ors,* Bunyād-e Bīdel-e Dehlavī, Tehran, 1395 H.S./[2016 A.D.].

«35»

Bīdel Dar Āyīneh-e 'Ors

Bunyād-e Bīdel-e Dehlavī, Iran, 1395 H.S./[2016 A.D.].

It is a collection of 24 articles on various aspects of life and works of Bīdel presented in three different international conferences in Tehran under the auspices of Bunyād-e Bīdel-e Dehlavī. It has the following 26 articles on Bīdel in Persian:

۱) بیدل و بهزاد؛ خسرو احتشامی هونه‌گانی.

۲) ترجمهٔ آثارِ بیدل به‌زبانِ ازبکی؛ دکتر ارکش ذاکراچل‌اف (ازبکستان).

۳) عرسِ بیدل؛ دکتر سیّد احسن‌الظّفر (هند).

۴) سهم اقبال در شناختِ بیدل در ایران؛ دکتر اخلاق آهن (هند).

۵) اندیشه‌های شاعری فیلسوف، بیدل دهلوی؛ دکتر فرهنگ جهانبخش.

۶) واژه‌گزینی و واژه‌سازی در شعر و نثرِ بیدل؛ دکتر اسدالله حبیب (افغانستان).

۷) بهار تازهٔ طرزِ فطرت؛ غلام حیدر یگانه (بلغارستان).

۸) فهرست کتابهای چاپِ سنگی بیدل دهلوی در ماوراءالنّهر، ازبکستان، دکتر ابراهیم خدایار.

۹) درآمدی بر شناختِ منابع شعر بیدل؛ دکتر ابوالقاسم رادفر (ایران).

۱۰) اندیشهٔ بودیسم و هندوئیسم در شعرِ بیدل دهلوی؛ خانم دکتر زی‌بانگ نگوین (ویتنام).
۱۱) پیرمیکدهٔ سخندانی و افلاطون خم‌نشین معانی (سبک‌شناسی غزلیّاتِ بیدل دهلوی)، نرجس سپهرنژاد.
۱۲) هم‌فکری میر محمّد علی رایج سیالکوتی (با ابوالمعانی میرزا عبدالقادر بیدل)؛ دکتر محمّد سرفراز ظفر (پاکستان).
۱۳) عوامل شاعرانگی در شعرِ بیدل دهلوی؛ دکتر پروین سلاجقه.
۱۴) وحدتِ وجود در کلامِ بیدل؛ دکتر سمیع رفیع.
۱۵) از روزنهٔ احساس تا پنجرهٔ تفکّر؛ گلنار طاهریان (طاهرادا)، (تاجیکستان).
۱۶) بیدل: شاعر از یادرفته؛ پروفسور افتخار عارف (پاکستان).
۱۷) معرفی آثارِ منظوم و منثور میرزا عبدالقادر بیدل در کتابخانهٔ سالارجنگ، حیدرآباد؛ دکتر علیم اشرف خان (هند).
۱۸) محیطِ وحدت (بررسی وحدتِ وجود ابنِ عربی در مثنوی محیطِ اعظم بیدل)؛ معصومه غیوری.
۱۹) معرفیِ نسخه‌ای خطّی انتخابِ کلامِ بیدل؛ پروفسور شریف حسین قاسمی (هند).
۲۰) اکنون باید معنیِ ما فهمید؛ دکتر علی رضا قزوه.
۲۱) بیدل و اهلِ قدرت؛ محمّد کاظم کاظمی.
۲۲) بیدل شاعر ـ شاعرِ حیرت؛ فائزه زهرا میرزا.
۲۳) مکتبِ پیروانِ بیدل و مراحل تحوّلِ سبکِ هندی در ادبیاتِ فارسی فرارود؛ دکتر نور علی نورزاد (نوراف).
۲۴) بحثی در پیکربندیِ مفهومِ «من» در شعرِ بیدل؛ دکتر شروین وکیلی.
۲۵) بیدل پژوهی در افغانستان، پیشینه و گستره؛ دکتر محمّد جعفر یاحقّی.

«36»

Ṭāvūs-e Bīdel Zār-e She'r: Radd-e Pāy-e Ṭarz-e Bīdel Dehlavī Dar Ghazal-e Aḥmad 'Azīzī

Walīpūr, 'Abdollāh; Himmatī Roqayya, *Adabiyāt-e Inqelāb-e Islāmī*, 2nd Volume, No. 1, (Bahār, 1396 H.S.)/[Spring, 2017 A.D.].

«37»

Āshtī Bā Bīdel

Included in a Collection of 9 Articles by Gholām 'Alī Ḥaddād 'Ādil entitled Ḥadīth-e Sarv-o-Nīlūfar

Sokhan Publication, 1st edition Zamistān, 1396 H.S./[Winter, 2017-2018 A.D.].

«38»

Ghālib's Thought, Dialectical Poetic and the Indian Mind

(غالب؛ معنی آفرینی، جدلیاتی وضع، شویتا اور شعریات)

Prof. Gopī Chand Nārang, a renowned Urdū scholar, has dedicated Chapter VI of his scholarly book *Ghālib, Ma'ne Āfrīnī, Jadaliyātī Waẓe', Shonītā Aur She'rīyāt* [Ghālib's Thought, Dialectical Poetic and the Indian Mind, Sāhitya Academy, New Delhi, 2013], to scholarly and critically evaluate and assess Bīdel's contribution to Persian literature and its influence on Ghālib. He has accomplished it under these headings:

1) Bīdel, Ghālib, 'Irfān Wa Dānish-e Hindī, pp.173-78.
2) Solūk-o-Taṣawwuf, pp.179-89.
3) Bīdel-o-Ghālib, pp. 190-219.
4) 'Irfān-o-Dānish-e Hindi, pp.220-37.
5) Bīdel, *Sokhan Aur Wāke*, pp.238.

«39»

Article on Bīdel: Encyclopedia of Persian Literature in Indian Sub-Continent (India, Bangladesh & Pakistan)

Ḥassan Anūsheh, published by Persian Academy, Iran, Tehran.

«40»

Mīrzā 'Abdul Qādir-e Bīdel Kī Shakhṣiyat aur Unkā Aslūb

'Abdul Ghanī, *Iqbāl*, Lahore, Vol. VI, No. 4.

«41»

Nigāhī beh Bīdel

Dr. Shafī'ī Kadkanī, An Article published in Rāhnumāy-e Kitāb, No. III, Tenth year of *Majallāh*.

Dr. Shafī'ī Kadkanī has reviewed the work of Ṣalāḥoddīn Saljūqī entitled «نقدِ بیدل».

«42»

Bīdelī Keh Mann Mī-Shanāsam

Dr. Asadollāh Ḥabībī, *Rūznāmeh-e Anīs*, No. 129-131 & 241-281.

«43»

Bīdel-Gerāyī Dar Afghanistan

(Conversation with Prof. Wāṣif Bākhtarī, the poet & research scholar of Afghanistan)

Īraj, Shehbāz, Quarterly *She'r*, Vol. 9, No. 29, Zamistān.

«44»

Beḥthī Dar Aḥwāl-o-Āthār-e Mīrzā 'Abdul Qādir-e Bīdel

Prof. Mīr Ḥusain Shāh, *Adab*, No. 5 & 6.

«45»

Bīdel Ke Ash'ār

Niyāz Fateḥpūrī, *Nigār*, Lucknow.

«46»

Ash'ār-e Bīdel

Niyāz Fateḥpūrī, *Nigār*, Lucknow.

«47»

Mīrzā Bīdel Ke Ta'alluqāt

Yāsīn Khān Niyāzī, *Oriental College Magazine*, Lahore.

«48»

Bīdel Kī Aik Jamālīyātī 'Alāmat

Dr. 'Abdul Ghanī, *Nigār*, Lucknow.

«49»

Bīdel

Shāh Walī-ur Raḥmān, *Nuqūsh,* Lahore, *Shakhṣiyat Number* 2, Vol. 9, No. 1-2.

«50»

Mīrzā 'Abdul Qādir-e Bīdel

Dr. Moḥammad Shafī', *Maqālat-e Dīnī-o-'Ilmī*, Lahore, Part II.

«51»

Ẕikr-e Bīdel

Niyāz Fateḥpūrī, *Nigār*, Lucknow.

«52»

Mīrzā Bīdel

Asrār Aḥmad Nadvī, *Nadīm*, Gaya (India).

«53»

Ārāmgāh-e Bīdel

Dr. 'Abdul Ghanī, *Nigār*, Lucknow.

«54»

Mīrzā 'Abdul Qādir-e Bīdel

Yāsīn Khān Niyāzī, *Oriental College Magazine*, Lahore, Vol. 8, No. 4.

«55»

Maktab-e Hind-o-Maktab-e Bīdel

'Abdul Ḥayī Ḥabībī, *Majallāh-e Kābul*, Vol. IV, Kabul.

«56»

Mukhtaṣar-e Afkār-e Bīdel

Faiẓ Moḥammad Zakarīya, Ministry of Publications, Kabul.

«57»

Mulāḥeẓātī Darbāra-e Realism-e Bīdel

A. Sandre Bausānī, *Adab*, Kabul, Vol. 13, No. 4.

«58»

Waṣf-e Ṭabī'at Dar Ash'ār-e Bīdel

A. Sandre Bausānī, *Adab*, Kabul, Vol. 13, No. 4.

He is the same Sandre Bausānī, an Austrian scholar who visited Afghanistan for delivering lectures on Bīdel in University of Kabul, Kabul.

«59»

Bīdel

Perviz 'Abbāsī Dākānī, Article in *Dānishnāma-e Jahān-e Islām*, Vol. 5, pp.132-135, printed in Tehran.

«60»

Article on Bīdel: Urdū Dā'eratul Ma'aref-e Islāmīa (Lahore)

Vol. VII, pp.919-923.

«61»

Bīdel: Sākhteyātī Fikr Kā Pīshraw (بیدل ساختیاتی فکر کا پیشرو)

'Alī Badāyūnī, *Alfāż*, Aligarh.

Bibliography

1. *A Catalogue of Arabic, Persian and Hindūstāny Manuscripts in the Libraries of the Kings of Oudh*; A. Sprenger, M.B., Calcutta, 1854, Vol. II.
2. *A Catalogue of Manuscripts in Ḥabībganj Collection* (ذخيرهٔ حبيب گنج) *in the Maulānā Azad Library*, A.M.U., Aligarh, 1981.
3. *A Catalogue of Manuscripts in Mas'ood Jhandir Library* (Pakistan); compiled by Dr. Syeda Nikhat Firdous KḥHn¯, Iran-Pakistan Institute of Persian Studies, Islamabad, 2005.
4. *A Catalogue of Manuscripts in National Archives of Afghanistan* (فهرستِ نسخ خطّی آرشفِ ملّی افغانستان); Mozammad A'Hm, Afaal, Mozammad Anwar M¯r, Kabul, Jadd¯, 1364, Vol. II, Part I (in Persian).
5. A Catalogue of Persian Manuscripts in Rampur Razḥ Library, Rampur, Vol. I, 1996, Vol. II, 1998.
6. *A Catalogue of Persian Manuscripts in the Library of Nadva-tol 'Ulemā Lucknow*; Persian Research Centre, Iran Culture House, New Delhi, 1365 H.S./1986 A.D.
7. *A Collection in the Maulānā Āzād Library*, Aligarh Muslim University Collection (AMU), Aligarh U.P., India, 1969.
8. *A Descriptive Catalogue of Arabic, Persian and Urdu Manuscripts in Mozzammil Library, Aligarh*; 'ASḥ Khursh¯d, Patna, 1995.
9. *A Descriptive Catalogue of Islamic Manuscripts in the Government Oriental Manuscripts Library*: T. Chandra Shekhran, Madras, 1950, Vol. II.

10. *A Descriptive Catalogue of Persian Manuscripts in Sālār Jung Museum and Library*; Mozammad Ashraf, Hyderabad, 1980.

11. *A Descriptive Catalogue of Persian Manuscripts in the library of Anjuman-e Taraqqī-e Urdu (India)*; Rouse Avenue, New Delhi, 1998.

12. *A Descriptive Catalogue of the Oriental Manuscripts* belonging to the Late E.G. Browne and completed by R.A. Nicholson, Cambridge, University Press, 1932.

13. *A Descriptive Catalogue of the Oriental Manuscripts in the Dargāh Library, Ūch*; Shar¯f, Bhḥgalpṭ r State, Dr. Gholḥm Sarwar (Aligarh), Urdu Academy, Bhawalpur.

14. *A Descriptive Catalogue of the Persian Manuscripts in the Banaras Hindū University Library*, Dr. Amr¯t Lḥl 'Ishrat, Banaras Hindṭ University, Varanasi, U.P.

15. *A Descriptive Catalogue of the Persian Manuscripts*; Maulḥnḥ ū zḥd Arabic and Persian Research Institute Rajasthan, Tonk, Vol. I.

16. *A Hand-List of 'Arabic, Persian and Urdu Manuscripts in Sharaf-ul Molk Library*; Madrasa Mozammad¯, Bḥgh-e D¯wḥn Sazeb, T.T.K. Road, Chenḥ'¯ (not published but available in the library).

17. *A Hand-List of Manuscripts in Moḥammadan Library*, Chenḥ'¯ (available in the library).

18. *A Hand-List of the Manuscripts of the Works of Bīdel in the National Archives of Afghanistan*; Kabul, provided by the Archives to me.

19. *A Union Catalogue of Persian Manuscripts in Pakistan*; Azmad Monzav¯, Iran-Pakistan Institute of Persian Studies, Islamabad, Pakistan, 1987, Vol. VIII.

20. *A Union Catalogue of Persian Manuscripts in Pakistan*; compiled by Azmad Monzav¯, enlarged, revised and edited by 'ū rif Naushḥh¯, Iran-Pakistan Institute of Persian Studies, Islamabad, Pakistan, 1997, Vol. XIV (in Persian).

21. *ACTA Bibliotheca R. Universitatis Upsaliensis*; Vol. III, K.V. Zettersteen, Upsala, 1930.

22. *Āwāzhāy-e Bīdel* (آوازهای بیدل); (a collection of B¯del's prose-works), edited by Akbar Behdḥrwand, Mṭ assaseh-e Inteshḥrḥt-e Negḥh, Tehrḥn, 1386.

23. *Catalogue of Books of the Fort William College Collection in the National Archives of India Library*; edited by Dr. R.K. Pert¯, National Archives of India, New Delhi, 1984.

24. *Catalogue of Manuscripts of the Fort William College Collection in the National Archives of India Library*; Dr. R.K. Pert¯, National Archives of India, New Delhi, 1989.

25. *Catalogue of Oriental Manuscripts in the Lucknow University Library*; Kḥl¯ Prasad, Lucknow University, Lucknow, 1951.

26. *Catalogue of Persian and 'Arabic Manuscripts in Ṣaulat Public Library* (Rampur); compiled by 'ū bid Reaḥ B¯dḥr, Āaulat Public Library, Rampur, U.P., 1966.

27. *Catalogue of Persian Manuscripts in the Austrian National Library and in the Austrian State Archives in Vienna*; ṣraj Afshḥr, Austrian Academy of Sciences Press, Vienna, 2003.

28. *Catalogue of Persian Manuscripts in the India Office Library*; Hermann Ethe, India Office Library and Records, Foreign and Commonwealth Office, London, 1980.

29. *Catalogue of Persian Manuscripts in the libraries of Bombay*, Iran Culture House, Mumbai (in Persian).

30. *Catalogue of Persian Manuscripts in the library of the India Office*; H. Ethe, Oxford, 1903, Vol. II revised and completed by E. Edwards, Oxford, 1937, Vol. I.

31. *Catalogue of the 'Arabic and Persian Manuscripts in the Khodā Bakhsh Oriental Public Library*; Khodḥ Bakhsh Oriental Public Library, Patna, 1988, Vol. III.

32. *Catalogue of the Persian Manuscripts in the British Museum*; C. Rieu, London, 1879-83, Vol. I-III.

33. *Catalogue of the Persian Manuscripts in the Bohār Collection*; S.M. ż asan and S.M. Islḥm, National Library, Belvedere, Calcutta, 1982.

34. *Catalogue of the Persian, Turkish, Hindustani and Pushtū Manuscripts in the Bodleian Library*; H. Ethe, Part I, Persian Manuscripts, Oxford, 1889; Part II, Oxford, 1930; Part III, additional Persian Manuscripts, A.F.L. Beeston, Oxford, 1954.

35. *Concise Descriptive Catalogue of the Persian Manuscripts in the Curzon Collection*; Asiatic Society of Bengal, Wladimir Ivonow, Calcutta, 1926.

36. *Concise Descriptive Catalogue of the Persian Manuscripts in the Collection of the Asiatic Society of Bengal*; First Supplement, Wladimir Ivonow, Calcutta, 1927.

37. *Descriptive Catalogue of 'Arabic, Persian and Urdu Manuscripts in the library of the University of Bombay*; Shaikh 'Abdul Qḥdir Sarfarḥz, Bombay, 1935.

38. *Descriptive Catalogue of Manuscripts of the Fort William College in the National Archives of India*; New Delhi, Noor Microfilms Centre, Iran Culture House, New Delhi, 2012 A.D. (in Persian).

39. *Dictionary of Indo-Persian Literature*; Nabi Hadi, Indira Gandhi National Centre for the Arts, New Delhi, 1995.

40. *Fakhnā: Fehrist-e Noskhehā-e Khaṭṭī-e Iran* (فخنا: فهرستِ نسخه‌های خطّی ایران); Information about the Manuscripts of the works of B¯del preserved in Iranian libraries have been drawn from this list.

41. *Fārsī Adab Be-'Ahd-e Aurangzīb* (فارسی ادب بعهدِ اورنگ‌زیب); Dr. Nṭ rul ż asan AnĪḥr¯, Indo-Persian Society, Delhi, 1969.

42. *Fehrist-e Āthār-e 'Ilmī-e Ostādān-o-Monograph-ha-e Moḥaṣṣilān-e Pohantun* (فهرست آثار علمی استادان و مونگراف‌های محصّلان پوهنتون; Mozammad Ibrḥh¯m, Sotṭ deh with the co-operation of 'Abdur Razmḥn, assistant librarian, Kabul, 1353 Khursh¯d¯.

43. *Fehrist-e Kotob-e 'Arabī, Fārsī-o-Urdu* (فهرست کتب عربی، فارسی و اردو; ū Īaf¯ya Sarkḥr-e 'ū l¯ Library, Printed by Akhtar-e Deccan, Hyderabad, 1332 A.H.

44. *Fehrist-e Kotob-e 'Arabī, Fārsī-o-Urdu* (فهرست کتب عربی، فارسی و اردو; a collection of ū Īaf¯ya Sarkḥr 'ū l¯ Library, Dḥrul ẕaba'-e Jḥmia-e Uthmḥnia, Sarkḥr 'ū l¯, Hyderabad Deccan, 1347 A.H., Vol. III.

45. *Fehrist-e Kotob-e Qalmī-e Sho'beh-e Makhṭūṭāt-e 'Arabī, Fārsī, Urdu* (فهرست کتب قلمی شعبۂ مخطوطات عربی، فارسی، اردو); NaŻriya Public Library, Phḥtak ż abash Khḥn, Delhi, compiled by ż aq¯r Mozammad Al-Mehd¯ Ja'far¯, NḥHm-e Kotobkhḥneh-e NaŻriya, Delhi, 1360 A.H.

NaŻriya Public Library has been shifted to Jḥmia Hamdard Library, Tughlaqabad, New Delhi-110062.

46. *Fehrist-e Makhṭūṭāt, Ẕakhīreh-e Aḥsan* (فهرستِ مخطوطاتِ ذخیرۂ احسن; Syed Mozammad ż usain Reaav¯, M.A. Library, Aligarh Muslim University, Aligarh, 1985.

47. *Taẕkirah-e Jawāhar-e Zawāhir, Fehrist-e Makhṭūṭāt-e Fārsī, Jawāhar Museum*; a collection in M.A. Library, Aligarh Muslim University, Aligarh.

48. *Fehrist-e Makhṭūṭāt-e Kotobkhāneh-e Al-Qarshiya-e Qil'ehdār*, Majalleh-e Kithḥbdṭ st, Qaum¯ Hijr Council, Islamabad, Pakistan, 1406 A.H.

49. *Fehrist-e Makhṭūṭāt-e Ẕakhīrah-e Aḥsan* (فهرستِ مخطوطاتِ ذخیرۂ احسن; by S. Mazmood ż asan Qaisar, M.A. Library, Aligarh

Muslim University, Aligarh, 1983.

50. *Fehrist-e Makhṭūṭāt-e Ẕakhīreh-e Shīfta* (فهرستِ مخطوطاتِ ذخیرۀ شیفته; by S. Mazmood ż asan Qaisar, M.A. Library, Aligarh Muslim University, Aligarh, 1982.

51. *Fehrist-e Nosakh-e Khaṭṭī-e Fārsī-e Institū-e Āthār-e Khaṭṭī-e Tājīkistān*; under the supervision of Syed 'Al¯ Mojan¯, Am¯r Yazdḥn 'Al¯ Mardḥn, Markaz-e Mothḥle'ḥt-e ū siḥ-e Markaz¯ wa Qafqḥz, Ministry of External Affairs, Tehrḥn, 1376 H.S./ 1997 A.D. Vol. I.

52. *Fehrist-e Noskhehā-e Khaṭṭī Kitābkhāneh-e Sho'beh-e Teḥqīq-o-Ishā'at-e Kashmīr-o-Kitābkhāneh-e Hamidiya Bhopal*, Persian Research Centre, Iran Culture House, New Delhi, 1364 H.S./1986 A.D.

53. *Fehrist-e Noskhehā-e Khaṭṭī-e Fārsī-e Dr. Ẕākir Ḥusain Library*; Jḥmia Millia Islḥm¯a, Persian Research Centre, Iran Culture House, New Delhi, 1377 H.S./1999 A.D.

54. *Fehrist-e Noskhehā-e Khaṭṭī-e Fārsī in Hardayāl Public Library, Delhi*; Persian Research Centre, Iran Culture House, New Delhi, 1377 H.S./1999 A.D.

55. *Fehrist-e Noskhehā-e Khaṭṭī-e Fārsī-e Kitābkhāneh-hā-e Torkiya* (فهرستِ نسخه‌های خطّی فارسی کتابخانه‌های ترکیه): Tauf¯q H. Sobzḥn¯, Markaz-e Nashr-e Dḥnishgḥh¯, Tehran, 1373 H.S.

56. *Fehrist-e Noskheh-hā-e Khaṭṭī-e Fārsī-e Kitābkhāneh-e Meghnīsā* فهرست نسخه‌های خطّی فارسی کتابخانۀ مغنیسا, compiled by Tauf¯q H. Sobzḥn¯, Markaz-e Nashr-e Dḥnishgḥh¯, Tehrḥn, 1366 H.S.

57. *Ganjīneh-e Khaṭṭī-o-Honarī-e Tālpūrān* (گنجینۀ خطّی و هنری تالپوران), Dr. Qḥsem Āḥf¯, Islamabad, Pakistan, 1383 H.S./ 2005 A.D.

58. *Gol-e Ra'na*; Lachhm¯ Nḥrain Shaf¯q, in *Tīn Tazkirey* (تین تذکرے, edited by Nithḥr Ahmad Fḥrṭ q¯, Maktaba-e Burhḥn, Urdu Bazar, Delhi, 1968.

59. *Hand-List of Persian Manuscripts*; G.M. Maredith-Owens, the Trustee of the British Museum, 1968.

60. *Hand-List of the Moḥammadan Manuscripts preserved in the library of the University of Cambridge*; E.G. Browne, Cambridge, 1930.

61. *Ma'āthir-e 'Ālamgīrī;* M¯rzḥ Mozammad Sḥq¯ Mosta'ed, Asiatic Society, Calcutta, 1871.

62. *Ma'āthir-ul 'Omerā;* Shḥhnawḥz Khḥn, Calcutta, 1890, Vol. II.

63. *Majma'-ul Afkār* (مجمع الافکار), edited by Prof. Chander Shekhar, National Mission for Manuscripts, New Delhi, 2016 A.D.

64. *Mīrzā 'Abdul Qādir-e Bīdel*; edited by Prof. Qamar Ghaffar, Jamia Millia Islamia, New Delhi, 2017.

65. *Mīrzā 'Abdul Qādir Bīdel, Ḥayāt aur Kārnāmey* (in two volume); Dr. Syed Azsan-uH Ṭafar, Rampur Razḥ Library, Rampur, U.P., 2009.

66. *Moraqqa'e Dehlī* (Persian Text with Urdu translation), Dargḥh Qul¯ Khḥn; by Khal¯q Anjum, Delhi, 1993.

67. *Moraqqa'e Dehlī*; Dargḥh Qul¯ Khḥn, English translation by Chander Shekhar and Shama Mitra Chenoy, Deputy Publication, Delhi, 1989.

68. *Mughals in India: A Bibliographical Survey of Manuscripts*; D.N. Marshall, Mansell Publishing Limited, London and New York, reprinted from Asia Publishing House, 1967.

69. *Nekāt-ush Sho'arā*; M¯r Taq¯ M¯r, Anjuman Taraqq¯-e Urdu, Auranghbḥd, 1929.

70. *Sair-ul Manāzil*; Sang¯n Beg, edited by Dr. Sharif Husain Qasemi with Urdu translation, Ghḥlib Institute, New Delhi, 1982.

71. *Supplement to the Catalogue of the Persian Manuscripts in the British Museum*; Charles Rieu, British Museum Publications Limited, 1895.

72. *Tashrīḥī-e Fehrist-e Makhṭūṭāt-e Fārsī* (تشریحی فهرستِ مخطوطاتِ فارسی; Anjuman Taraqq¯-e Urdu-e Hind Library, Aligarh, Maulḥnḥ Mozammad Abrḥr ż usain Fḥrṭ q¯ Azhar¯, Aligarh, 30th January, 1951, Vol. I.

73. *Ta'aruf-e Makhṭūṭāt-e Kotobkhāna-e Dārul 'Ulūm*, Deoband, Maulḥnḥ Muft¯ Muzammad Ṭaf¯rudd¯n, Dḥrul 'Ulṭ m, Deoband, 1973, Vol. II.

74. *Taẕkireh-e Makhṭūṭāt* (تذکرۂ مخطوطات); (A Descriptive Catalogue of Urdu, Persian, 'Arabic and Hind¯ Manuscripts preserved in the library of the Idḥra-e Adabiyḥt-e Urdu, Hyderabad), India, compiled by Dr. S. Moz¯udd¯n Qḥdr¯ Zore, Bureau for promotion of Urdu, New Delhi, Vol. II, 1984, Vol. III, 1985.

75. *The Catalogue of the Persian Manuscripts in the Bursa Library*; Dr. Tauf¯q H. Sobzḥn¯, G¯lḥn University, 1368.

76. *Ẕikr-e Jamī'-e Aulīya-e Dehlī* (ذکر جمیع اولیای دهلی) ż ab¯bollḥh, edited by Dr. Sharif Husain Qasemi, Arabic and Persian Research Institute Rajasthan, Tonk, 1988.

Index

Persons

Scribes

Places